A Book Too Risky to Publish:
Free Speech and Universities

James R. Flynn

A Book Too Risky to Publish: Free Speech and Universities

James R. Flynn

Academica Press
Washington – London

Library of Congress Registration Information

Name: Flynn, James R., author. 1934 –
Title: A book too risky to publish : free speech and universities
Description: Washington, DC : Academica Press, 2020. | Identifiers:
LCCN: 2019952687 | ISBN 9781680532043 (hardcover : alk. paper) |
ISBN 9781680532197 (paperback : alk. paper)
LC record available at https://lccn.loc.gov/ 2019952687

He who dares not reason is a slave.
(Sir William Drummond, 1585 – 1649)

If liberty means anything at all, it means the
right to tell people what they do not want to hear.
(George Orwell, original preface to Animal Farm, 1953)

Someone had said that there was nothing
that tasted so good as one's own ear wax.
(Kōbō Abe, The woman in the dunes, 1966, p. 280)

Looming over this whole debate is a terrible temptation:

the assumption that since you know that virtue is on your side,

truth must be on your side – and that an honest effort to

perceive the truth is immoral (Flynn, 2019)

Contents

Preface ix

List of Boxes xiii

List of Tables xiii

Acknowledgements xv

Introduction 1

Part 1
Knowledge and Right Opinion 5

1
John Stuart Mill and the mission of the university 7

2
Middlebury and my mind 31

Part 2
What others do to academics 55

3
The era of conservative oppression 57

4
The transition 83

5
The era of radical oppression 89

6
The struggle for control 115

7
Chicago and Yale and Harvard 129

Part 3
What academics do to themselves 151

8
Black studies 153

9
Women's Studies 167
10
The Walden Codes.. 183
Part 4
What academics do to students 209
11
The teaching of teachers 211
12
The whole man: Critical skills.. 227
13
The whole man: Critical minds 245
Part 5
Justification and advice.. 273
14
In praise of autonomy 275
15
The three frogs.. 289
References 301
Index 319
Name Index 319
Subject Index.. 326

Preface

A publishing house in the United Kingdom had scheduled this book for publication but then e – mailed that they would not proceed:

Dear Professor Flynn:

I am contacting you in regard to your manuscript "In Defense of Free Speech: The University as Censor." [We] believe that its publication, in particular in the United Kingdom, would raise serious concerns. By the nature of its subject matter, the work addresses sensitive topics of race, religion, and gender. The challenging manner in which you handle these topics as author, particularly at the beginning of the work, whilst no doubt editorially powerful, increase the sensitivity and the risk of reaction and legal challenge. As a result, we have taken external legal advice on the contents of the manuscript and summarize our concerns below.

There are two main causes of concern for [us]. Firstly, the work could be seen to incite racial hatred and stir up religious hatred under United Kingdom law. Clearly you have no intention of promoting racism but intent can be irrelevant. For example, one test is merely whether it is "likely" that racial hatred could be stirred up as a result of the work. This is a particular difficulty given modern means of digital media expression. The potential for circulation of the more controversial passages of the manuscript online, without the wider intellectual context of the work as a whole and to a very broad audience – in a manner beyond our control – represents a material legal risk for [us].

Secondly, there are many instances in the manuscript where the actions, conversations and behavior of identifiable individuals at specific named colleges are discussed in detail and at length in relation to controversial events. Given the sensitivity of the issues involved, there is both the potential for serious harm to [our] reputation and the significant possibility of legal action. Substantial changes to the content and nature of the manuscript would need to be made, or [we] would need to accept a high level of risk both reputational and legal. The practical costs and difficulty of managing any reputational or legal problems that did arise are of further concern to [us].

For the reasons outlined above, it is with regret that [we have] taken the decision not to publish your manuscript. We have not taken this decision lightly, but following senior level discussions within the organization, and with the additional benefit of specialist legal advice. I realize that this decision will come as a disappointment to you and hope that you will be able to find an alternative publisher with whom to take the work to publication.

The reader can evaluate the above after reading the book. The text in front of you has not been sanitized – all changes have been made simply to clarify passages or eliminate typos. The text does not deviate from my practice in seventeen previous books: all comments on named persons are based on citations of published sources or material in the public domain. This is not merely my opinion but also that of several leading scholars and two American presses that were asked whether it posed legal problems. Historians or journalists that wish to verify the facts should contact the author to receive the original copy of the book. In light of the circumstances I have altered the title from *In Defense of Free Speech: The University as Censor* to *A Book Too Risky to Publish: Free Speech and Universities*.

The UK publishing house's fears are typical in that country and pose a question: does the climate of opinion in Britain even approximate what might be called free speech? Since the rejection became public in *Quillette* (Flynn, 2019), fifteen other presses approached the author: nine in the United States, one in the UK (a non – royalties paying press), three in Europe, and two in Brazil. Confidential communications revealed that two other UK presses were terrified. None of the non – UK presses seemed to fear legal consequences. Among the American presses, right – leaning ones were very receptive: they were happy to use the book's withdrawal from publication as evidence of liberal intolerance. At least one (self – described) left – leaning press wanted changes that would prevent the book from being "weaponized" by the right, and also wanted "incendiary" passages qualified. Two others felt that their readers were not quite ready for this kind of book.

I can hardly generalize, but it looks as though freedom of the press is endangered, at least in Britain. American presses seem to be politicized but collectively allow a range of views to be published, not because they endorse free speech but because they wish to vindicate their own politics. Academica Press, the ultimate publisher of this book, was the notable exception and has no ideological leaning.

A number of scholars and journalists, all of whom read the original manuscript, wish to put on record their view that this book should not have been withdrawn from publication. With their permission, their names are listed here:

Joshua Aronson – Associate Professor of Psychology, New York University

Thomas J. Bouchard – Professor Emeritus of Psychology, University of Minnesota

Roberto Colom – Professor of Psychology, Autonomous University, Madrid

Gilberto Corbellini – Professor Bioethics & Medicine, Sapienza University, Rome

Ian J. Deary – Professor of Psychology, University of Edinburgh

William T. Dickens – Distinguished Professor of Economics, Northeastern University

Linda Gottfredson – Professor Emeritus of Psychology, University of Delaware

Jonathan Haidt – Professor of Ethical leadership, New York University

Aynsley Kellow – Professor Emeritus of Government, Univrersity of Tasmania

John C. Loehlin – Professor Emeritus of Genetics and Psychology, University of Texas

Austin Mitchell – Former MP and Whip of the British Labour Party

Charles Murray – Fellow of the American Enterprise Institute (US)

Richard Nisbett – Distinguished Professor of Social Psychology, University of Michigan

Mark Olssen – Professor Emeritus of Political Theory & Education, University of Surrey

Steven Pinker – Distinguished Professor of Psychology, Harvard University

Peter Singer – Distinguished Professor of Bioethics, Princeton University

Thomas Sowell – Senior Fellow, Hoover Institution

Thijmen Sprakel – Educator and Editor – in – Chief, EduKitchn.nl

Ramesh Thakur – Professor Emeritus, Australian National University and Former Assistant Secretary General of the United Nations

The names of three others that could not be located appeared in an early printing. This list is definitive.

List of Boxes

Box 1. Books about free speech on campus....24

Box 2. Jensen and Factor X...34

Box 3. Black subculture and the IQ debate...190-191

Box 4. Subjectivity and objectivity in ethics...199-200

Box 5. How to give a decent lecture in the humanities...239

Box 6. FISC items and concepts: Gene Debs...252-253

Box 7. FISC performance by subtest, total score, and realist vs. postmodern...257-258

Box 8. Israel and Arabs...279

Box 9. Flynn versus Murray...295

List of Tables

Table 1. Caliber of university intake for selected years...229-230

Table 2. Gains in critical thinking at university...235

Acknowledgements

I owe thanks to all of the scholars who read drafts of the text as listed in the preface. I have used material from my previous books but the major borrowings are as follows:

Chapter 14 from *How To Improve Your Mind: Twenty Keys to Unlock the Modern World* (London: Wiley – Blackwell, 2012). That book describes the FISC (Flynn's Index of Social Criticism) and uses it to evaluate "Gene Debs University."

Chapter 15 from from *The Torchligth List: Around the World in 200 Books*; *The New Torchight List: In Search of the Best Modern Auhors*; and *Fate and Philosphy: A Journey Through Life's Great Questions*. Wellington, NZ: AWA Press (2010, 2016, 2012, respectively).

My sincere thanks to William van der Vliet for all his help in formatting.

Introduction

This book is about the ways in which legislators, students, academics, and university curricula censor the range of ideas that ought to be heard in a university and impede the proper education of students. I will begin with a pledge to the reader: throughout I will say exactly what I believe to be true; I have not altered one sentence to be politic. This is not a confession that my previous books are remiss. As Aristotle said, "Plato was a friend to us all, but an even better friend must be the truth." My colleague Charles Hansel called my attention to these words sixty years ago. His honesty was so manifest that it was humiliating not to try to imitate him.

A Book Too Dangerous To Publish assumes that the great goods of humanity include human autonomy and the liberation of the human mind. It argues that this is possible, or at least likely, only under certain conditions, one of which is that free speech prevails. It also assumes that the university has a peculiar mission: the good society has designated it as an institution that, above all, not only seeks truth but also graduates people whose minds are prepared to seek the truth. I am not sure that there are many good universities today. Rather than feeling free to debate, professors and students walk about, and indeed, even off of campus are apprehensive of making slips of the tongue or behavior and being sent to mind – cleansing sensitivity training, harassed by mobs of their angry fellows, pilloried on social media, or brought before nebulous administrative tribunals with the power to punish them with consequences up to expulsion or termination of employment.

I will address the situation primarily in the humanities and social sciences. This omits one potent force that stifles the integrity of the university. That is when the administration pressures scientists to suppress research because outside donors (or governments) might be affronted. I can only claim battle fatigue and await a book that analyzes the sciences in the same way.

This book is divided into five parts. The first part is "Knowledge and Right Ppinion." Chapter 2 uses John Stuart Mill's *On Liberty* to describe what liberty means for thought, speech, and behavior, distinctions that will inform us about what we ought to do. For example, sometimes a university does behave in a way that affects the outside world adversely (e.g. invest its funds in corporations that are believed to do the world harm) and this can cloud its primary mission. It also asserts that the university is quite different from the rest of society's institutions and defends that assertion against critics like Jeremy Waldron.

Chapter 3 drives home a point implicit in Mill, namely the distinction between knowledge, being knowledgeable, and right opinion. When faced with plausible objections to your beliefs, one must be able to answer them or forfeit a claim to *knowledge*. The word "plausible" adds common sense qualifications: you cannot answer objections no one has thought of (including yourself). Then there are objections that one can dismiss by *your awareness of the accumulated knowledge* of various disciplines. Even this involves a kind of knowledge in the sense that you must not exaggerate (or underestimate) what has been overwhelmingly evidenced (for example, that psychology has reached firm conclusions about race and IQ). However, when you simply refuse to acquaint yourself with objections or make ignorant assumptions about a discipline, the best you can hope for is *right opinion*: You have to hope that you are lucky enough to hold opinions that knowledgeable people can show to be true. Chapter 3 also offers a contemporary example – that of Charles Murray at Middlebury, a case in which students acted violently to prevent anyone including themselves from transcending ignorance about their principles. It also uses myself as an example of how little a critical intellectual would know if these students had "shielded" me from listening to Charles Murray and other thinkers whom they find obnoxious.

The second part is titled "What Others Do To Academics." Chapter 4 sketches the period before 1965 when conservatives used government and compliant university administrators to intimidate free speech on campus and off. Chapter 5 describes the swift transition from conservative oppression to radical oppression. Chapters 6 and 7 focus on the period from 1965 to the present, a time when student "radicals" began to use intimidation to banish free speech. Chapter 8 compares three great universities in terms of their resistance to radical oppression.

The third part is "What Academics Do To Themselves." Independently of student or administrative pressure, many academic departments adopt a "Walden Code," a code of conduct that sends academics to Coventry if they try to include in their research or their courses anything that deviates from the "party line" about what is relevant or permissible. Chapters 9 and 10 list Black Studies and Woman's Studies as obvious offenders. Chapter 11 argues that this form of self – censorship extends to a lesser but significant degree to Anthropology, Sociology, Education, Psychology, Political Science, Philosophy, History, and similar disciplines.

"What Academics Do To Students" is part four. Chapter 12 analyzes why Teacher's Colleges and Colleges of Education indoctrinate their students with an ideal, the super teacher, and an ideology, progressive education, that damage schools. Chapters 13 and 14 assess a claim every university makes: its primary purpose is to foster critical skills and educate the whole individual so that he or she can become an intelligent citizen. There is evidence that they fall short of developing even those narrow critical skills which students need in the world of work and thus deprive them of the ability to be good citizens. Few graduates can test current opinion, which is to say the opinions foisted on them by politicians and the media. They are about as equipped to transcend their time and place as a medieval peasant was equipped to transcend the role of serf. I use my test "The FISC" (Flynn's Index of Critical Thinking) as evidence.

The fifth part defends human autonomy, one of the great goods of human existence. Chapter 15 analyzes it on three levels: ontological, sociological, and psychological. The search for autonomy is difficult and indeed almost impossible without free speech. Chapter 16 summarizes the problems of any university that hopes to be a free speech university. I also collect the solutions foreshadowed throughout the book.

A nephew recently asked me what was the point of reading widely and of a non – vocational university education. I could only respond because one wants to be a free man with a cultivated mind. The university has been my home as a professor for sixty years, and I owe it most of the autonomy I have. Herein I try to do something to repay that debt.

Part 1
Knowledge and Right Opinion

1
John Stuart Mill and the mission of the university

John Stuart Mill's essay *On Liberty* (1859) is the starting point for anyone who wants to be able to defend free speech. Mill begins by defending freedom of thought, the principle that one's thoughts are one's own and that society has no right of access to them. Speech, however, is a kind of behavior often intended to influence the action of others. Sometimes this threatens grave injury. One could not give a speech against the Corn Laws, to take an example Mill would have recognized from a great national debate over free trade during his lifetime, in front of a corn dealer's house urging an inflamed mob to take action against him. The United States Supreme Court has recognized this in its clear and present danger test: speech is not protected when it is used to threaten the death or physical injury of others, such as to incite a lynch mob or plan the assassination of a public official. Sometimes free speech is rendered impossible by a breakdown in public order, as was the case in pre – Nazi Germany. Major political parties competed in terms of who could disrupt everyone else's meetings. Politics became a contest to see who could put the largest mob in the streets.

But in many countries, speech occurs in less fraught circumstances: a discussion of religious, moral, political, or social issues in a democratic atmosphere. It is an ever – present temptation for a government or majority public opinion to suppress speech because they consider its content to be false or pernicious. Often they use as an excuse that a democracy is on the verge of revolutionary change when it is not. The American Communist Party was not a danger when it was persecuted. The Cold War atmosphere of the 1940s and 1950s had decimated it at the very time it was called a menace.

Mill's case for free speech

Mill makes four points in favor of free speech. First, even if a doctrine is largely false, there may be a grain of truth that would be lost if it were suppressed. The most noble of the Roman emperors, Marcus Aurelius, thought he was justified in suppressing Christianity. Here, he believed, was a typical Eastern superstition speaking of a resurrected god and virgin birth that preached pacifism at a time when Rome's armies were struggling to hold off barbarian hordes. Today, most would feel he was mistaken. However skeptical we may be about Christian dogma, they were preaching that all people had a soul and were precious in the sight of God, and that pagan criteria of who was higher or lower were arbitrary. As we will see in the next chapter, Arthur Jensen's case that there is a genetic component in the black – white IQ gap raised many points from which we can learn, even if we think him mistaken, and these are points that probably only someone who believed in a genetic component would think to raise. Even in Hitler's *Mein Kampf*, there was a diagnosis of the frustrations of Germany's middle class that other parties overlooked to their peril.

Second, truth unopposed loses much of its vitality. When every Christian was a convert, it was a vibrant faith. Now that one inherits one's church as one might inherit a family legacy or membership in a club, much of that vitality is lost. The Romans marveled at how the Christians in their midst loved one another. As Mill remarked, "No one is likely to say that today."

Third, truth undemonstrated or unevidenced is at best what Plato called right opinion rather than knowledge. Unless you can give reasons for the truth (or some other knowledgeable person can), you must simply hope that what you happen to believe is the truth. And the best way to accumulate reasons is to debate with opponents who believe the opposite. This line of thought persists. Karl Popper argued that we must do everything we can to falsify the truth of whatever we believe, and that this is never – ending in that evidence only discovered in the future may falsify it. It may be that we will never be certain of the truth. Human beings may not be bright enough to understand the full complexity of the universe. But at any given time, the only claim we have to know our theories are closer to the truth than opposing theories is that ours have thus far survived falsification while others have not.

Fourth, when trying to suppress a doctrine, one must hope to succeed, which means suppressing it permanently. This entails an assumption that goes beyond a claim to subjective infallibility (certainty in your own mind that something is false). It is to claim a prescriptive infallibility, as if you were an omnipotent god − emperor decreeing that something never be heard or weighed by others for the remainder of human history. As we will see, this kind of prescriptive certainty is a common characteristic of the enemies of free speech.

Fundamentally, Mill argued that open debate is a better method of attaining truth than a struggle for power. It is hard to disagree. When government and public opinion shut me up, it is because they are stronger than I am, which has little to do with truth. History is littered with doctrines once thought unpopular or ridiculous that later became accepted. When scientists were trying to discover whether an object was lighter (because it had lost phlogiston) or heavier (because it had combined with oxygen) after combustion, parliamentarians ridiculed them because "they were trying to weigh air."

Freedom of thought

Mill's argument for freedom of thought is one I do not share but, fortunately, the argument is unnecessary. I think he is saying that my thoughts are my own property and thus, I have a natural right to them that no one can abridge. I do not believe in natural rights, although I do believe in human rights that can be justified because they contribute to some great good for humanity. If fear forces me not to think as I normally would, if others persecute me unless I disavow thoughts they think pernicious, I dare not get my own thoughts in order to take an independent stand when I speak. In other words, if I can justify free speech, I will have justified free thought as its prerequisite.

This is not just an academic issue in that during my lifetime, the US government used sanctions to make its citizens take loyalty oaths. For example, when you entered the US armed forces you were supposed to swear that you did not advise the overthrow by force, violence, or other unlawful means, of the Government of the United States of

America; that you did not belong to a list of organizations the Attorney General had labeled disloyal; and that you were not withholding the names of any family or friends you suspected of belonging to these organization.

Knowledge of these external penalties discouraged people from weighing the message of revolutionary organizations and made the prospect of agreeing with them daunting. Anyone who tried to recruit people for left – wing organizations during the McCarthy period (Senator McCarthy led the "anti – subversive" campaign from 1948 to 1956) can attest to this. As a measure of the potency of this negative reinforcement, consider how difficult it is to consider an issue objectively even when the "intimidation" is strictly internal: I have always had to guard against being biased on the race and IQ issue, simply because I do not *want* to show that individuals of African descent may have genes that determine lower IQ.

These loyalty oaths had the usual effect of all such interferences with freedom of thought by singling out the best of people for sanctions. All of us on the left at the University of Chicago when I was there (1951 to 1957) knew that certain students were in the Labor Youth League, which was controlled by the Communist Party. People were expected to name them when you took the Loyalty Oath. Most people took the oath and simply lied, assuming it was unlikely anyone could prove anything against them. Only the best refused to take the oath as compromising their integrity and thus felt its penalties (see the case of Don Anderson in Chapter 4). Mill points out that there was only one effect of refusing to allow someone to testify in Court unless they believed in God: atheists who were liars testified, while atheists who were truthful were excluded.

Amplifying Mill's case

I will take some of Mill's arguments and add to them. You will recall that there is an implicit distinction between knowledge and right opinion. First, there are those who have debated their way toward their convictions and can give reasons for them and thus have a claim to the best knowledge available at the time. Then there are the holders of right opinion who are fortunate enough to share the conclusions of the knowledge – holders, conclusions that just happen to dominate the general opinion of the time. The latter are bereft of autonomy, of course. They just happen to be lucky in terms of whoever has programed them. They may believe in the same conclusions but these are a dogma based on faith in the sense that they cannot defend them as demonstrable.

As Freud pointed out in *Future of an Illusion* (1927; 1990), dogmatists are always on the verge of launching persecution. They hold something sacred but have no voucher for it except the passionate intensity of their faith. Anyone who disagrees with them is seen as having a false and pernicious faith and threatens the very foundations of their belief. Any dissident threatens to expose *that faith alone is not enough*. Dissidents cry out for suppression. How can they be banished from existence? Not by reason because you have no reasons; therefore they must be banished as heretics. You have a sneaking sense that this is not enough because they may still disagree with you but at least you can shut them up – and no one explicitly questions your faith. Ideally, in the current climate, how heretics "feel" can be changed by sending them to sensitivity sessions which are judged successful only if they at least pretend to agree.

Heretics are likely to accumulate over time. Since your beliefs are dogma they cannot be altered in the light of reason. Knowledgeable people are likely to complicate things, if only through qualifications, and you see these as heresy. The fact that anyone continues to investigate the truth of the dogma can only be seen as a lack of faith – if there are no doubts, why investigate? Dogma moves at a glacial pace and freezes minds. In sum, dogma makes tolerance a sin.

Speak truth to power

On the left, there is a critique stemming from Herbert Marcuse that would smile at my analysis as naïve. Are we interested in what would emerge as truth from a debating society or in the actual accumulation of truth? Society indoctrinates people in a way that biases the debate. Imagine we had a perfect reign of free speech in America. The left is free to say and publish what it wants in its newspapers and conversations. Conservatives, privileged parents, the media, and the government propagandize the audience. When we have a society in which oppressive power has been eliminated, we can have a real debate.

For now, it is perfectly justified to silence the voices of those who support the status quo and bolster the voices of those who are trying to eliminate whatever dehumanizes human beings.

In fact, this analysis is utterly naïve: it assumes the left has already won. The fact that the Romantic left has bullied a number of universities has gone to its head. If the left makes clear that it does not believe in free speech, in the "interim" before the left triumphs, this can only lead the defenders of the status quo to take them at their word. The Communist Party pleading for free speech in America and rationalizing its utter absence in the USSR was not very convincing (of course, the *real* new society would not be like the USSR). If the conservative forces all abandon free speech, the left will find out how quickly the larger society will swat the fly. They would do well to ponder Chapter 4, which details what things were like when civil libertarians among conservatives were few and far between. I want conservatives to ponder it, too, as an antidote against backsliding. Are they really converts to free speech; or are they temporary adherents because of what is happening on many college campuses?

However unequal the debate between left and right, the choice is between a conservative society that allows you to speak and one that uses repression. As Erich Fromm says, the powerless man's only weapon is the truth. No matter who is in power, the best road to truth is to allow your critics to speak and try to refute what they say (or adjust your views if they are correct). Even if everyone recognizes this, and we are united by a concern for attaining as much of the truth as possible, it will not be like a debating society. But history shows that it is the best we can do.

Truth versus other great goods

In teaching Mill, it is important to point out an oddity. He assesses free speech entirely in terms of whether it is productive of truth. As a utilitarian, he ought to defend it as productive of human happiness. In fact all good societies seek at least six great goods: happiness, justice, the pursuit of truth, the creation of beauty, human autonomy, and tolerance (or delight in human diversity). Even within the best society, there will be different balances of the great goods. There are inevitably trade – offs between them: whether the city should spend less on the art gallery (beauty) and more on pensioners (happiness) (see Flynn, 2012c and 2018).

The good society tries to minimize trade – offs by distributing these goods among separate social institutions. The corner pub is mainly devoted to happiness or conviviality, and anyone who would launch a debate about race and IQ just does not understand what a pub is all about – the same for someone who tried to introduce the subject into the annual meeting of a sporting club. The court system has its own peculiar role in seeking justice. The artistic community and its patrons, and the galleries and concerts that make art accessible to the public, promote beauty. Tolerance is much more difficult in that it should be present everywhere and one can only gentle mores in that direction, with the proviso that if tolerance is based on fiction it has a fragile foundation. The pursuit of truth should be the task of a responsible media, but we know how well it performs that role.

The good society designates the university, above all, as its primary institution to pursue truth, with the added role of graduating students who have full autonomy and can seek the truth throughout their lives. Sometimes this conflicts with promoting the general happiness on campus.

Today, the greatest tension is between truth and avoiding speech that may offend some ethnic identity, religious group, or gender. Just as the pursuit of truth should give way to conviviality at the corner pub, so group sensitivity should give way to truth and autonomy at university. In so far as group attachments are reinforced by dogmatic beliefs, insofar as they limit the autonomy of young people to follow their own star against the pressure of group opinion, students *should* become less attached to their groups during university. In 1936, Robert Maynard Hutchins wrote that education frees a person "from the prison – house of his class, race, time, place, background, family, and even his nation" (Levine, 1996, p. 29).

I will be brief about the autonomy of choosing your vocation because here I think group pressure is diminishing. When I was young, there was unrelenting pressure to embrace Catholicism as a badge of Irish patriotism. The determination of religious belief is central to the examined life and must not be compromised. As for vocation, a bright Irish lad was encouraged toward the priesthood or law and away from philosophy (with all of its agnostics and atheists).   Young Jewish Americans had to fight off the push to become a rabbi or doctor. After my (Jewish) mother – in – law met me, she was impressed by my Ph.D. But she added, "You know with his brains, he could have become a real doctor." Blacks are still subject to great pressure. A black artist or singer or novelist is not necessarily a "traitor" when he or she chooses non – racial themes rather than black themes. A black should be free to integrate his or her life with the dominant culture, something parents might feel would benefit their children. This should be a personal choice without recrimination.

More important, let me list some of the things that may upset members of various groups as they become properly educated. I am not saying that all of these things are true, but outstanding scholars have supported them (see particularly the works of Thomas Sowell). They raise important issues and we should be able to assess them for ourselves rather than be censored by group – think.

Blacks: That the race and IQ debate is an evidential question, which like other group differences must allow both genes and environment as possible causes; that the contribution of Egypt and the northern coast of Africa have nothing to do with black Africans south of the Sahara; that black African rulers were deeply complicit in the slave trade; that single – parent homes are not simply a direct effect of slavery because in fact intact black homes were far more common one or two generations ago; that even when black parents are equated with white parents in socio – economic status (SES), there is evidence that black homes are less efficient in encouraging the cognitive skills America values; that black teenage subculture is not just different but causes substandard academic achievement; that affirmative action beyond a certain point is counterproductive; that whites are not by definition racist or blacks by definition non – racist; that "white" social science is necessary to base any program for the enhancement of blacks on a sound social and political analysis of American society.

Since I cannot cover all ethnic groups, I will use my own ethnic group, Irish – Americans, to indicate that not only blacks but also other groups carry into (and sadly carry out of) university baggage of fiction and illusion. The British did not simply use the Great Hunger of the 1840s as a tool for ethnic cleansing or genocide; Queen Victoria's refusal to allow the Turks to provide aid during the Great Hunger was based on vanity not viciousness; that some of those on the list of Irish Martyrs had something to answer for; that anti – Irish prejudice ("no Irish need apply") was more than Anglo – Saxon bias – it had something to do with the fact that Irish history had sent to American a people more likely than average to be violent, lawless, alcoholic, and lacking in skills.

Religious groups: born – again Christians should learn that intelligent design is not an alternative hypothesis to evolution because it puts forward no real hypotheses to be falsified – and it encourages a lot of bad science to try to find "evidence" for the occurrence of Biblical events. Mormons should ask themselves whether the Battle of Cumorah really took place (I am aware of the endless attempts to square it with the lack of archeological evidence). Orthodox Jews should face up to the image of Jehovah in Leviticus where he chastises the Israelites for sparing women and children and advises them on how to melt the resistance of sex slaves. Christians in general should note that Christ referred to the gentiles as "dogs" and that Jewish historians argued that Christ never claimed divinity.

Women should ask: whether the lower wages of American women are really mainly due to gender bias or whether there is evidence for genetic differences between the genders affecting types of intellect and character; whether rape is simply a crime of violence; whether all rape allegations be accepted as factual (black women certainly question the credibility of some white women who claim that black men raped them); whether women really have an alternative to the scientific method; and how far we can get with a program to benefit women without using "male" social science to analyze American society?

American patriots and other patriots have too many myths to take time to exemplify. All Americans should ask whether US policy from Vietnam to the present is really a mix of national interest and good intentions, or whether America can be classified as a "rogue state." Those who believe Israel is blameless should read her new historians on what massacres really took place during its War of Independence; those who see Israel as automatically worthy of extinction should ask why Egypt and Saudi Arabia are effectively Israeli allies.

Choice of the road to truth

However complex the university, it must never lose sight of Mill's fundamental point. Free speech may often blur the truth, but the only alternative is far worse: determining "truth" by a struggle for power, a test of strength, or the ability to inflict the most pain. Might makes truth is just is false as might makes right. The left should closely examine what its dominance on campus actually does to the search for truth. The next chapter will offer the example of Middlebury University. I will argue that the main result of the behavior of the student mob was to make them more ignorant.

A lot of the items of on my list are debatable, and that is the point: would anyone call a graduate an educated person who had not confronted them and had not developed the habit of setting anger aside when they are discussed? I defy anyone to suggest how that could be done without today's students "feeling uncomfortable," or if you prefer, without speech they feel undermines their dignity. A large number of these issues are included in my courses, which range widely. I wonder how long I would last at a typical US university – and I would not even apply to one that had a speech code that that encouraged students to report me for "hate speech." In New Zealand, I have had only one complaint to the dean: four born – again Christians objected to having to read Nietzsche. Neither the dean nor I apologized but gently explained that students ought to read people who disagree with them.

The university as censor

Free speech in society includes *almost* everything that is sayable, however ignorant or infuriating. However, part of the very role of the university is to upgrade uninformed debate to informed debate. Therefore, it always has the role of censor in that the courses it offers do not endorse sheer ignorance as true (ideally). This presents a temptation to be resisted: classifying opinions as ignorant that are not at all ignorant simply because academics or students do not like to hear them. Outside the classroom, the university has no business banishing either ignorant or infuriating debate, however apt the adjectives may be.

The good university offsets whatever harm it may do as a censor in four ways. First, accustoming students and staff to tolerate free debate however disturbing. Second, forcing them to face objections to their own beliefs that they would not normally hear (outside the university). Third, making them realize that you can have knowledge rather than mere opinion only if you can defend your beliefs against all plausible objections that can be put to them. Fourth, giving students the kind of knowledge and intellectual skills they need to be intelligently critical, not only of their own views but also the conventional views they are bombarded with by politicians and the media. Sadly, very few (if any) universities meet these standards, at least in the United States. I will have less to say about the rest of the English – speaking world, but some examples indicate that things are not much better there.

Jason Stanley

First, however, let us hear from voices whose message is contrary to my own. On March 1, 2016, Jason Stanley took part in a debate at Yale on the motion "Free speech is threatened on campus." He was baffled to hear that student protestors are silencing and intimidating people. His philosophy classes include debates about controversial and contentious topics all the time. He concluded that on the Yale campus, these discussions are taking place everywhere: in the dining halls, classrooms, and residential colleges. "I am glad that robust discourse … is taking place on our campuses" (Gonzalez, 2016).

In Chapter 8, I investigate the status of free speech at Yale in detail and will be happy for the reader to compare my account with that of Stanley. The most remarkable thing about Stanley's assertions is that he made them at the time of the great Halloween debate, and that he lists the residential colleges as an area of free debate. Here is a brief summary for now.

(1) Origin of the debate: Erika Christakis was associate master of a Yale residential college called Silliman and her husband Nicholas

Christakis was the master. On October 30, 2015, she sent an email to the residents arguing that Halloween is a time of exuberance and that insensitive costumes (wearing Indian headdresses by non – Indians) should be allowed.

(2) Rules of the debate – **allowable**: Over 740 Yale undergraduates, graduate students, alumni, faculty, and even students from other universities sent an open letter to Christakis telling her that her offensive email invalidated the voices of minority students on campus. She was castigated at a meeting of 350 people in the Afro – American Cultural Center. Rules of the debate – **borderline**: The day after the letter, 100 students confronted Nicholas Christakis, who had said nothing about the costumes, in the courtyard of Silliman College. Their tone was very angry. A student told him that it was his job to create a place of comfort and home, and when he demurred, shouted, "Who the fuck hired you." Rules of the debate – **vicious**: Calls for their dismissal, threatened violence, and violence.

On November 6, 2015, there was a forum on campus on free speech. At 4pm, the academic rights activist Greg Lukianoff said: "Looking at the reaction to Erika Christakis's e – mail, you would have thought someone wiped out an entire Indian village." His words were posted online almost immediately, and at 5:45pm, as the participants left, a crowd of 100 students gathered chanting, "Genocide is not a joke." Several attendees were spat on as they left, and one was told he was a racist. Neither Nicholas nor Erika Christakis taught in the semester following the Halloween controversy. During that semester, students marched on their house, scrawled angry messages in chalk beneath their bedroom window, and shouted insults and epithets. On May 25, 2016, the Christakises resigned from their posts at Silliman College. Yale had a bad conscience about the whole affair. Three years later, Nicholas Christakis (still a professor) was awarded the university's highest faculty honor, the Sterling Professorship

(3) The campus community intimidated: On November 6, 2015, Yale's president Peter Salovey sent an e – mail to all members of the Yale college community that contained not a word about how people should debate with Christakis rather than want to fire her. The body of

QTY	PRODUCT	DEPT	PRICE
1 >	A BOOK TOO RISKY	999000	29.95

	TOTAL SALE	$29.95
>	SALES TAX	$2.47
03780	NET SALE	$32.42

| 1 | CHARGE AMOUNT | $32.42 |

** CUSTOMER COPY *** CUSTOMER COPY **

WEB INTERNET SALES - DRUPAL
A/R CHARGE THE CC SALES
ACCOUNT NUMBER 108943

00001 70-011 LAM 1/15/21 10:26 AM

THANK YOU FOR SHOPPING AT BOOKPEOPLE
THE LARGEST INDIE BOOKSTORE IN TEXAS
PLEASE SAVE RECEIPT FOR RETURNS WITHIN
30 DAYS AND AUTHOR SIGNINGS.
RESTRICTIONS APPLY.
TRAVEL BOOKS MAY BE RETURNED WITHIN 7
DAYS. NO RETURNS ON MAGAZINES, TEST
PREP, CLEARANCE OR MARKDOWN GOODS.

the email actually reinforced the rationale of those who felt that Christakis has committed some great sin. To my mind, it had the tone of a missionary sitting in a pot of boiling water surrounded by cannibals.

Salovey should have said: "The debate between Erika Christakis and the Intercultural Affairs Committee is moderate in content and language and exactly the sort of debate Yale wants. I would no more dream of taking sanctions against her than firing the Committee." To be fair, after the furor died down, his e – mails got better.

The faculty's state of mind was revealed when Professor Douglas Stone drafted a letter of support. He was warned he was putting himself at risk, and relatively few humanities professors signed it. Journalists who interviewed academics found that they were unwilling to be identified, whatever their opinions. As for the students, in April 2017, a survey of 872 undergraduates asked, "How comfortable do you feel about voicing your opinions on issues such as politics, race, religion, and gender?" Only 29 percent of conservatives said that they were comfortable, compared to 74 percent of liberals.

When I was a CORE (Congress of Racial Equality) chairman in the south in 1960 – 1961, I was called a "nigger lover," suffered some violence, some of my friends were intimidated, and I was eventually dismissed from my university post. There was, indeed, more discussion about racial segregation. However, this was not enough to make me welcome the situation as an example of "robust discourse."

Professor Stanley's classes sound wonderful. But has he sampled other classes and reading lists, for example, in Yale's Department of African American Studies or in its program of Women's, Gender, and Sexuality Studies?

Jeremy Waldron

Jeremy Waldron is an eminent scholar whose intelligence and integrity are beyond dispute. In 2012 he published a book, *The Harm in Hate Speech*, in which he described things that cause distress and even fear, particularly among minorities who have suffered historical trauma or systematic exclusion. Waldron endorsed law as an antidote, although he does not much like the term "hate speech" as an alternative to group libel or group defamation. He began with an account of a Muslim man out walking with his two children "on a city street in New Jersey," confronting a sign saying: "Muslims and 9/11! Don't serve them, don't speak to them and don't let them in." McConnell (2012) accused Waldron of never actually saying whether law should forbid this sign, but Waldron clearly sided with the Supreme Court in condemning a racist leaflet. He also cited (with seeming approval) Austria's jailing of the convicted Holocaust denier David Irving.

Naturally we feel for the children, and for the father, and wish they did not have to suffer this indignity. The father should say to them, "there are some people in America that mistakenly believe Muslims have committed all sort of crimes, which of course we have not, and we have powerful allies who are on our side." When Irving visited New Zealand, I and a few others used his absurd contentions to inform people about the dynamics of dictatorships and the details of the Holocaust.

But that aside, for every item added to the list of what counts as group libel, we must compile another list: the list of official truths or falsehoods. As to what might be on it: That no particular ethnic group (or religion) undermines or represents American society or culture; broadly there is a history of Nazi Germany, and perhaps a history of Turkey (remember what they did to the Armenians), and certainly a history of what white Americans did to Indians that is official; that being gay is not a choice and does not arouse God's wrath; that miscegenation is not bad; that there are no significant genetic differences accounting for intelligence that negatively effects blacks or women; and so forth. Those who take the oath of citizenship should be told what it means when they promise "to uphold the law."

Whatever is to be on the list, I do not even want to see it get started. Every possible item it might include removes a subject from the sphere of freely contested debate to the arena of a test of force, a coercive act of the US government. I would far prefer that the oath mirror what the University of Chicago now encourages in its entering students: "when you come here you must tolerate ideas you hate for the sake of open discussion."

As for racial epithets, I see a case for their selective prohibition. They are not, of course, an argued – case for anything, they are simply meant to injure or enrage. Frankly, I do not believe they merit being cited in speech codes, except that students must treat one another with ordinary civility. What campus has students who regularly and publicly use the epithets quite common sixty years ago?

Rare students who find themselves exposed to a racial epithet have a remedy: he or she can simply walk away. If the offender is a roommate, rehousing can be arranged. If anyone shouts epithets at students they happen to meet on campus, they should be told that they are becoming a nuisance and the university will seek a remedy in law. There are plenty of judicial statutes that forbid personal harassment, defined as a course of conduct that annoys, threatens, intimidates, alarms, or puts a person in fear for their safety. In cases of genuine harassment, the university can provide assistance and funds so that wronged students can go to court. I have not found a case where epithets of this sort have come before the courts. But sometimes their language seems ambiguous as to whether habitual use of racial epithets can be called harassment.

University speech codes usually include prohibitions on harassing language. However, at present, they are widely abused to cover any speech that offends students. The real problem is not that such codes should be strengthened with language borrowed from laws against group libel, but how to keep their present language under control. I think that putting such laws in the civil code would be a disaster. I will try to show that the fact that the courts continually refer to "anti – hate speech rhetoric" is welcome. It makes them into an institution that checks the worse tendencies of university speech codes.

The most endangered minority

The most endangered minority on campus is a group Waldron does not mention: those who use reason or science to seek the truth. They have a history of persecution as old as universities themselves, and they are in far more danger of being excluded (and indeed at this very moment are being excluded) from campus than any other minority. Their opponents dominate a number of departments that are sacred cows and have great influence, including, for example, black studies and women's studies. Throughout the university, other humanities and social science departments may pay lip service to science and free debate, but they are riddled with those whose hyper – egalitarian ideology makes them reject a whole range of views as things that simply cannot be true. In America today, what is more likely: that the Ku Klux Klan will get the Civil Rights Act rescinded, that pornographers will put women back into the home, that "family values" proponents will reverse the constitutionality of gay marriage, or that universities will find new ways of repressing freedom of expression?

When the marginalized ask for dignity for themselves, they often resort to anger: "You say you lament the Klan – that is supposed to show you are a progressive! You promote ideas that do 100 times the harm of a Klansman. You hide behind a science that has been defined by white males and a truth that is no more than a political weapon. You are a privileged elite, mainly male, mainly white, and blind to the pleas for dignity made by the less fortunate. The students know who their enemies are. We look forward to the day when you are gone, and we have a well ordered campus free of those whose words and deeds visibly undermine the well – being of our students."

Waldron (2012, pp. 95 – 96) wrote:

> Of course we ought to be able to speak out in favor of our most fundamental commitments. But presenting them as propositions up for grabs in debate – as opposed to settled features of the social environment to which we are visibly and pervasively committed – is exactly what the speech in question aims for. Its implicit message to the members of vulnerable minorities is something like this: 'I know you think you are our equals. But don't be so sure.'

There is a parallel to this on many US campuses today. When speech codes or class "monitors" or dismissals are used against staff based on the *content* of what they say, there is an implicit message to the vulnerable minority who hold unpopular views: "I know you think you are safe, but shut up or we will soon get around to you."

Waldon is referring to extreme cases of group libel, and I do not for a moment think he would approve of campus excesses. He is quite clear that merely taking offense is not enough: a group must perceive that its dignity and peace of mind are threatened. Sadly, that is exactly the language that offended groups use. From the Halloween debate: "your offensive email invalidated the voices of minority students;" "your job is to create a place of comfort and home" for minorities.

I think Waldron underrated the unrelenting pressure in an egalitarian society to expand the sphere of "the features" of the social environment to which we "are all committed" at the expense allowing "anti – egalitarian" propositions to be a legitimate topic of debate. In the past, those beyond the pale (the enemies of a "well – ordered society") ran from non – Christians to atheists to those who criticized sexual mores to those who rejected capitalism as a form of class domination to those whose patriotism did not extend to foolish wars. As Plato said, every society, democracies included, is like a great beast that requires its intellectuals to respond to its mood and wants.

How are the minority who use science to seek the truth to plead for tolerance? To accuse their enemies of being epistemological fools, or of being under the spell of dogmas that endanger the search for truth? The only argument that Waldron seems to allow is to fly in their face: do you *really* believe that your dignity or security is threatened? That is an argument that I am sure to lose. The only argument left is to appeal to Mill's great essay: using the *content* of speech as a criterion to forbid speech opens up a can of worms; far better to use good speech to counter bad speech. Gentle reader, I will ask for your patience. I believe my contentions and examples will take on substance as you read this book. If they do not, then I have no case.

As for the sign Waldron castigates, I do not deny that it might inspire fear. It is horrifying that in 2007, there were 63 reported cases of mosques targeted with threats, vandalism, or arson, five in New York City alone (Coleman, 2007). If things escalate, there might be something close to the anarchy of Nazi Germany. At a certain point, a court might have to ban hateful signs on the basis of a clear and present danger, even though they do not explicitly urge burning Mosques. If there are similar conditions at a university, mosques burned, Muslim students hassled on campus, anti – Muslim rhetoric could be banned by law.

What should we do about the Klan? If I were a university president, I would say: (1) Send someone to distribute your leaflets – I will assign two campus police to protect him; (2) You can put posters on the usual notice boards – campus police will be assigned to put up a replica if it is removed; (3) If you want to burn a cross, the courts have held that it must be in an area in which its presence does imply a direct threat to students (not near hostels, not near clubrooms, etc.); (4) If you want to speak at a campus venue, we will play it by ear. If the cost of policing is going to be huge, we will shift you to a near – by venue and shift the cost to the local police; (5) In effect we will do as much as we can, but as to the content of your material, you must avoid crude racial epithets. In addition, I would tell students in advance what was likely to take place, tell them why, and tell them to simply avoid the presence of the Klan events and material, unless they are curious in which case they are expected to behave.

> **Box 1.** *Free Speech on Campus* by Sigal R. Ben – Porath (2017); *Free Speech on Campus* by Erwin Chemerinsky and Howard Gillman (2017); *We Demand: The University and Student Protests* by Roderick A. Ferguson (2017); *Safe Spaces, Brave Spaces* by John Palfrey (2017); *The Case for Contention* by Jonathan Zimmerman and Emily Robertson (2017). I list them because they all moderated my views to some extent. They are by a school principal, lawyers, various academics, a philosopher, and a vice – chancellor respectively.

Exclusion and happiness

Concerning universities, Waldron's book is less relevant than his recent review essay in the *New York Review of Books* (Waldron, 2018), which address titles in Box 1. In it, Waldron discusses two key questions that affect the balance between free speech on campus and the sensibilities of students: that many students on US campuses have a history of exclusion that renders them sensitive to speech that insults them, labels their group as inferior, or makes them feel that their place on campus is insecure; and that the contention that colleges and universities hold a unique place in the conversation about speech is often unsound.

Blacks as a group certainly have a history of exclusion not only from universities but also from mainstream American life, and no doubt blacks on campus are alert to reminders of their history and find discussion of certain issues (the race and IQ debate, legacies of slavery and slave owners, Confederate commemoration) disturbing. Waldron chastises some authors for the fact that, when the chips are down, they do little to address these concerns. I will address them by encouraging them to favor truth over falsehood. The facts, as I see them, are:

Since black and other minority students are now enrolled in universities in large numbers, it is self – evident no one has excluded *them*. To the contrary, in the United States university admission officers (who are increasingly administrative employees rather than faculty members) are legally permitted to consider minority racial origin as a factor favoring admission even for candidates with lesser academic achievements, and, as the recent Harvard case has shown, to consider race as a factor in limiting enrolment of minority Asian students with strong academic records. The admissions departments generally do this enthusiastically and unapologetically in the name of "diversity," which is held out as a value per se, and to deflect accusations of racism, notably without regard for the discrepancy between minority admission rates and minority graduation rates. As for feeling insecure about their continued presence at universities, they need have no worries. To be expelled, like all other students, they have to be found to have severely unperformed in their studies, committed serious academic dishonesty, engaged in major criminal behavior, or, by very loose standards of evidence that ironically affect minority students disproportionately more frequently than white students, perpetrated sexual harassment. White students, however, suffer the additional risk of being expelled after accusations of violating a speech code, while white professors can be dismissed on the basis of one student's complaint without the option of explaining themselves or apologizing. In the United States, at least, such accusations are generally handled by the same administrative bodies that address sexual harassment allegations (all under the umbrella of "discriminatory harassment") on the basis of low standards of evidence.

There is the question of social or psychological exclusion: some students arrive on campus and feel like "alien corn" – out of place, reluctant to speak up. I am sure that an African – American student in a mainly white university class may initially feel like this – as does a white student in a Black Studies class who would like to challenge what a black has just said – or a man in a Women's Studies class who would like to challenge what a woman has just said – or a student from a poor or rural background surrounded by young city sophisticates. I have found that the primary reason students do not participate in class (assuming the professor has not already stigmatized them as participants) is fear of revealing ignorance. For social, and historical, and economic reasons, blacks are more likely to enter university with a knowledge deficit. If that deficit is erased over four years, this will do far more to enhance participation than the distraction of shouting down speakers, however controversial, who can, in any case simply be ignored. They will begin to walk in the footprints that so many students have left behind them. With growing knowledge they begin to think: "that does not sound right" and speak up, walk away, or lead their lives uninfluenced by opinions with which they may disagree.

The only groups with a real case for exclusion, as the Harvard case shows, are high achieving Americans of East Asian descent, primarily Chinese, Japanese, and Koreans who are excluded on grounds of "diversity," much as Jewish Americans once were. These groups are relatively absent among student protesters, though not entirely: some resent suggestions that they are probably good at mathematics as racial stereotyping or are simply of a leftist political orientation and overlook strong evidence of their own race's potential exclusion for a larger cause.

As for white students, in many cases, the best remedy for their "insecurity" is to stop being so silly. To anticipate a later chapter, Vassar invited a Cornell University law professor to speak on October 25, 2017. His subject, that there is no Constitutional protection against "hate speech," was so threatening that students put together a safety plan: Vassar's library would be a safe place and provide coloring books, zine kits (a toy you can use to create images), markers, and construction paper. Designated students with glow sticks would mark off even safer places. There would also be emotional support teams (Jacobson, 2017).

This kind of pathological hysteria rivals the atmosphere surrounding young women who testified at the Salem witch trials of

1692 (Starkey, 1949) and claimed to be possessed by the devil when confronted by those whom they had accused. It is an extreme case, but it is a common plea that the very presence of certain speakers on campus is threatening. We must ask just what it is that threatens the affronted students and how we can cope with their disordered responses. No student is forced to listen to a visiting lecturer or to read what they have to say; they can refuse or discard a pamphlet after first glance, or move on quickly from a poster on a bulletin board. Imagine that something even more horrible had occurred at Vassar: a full – scale Flynn/Murray debate on race and IQ. Apparently, it is the mere awareness of such an event and its proximity that is disturbing. What if they became aware that such debates took place in Washington and New York – in the corridors of national political power and judicial authority? Do they lack imagination? Even if Murray is not on campus today he is likely *somewhere* giving a talk (Flynn has not yet reached the un – person status of Murray: "un – person" defined as a person so tainted he cannot speak on even the most innocent of topics).

What of the awareness that Murray's books (and Flynn's books) are available in the campus library? What if Murray's *Bell Curve* has been assigned in a large first year course? Then they would *know* that at this moment hundreds of students nearby might actually be reading it. What if, without a trigger warning, they find their roommate is sitting next to them reading it?

You may think this fanciful. But let us recall that in 2008, at Indiana – Purdue University at Indianapolis, a student employee was reading a book on lunch break entitled, *Notre Dame vs. the Klan: How the Fighting Irish Defeated the Ku Klux Klan*. The book was a historical account of a 1924 incident in which a group of University of Notre Dame students fought in the streets *against* members of the Klan. But two coworkers only saw the title and complained. The Affirmative Action Officer determined that the student reading it was guilty of racial harassment because of "openly reading the book related to a historically and racially abhorrent subject." Months later, after the American Civil Liberties Union had intervened and the *Wall Street Journal* publicized the case, he was reinstated with an apology and told that the accusatory letters had been removed from his personnel file (Associated Press, 2008). But the damage to his reputation and general life had been done.

What is to be done about the fact that Murray's books and mine are in the library? Should all "offensive" books be segregated in a safe place, surrounded by warnings so that no one may stumble on them unawares and suffer serious psychological or emotional harm? Students who see the warning signs and feel menaced thereby could then be provided with coloring books, zine kits, markers, and construction paper, until they recover. Or should they simply be removed and burned, as another group of university students did in different circumstances?

As to Waldron's second point, whether "colleges and universities hold a unique place in the conversation about speech," he answers this by raising questions about whether it is the business of the university to teach civics courses to improve the moral quality of its students and prepare them for citizenship. Let us put the question another way. Jeremy Waldron, above all, has learned to control his anger during debate and pursue the truth using a wide range of accumulated knowledge. Do we want to graduate more of him or fewer?

At our university, we all remember him as a student who had serious doubts about the legitimacy of prisons as an institution. Our conversations inevitably led to their effects on the poor and the Maori (New Zealand's indigenous minority). The discussions were wide – ranging and strayed into why Maori tended to commit more crimes, be more prone to family violence, and more likely to underperform at school. I did not accept the thesis that it was purely a matter of lower SES (socio – economic status). I advanced the "dangerous" idea that Maori were less disadvantaged than American blacks because they were more assimilated. For example, they have a much higher rate of marrying outside their race. In the America of today, I have no doubt I would have been hauled before the dean for violating a speech code and sent to sensitivity training or sanctioned in some career – damaging or even career – ending way.

As the reader knows, I answer Waldron's question as follows. Of course, the university has a special mission. Again, it has the special task of upgrading debate in the classroom, pressing the limits of free speech throughout the campus community, and habituating students (and giving them the skills) to ignore emotion in favor of reason as they pursue truth throughout their lives. Waldron is correct that freedom of inquiry in the hard sciences has not suffered much from current campus behavior: their integrity is threatened by something else, namely, the sources of their funding (and government). But a university free merely to pursue vocational training and hard science would betray its mission in a way that used only to be found in totalitarian nations.

About Charles Murray

Waldron (2018, p.1) refers to Charles Murray as coauthor of *The Bell Curve*, "*a discredited study* [italics mine] of the correlation between race and intelligence." No one should label Charles Murray "discredited." *The Bell Curve* shows that Murray has learned the methodology of his trade and that he is mindful of evidence. Ceci and Williams (2018) have listed the responsible scholars who have defended *The Bell Curve*. I would like to see a careful analysis of his book set against the mountain of unwarranted criticism that is tolerated only because it is on the "right" side of race/class/gender debates.

If Murray is discredited, rather than simply being critiqued and sometimes rebutted like any other scholar, then God help the rest of us. Naturally, I think I make fewer mistakes than he does, but I would not bet my life on it. If scholars adopt criteria that cast both of us in the shade methodologically, they have set a standard so high that most of the staff of Black Studies, Woman's Studies, Anthropology, Sociology, Education, and Politics, to name a few, would be decimated (see Chas. 9 – 12) if they, too, were on the wrong side of the political debate. As for my take on the significance of Charles Murray and Middlebury, please go on to the next chapter.

2
Middlebury and my mind

Middlebury is an outstanding liberal arts college. It is ranked in a tie with Swarthmore for fourth place among institutions of its kind. Only 25 percent of its students have an SAT Reading score below 630 (old scale), about the same as students at Cornell University, a major Ivy League University. It is situated in the beautiful Green Mountains of Vermont with a student body described as athletic, artistic, environmentally minded, and sociable. When Charles Murray visited Middlebury on March 2, 2017, he was understandably unprepared for what followed. He was scheduled to give an address entitled "Coming Apart," which summarized his book about increasing social segregation between classes and groups in America.

Murray and Middlebury

The best accounts of what occurred appeared in *Commentary* magazine (Jonathan Marks, 2017), and the local *Daily Mail* (Cheyenne Roundtree, 2017). Prior to Murray's appearance, a letter signed by hundreds of alumni described Murray's invitation to speak as a "threat" to students, and urged cancellation. Middlebury's president Laurie Patton not only refused to cancel the event but spoke prior to Murray's taking the stage. The "very premise of free speech on this campus," she said, "is that a speaker has a right to be heard." She made it clear that protecting a speaker's right to be heard did not entail an endorsement of his views. Bill Burger, vice president of communications, then pointed to Middlebury's Code of Conduct, which forbids "noise or action that disrupts the audience's ability to hear" at community events. Students were told that potential penalties for violating the code included suspension.

As Murray began to speak, students turned their backs on him and chanted, "Who is the enemy? White supremacy;" "Racist, sexist, anti

– gay, Charles Murray, go away;" "Your message is hatred. We cannot tolerate it." Faculty members observed this behavior, but none rose to chastise the students. Murray said that the students radiated rage but what he found most disturbing was a young woman who reminded him of his daughter: her gaze was devoid of hate but had the look of one who felt called upon to do her civic duty. He notes that accusing him of being "anti – gay" was an innovation: presumably it was thrown in to make up the rhyme.

After 25 minutes, Murray was moved to another room to have his talk recorded. After the recording session, when Murray and his interlocutor Professor Allison Stanger left the student center, a group of protesters converged on them. One pulled Prof. Stanger's hair and twisted her neck. She later went to Porter Hospital and was fitted with a neck brace. Public safety officers managed to get Stanger and Murray into their car, but the protestors rocked it, pounded on it, jumped on it, and tried to prevent it from leaving campus. At one point a large traffic sign was thrown in front of the car. Public Safety officers were able, finally, to clear the way to allow the vehicle to leave campus.

Protecting the students

The rallying cry of the protesters was to prevent their university from providing a platform for hate speech. I can attest that Charles Murray is devoid of hate, as much as anyone I know: perhaps the demonstrators knew him better than I do. Others ignore the man and attack his works. On its web page, the Southern Poverty Law Center (SPLC) calls him a white nationalist who "links social inequality to genes . . . based on the work of explicitly racist scientists."

Presumably the organizers of the protest, particularly the staff, concurred with the alumni that Murray was a "threat:" students might hear his talk or read his books and be endangered thereby. Here I wish to introduce a digression about what reading such books did to me, and let the reader judge the kind of thing I was being protected against. I will focus on three "discredited" thinkers that affected me most: Arthur Jensen, Richard Lynn, and Charles Murray. Lynn has never been threatened by violence (to my knowledge) although students at the University of Ulster disrupted his lectures and demanded his dismissal.

Like Murray, he has not escaped condemnation from the Southern Poverty Law Center web page: "For 50 years, Richard Lynn has been at the forefront of scientific racism."

Arthur Jensen I

In 1978, I was writing a book that was eventually published under the title *How to Defend Humane Ideals* (Flynn, 2000). I thought I should include a brief passage dismissing those who thought there was a significant genetic difference between black and white. But I had a vague feeling that there was a scholar who disagreed and I discovered that his name was Arthur Jensen. Naturally, I knew I would have to answer his case to be plausible, and it never occurred to me simply to accept what others said of him. When I read his early books, Jensen (1969, 1972, 1973) had two arguments that troubled me.

The first was that when you equated American blacks and whites for SES (socio – economic status), this did not eliminate the 15 – point IQ gap. At most, allowing for SES and a few minor factors cut it to ten points.

The second was an argument about correlations. Jensen seemed to show that no environmental explanation of the IQ gap was possible. The argument ran as follows: (1) Twin studies (and other kinship studies) show that genes are highly potent in explaining IQ differences between individuals; (2) Indeed, the correlation between environment and IQ is low, at best about 0.33; (3) Which means that there is a one to three ratio between IQ gap explained and environment. Since blacks are one SD below whites for average (IQ (15 IQ points), they would have to be three standard deviations apart for environment.

Then you look at the facts. When you read a Table of Values under a normal curve, you see what *kind* of difference a three SD environmental deficit would amount to – and you find that the necessary black and white environmental gap is far too large to be plausible. At three SDs below the white mean, the average black environment would have to be so bad that only about one – fifth of one percent of whites fell below it or, conversely, that only one – fifth of one percent of blacks are above the average white environment. How could anyone believe such a thing? See Box 2.

> **Box 2.** Worse still, to evade Jensen's point, one might have to posit: either an environmental handicap that afflicted every black to the same degree; or an environmental asset that favored every white – a strange Factor X. I will not address this complication here, but only say that this absurdity was entailed by Jensen's assumption that the same arithmetic was appropriate both within and between groups.

Arthur Jensen II

By 1982, I had read a lot of Wechsler and Stanford – Binet IQ manuals and these all showed that representative samples of Americans had made massive IQ gains over time: 14 IQ points over the 46 years between 1932 and 1978 (Flynn, 1984). A subsequent analysis of data from 14 nations revealed that American gains were representative of most developed nations on all kinds of IQ tests, whether verbal, performance, or culturally reduced tests like Raven's Progressive Matrices (Flynn, 1987). The most striking results were from impeccable samples of 18 year – olds in the Netherlands: they had gained 20 IQ points (1.33 SDs) on Raven's between 1952 and 1982. Aside from its intrinsic interest, this showed that something was the matter with Jensen's arithmetic. If environment and IQ correlated at only 0.33, the environmental gap between the Dutch of 1952 and the Dutch of 1982 had to be four SDs (1.33 SDs of IQ divided by .33 = 4 SDs environment). This was even worse than three SDs: you had to assume that virtually no Dutchman in 1982 (even most of the mentally handicapped) was below the average environment of 1952.

The answer was absurdly simple but took 14 years to be identified (everything looks simple after the event). Identical twins are of the same age, and all of them had been tested at the same age. Therefore, they showed only that environment was "feeble" within a generation. However, Jensen was using that estimate to measure the potency of environment between generations; and a within – generation estimate was totally irrelevant to measuring potency between generations. His argument rests on a fallacy: that when two things correlate or match, one of them disappears.

Let us stay for the moment within a generation where environment is supposed to be feeble. Take my son. He was born with a great aptitude for mathematics. When he was seven, he came to me and said, "there is an infinity of numbers; but there is also an infinity of even numbers, so one kind of infinity has twice as many members as the other." I did not know much mathematics but was good at it. I said, "that means you can actually do arithmetic with different kinds of infinity; if you subtract the infinity of even numbers from the infinity of all numbers, you get the infinity of odd numbers." His teachers immediately saw his promise and gave him extra work. Slowly, the quality of his current environment began to match the quality of his genes. By age 22, he was doing a Ph.D. in mathematics at Trinity College, Cambridge; today he is Professor of Pure Mathematics at New College, Oxford.

Does his case show that environment was impotent? After we recognized his promise, neither his teachers nor I jumped out of a window. We stayed around and played the causal role of making sure that his quality of environment began to match the quality of his genes. Imagine there is a sleigh called "performance" pulled by two horses named "genes" and "environment." By maturity, the environmental horse has learned to follow the gene horse and only the latter need be taken into account to predict performance. But both horses add to the speed of the sleigh: both are potent, it is just that the potency of the environmental horse has been masked by its almost perfect correlation with genes. They are pulling together in the same direction.

Environment is still there, and it is ready and waiting for a situation in which genetic differences are absent. That is the situation between generations. This is because there is no appreciable upgrading of genes from one generation to the next (we do not execute everyone with an IQ below 100 to keep them from reproducing). An improvement in performance has to be explained by enhanced environment between the generations because nothing else is operative. It is as if our sleigh has had the gene horse cut loose and only the environmental horse is left. When that occurs, the environment, no longer masked by its correlation with genes, can show its true potency. The Dutch show how explosive that is: social progress caused a 20 – point IQ gain in only 30 years.

By social progress, I mean that a variety of factors operating between generations trigger IQ gains: smaller families (a lower ratio of adults to children in the home) and the growing practice of hot – housing children's intellectual development (more attention, books, games) means that school can be more demanding. More jobs are cognitively demanding, dictating an explosion in the average number of the years of schooling well into adulthood. Leisure, too, has become more cognitively demanding. Better health and a more active life among the aged works in favor of higher IQ. Jensen's mathematics really begs the question. Over 30 years, it was as if we graduated from one culture to another. If there are cultural differences between two groups that cause a large IQ difference, that is that. We cannot use a formula to conjure those differences away.

Let us return to black and white Americans. Either they belong to the same culture or blacks have a distinct subculture. Either their subculture is different in a way that handicaps them on IQ tests or it is not. The answers to these questions, however politically incorrect, will determine whether genes or environment explain the racial IQ gap. Jensen has, however, given us a lead. To offer cultural differences as an explanation, we will have to do more than cite differences in socio – economic status (SES).

It may seem from the above that an individual's life history is entirely the product of the correlation between genes and environment, and that this leaves no room for human autonomy. We will examine this conclusion in Chapter 15; for now, I will only say that it is mistaken.

Arthur Jensen III

Jensen often complained that the "Flynn effect" (massive IQ gains over time) was thrown at him as a sort of mantra that settled the IQ debate. He was quite right. It is entirely possible that the environmental differences between black and white are not nearly as potent as the environmental differences between generations. To make a real case that blacks are at a profound environmental disadvantage entails the claim that they live in a subculture capable of robbing them of cognitive stimulation. Oddly enough, some of the best evidence that this is so emerges from a critique of another of Jensen's own arguments: his use of the method of correlated vectors (Jensen 1998).

The value of this method is that it shows that the black/white performance gap increases in accordance with the extent to which IQ subtests have a greater "g loading." This is to say that the black/white gap increases the greater the cognitive complexity of the task. As Jensen puts it, this "g pattern" mimics a maturity gap. When you compare ten and twelve – year old whites, the latter (understandably) open up a greater gap the more complex the task. The younger ones do almost as well on the easier items and fall further and further behind on the more challenging ones. This point shook Sandra Scarr, who had always been a strong proponent of genetic equality between black and white Americans: "Black children matched . . . white children two years younger ... The implications of these studies are truly frightening." (Scarr, 1998)

I have offered a rebuttal in three steps, always emphasizing that it does not yet offer the kind of evidence that makes it more than probable. The first step is to show that the g pattern is a product of environment rather than genes. In Germany after World War II, American soldiers fathered either half – black or all – white children. IQ comparisons between these two groups showed that the g – pattern entirely disappeared (Flynn, 2008). In other words, when blacks are raised in America's black subculture, they fall farther behind whites the more complex or g – loaded the subtests. But when blacks were raised in Germany, where there was no black subculture, and where they were raised simply as dark – skinned Germans, they did not fall behind. This poses a hypothesis: where a black subculture exists, it makes lesser demands in terms of cognitive complexity than white subculture makes on whites. In passing, it is not easy to disentangling environmental and genetic factors. Half – black girls did better than half – black boys and one can posit that having a black biological father was an advantage for girls but a disadvantage for boys (Loehlin, et. al., 1975, p. 129).

The second step addresses Jensen's point that equating black and white for SES does not eliminate the racial IQ gap. Elsie Moore (1986) studied a pool of 46 adoptees, all of them black. Half were raised by white parents of high SES and half were raised by black parents who equalled the whites for SES. The blacks reared by the whites had an advantage of 13.5 IQ points by age 8.5. Moore also found that maternal attitudes toward the child's problem – solving skills were overwhelmingly positive among white mothers but negative among black mothers. Whatever cultural differences cause the racial IQ gap, they are far subtler than SES differences. Since Moore's study, now a generation in the past, improved black parenting practices may have caused most of the recent black IQ gains on whites: 5.5 points between 1972 and 2002 (Dickens & Flynn, 2006).

The third step is to provide an analysis of black American subculture that suggests how each succeeding environment blacks encounter offers less cognitive stimulation than each successive white environment (Flynn, 2008). The assertion that the black/white IQ gap is 15 points is an over – simplification. By 2002, the gap both varied and rose with age. With whites set at 100, the black IQ values were: 99.0 at 9 months (these tests are crude: using or not using a rod to pull toys toward you); 95.4 at 4 years; 92.4 at 9 years; 89.4 at 14 years; 86.4 at 19 years; 83.4 at 24 years.

Each successive black environment offers less cognitive stimulation than each successive white environment. Elsie Moore (if still valid) takes us to almost age nine. Even high SES black parents have a negative response to problem solving. To this, we must add that over 70 percent of black children are being raised in single – parent homes, often below the poverty line. They are mainly exposed to child – to – child speech rather than hearing adult – to – adult speech. Some of these black mothers ration their own verbal interaction: why talk to him if he can't talk back. Many blacks then go into majority – black schools where initial skills and standards and expectations are lower than in majority – white schools. Even before they are teens, they encounter black teenage subculture, which tends to emphasize dressing sharp and sexual prowess and ostracize academic achievement. Between age 18 and 24, a majority of women recommence the cycle of isolated single – parenthood. When I visited black homes for a civil rights group operating in Chicago, I met a woman who lived ten blocks from Lake Michigan but had never seen the

Lake. As for the young men, a higher percentage of them are convicted of felonies than attend college.

Where an overseas black culture dominates (different from that usual in America), the results are sometimes surprising. In 2010, there were 260,000 Nigerians in the US, which was 0.75 percent of the black population. Yet in 2013, 20 to 25 percent of the 120 black students at Harvard Business School were Nigerians. Nearly 25 percent of Nigerian households have incomes exceeding $100,000 (Sowell, 2015). These immigrants are of course from an elite group within Nigeria. However, note how much better they fare than the blacks who are the most elite of those produced by black American subculture (those of elite SES). These data are not decisive: Nigerian Americans may be fixated on Harvard Business School while black Americans in general aspire to a wider range of professions and universities.

Richard Lynn I

We now turn to Richard Lynn, who offered an evolutionary scenario called the "ice – ages hypothesis" (Lynn, 1987). It suggests that the IQ differences between the races must be genetic in origin. Modern man (*homo sapiens*) evolved in Africa, and migrated in the remote past to populate Europe and Asia. During the last Ice Age, some 20,000 years ago, those who remained in Africa enjoyed an environment that remained tropical or temperate and presented no new problems of survival. They are the ancestors of today's blacks. Those who left found themselves either north of the Alps or north of the Himalayas. The new conditions were far more rigorous and put a premium on intelligence to survive and reproduce. However, conditions on the Tibetan plateau were significantly more rigorous than in Northern Europe; and natural selection enhanced the intelligence of those who evolved into East Asians (those who eventually populated Japan, Korea, and China) more than it did those who evolved into Caucasians.

Thus we have a genetic hierarchy for the races which runs from: blacks – mean IQ of about 70 in Africa; blacks – mean IQ of 85 in America (higher than Africa thanks to interbreeding with Caucasians and a better environment); whites – mean IQ of 100; East Asians – mean IQ of perhaps 105. There are a number of problems with this scenario, including for example, identifying just where the ancestors of Koreans and Japanese were during the last Ice Age. But it generates predictions that we can test against data from modern China and from Chinese – Americans.

The Chinese are really two distinct groups, one of which originally settled north of the Yangzi River and the other south of the Yangzi. The two have intermixed but genetic markers show whose genes are most prominent: Southern genes are relatively absent in the North and become dominant as ones goes South, particularly to Southeast provinces like Guangdong. While the Northern Chinese may well have been north of the Himalayas during the last Ice Age, the Southern Chinese took a coastal route from Africa to China. They went along the Southern coast of the Middle East, India, and Southeast Asia before they arrived at the Yangzi. They never were subject to extreme cold and therefore, we have a firm prediction: the mean IQ of Chinese should drop as we go from North to South.

The island republic of Singapore is a city – state. A large majority of its people are Chinese from Guangdong, the most southeast of China's provinces. According to Lynn, Singapore has a mean IQ of 108, but among its Chinese population, the mean IQ is 114, compared to 105 in mainland China. We now have an IQ map of China proper, which shows no tendency for mean IQ to fall as we go from North to South (Flynn, 2012a, pp. 52 – 53).

Many have pointed to the outstanding achievements of Chinese – Americans as evidence of superior genes. By the 1980s, young people whose parents had come from East Asia comprised about two percent of the population, but 14 percent of students at Harvard, 16 percent at Stanford, 20 percent at MIT, 21 percent at Cal Tech, and 25 percent at Berkeley. Flynn (1991) analyzed the class that graduated from high school in 1966. During their senior year, the Coleman Report confirmed that they had no higher IQs than their white counterparts. However, they could concede whites 4.5 IQ points and match them on the SAT, and concede them almost seven IQ points and match them for high school grades. This meant that they could secure entry to the same universities as whites despite lower IQs. In the fall of 1966, Chinese entering Berkeley had an IQ threshold seven points lower than whites.

Their lower IQ threshold partially explains why they were vastly overrepresented at universities. In addition, 78 percent of those who could qualify actually went, while among whites it was only 60 percent. In other words, it was not higher IQ scores but family sociology that explains the remarkable academic achievements of Chinese – Americans students. Their parents create children atypical of even white society; that is, children who accept cognitive challenge more readily and have an extraordinary passion for educational excellence.

The best data about the offspring of the class of 1966 comes from the class of 1990. As young children, at an age when family environment is potent, they have a mean IQ of 108.6. As family influence fades, however, they fall to 104 at age 10.5 and to 103 at age 18 (Flynn, 2007, p. 121). Thanks to the achievements of their parents, the class of 1990 came from homes high in occupational status. The fact that Chinese – Americans average three IQ points above white Americans is a good measure of the effects of their distinctive subculture.

I am not claiming that this settles the question of whether Chinese have superior genes for IQ: the best verdict about East Asian genetic superiority is to say that it is unproven. I believe I have debunked one evolutionary scenario, but others may be forthcoming. I will only say that I am suspicious of these because none of them can go back and really evaluate environment and mating patterns.

Given free rein, I can supply an evolutionary scenario for almost any pattern of current IQ scores. If blacks had a mean IQ above other races, I could posit, for example, that they benefited from exposure to the most rigorous environmental conditions possible, namely, competition from other people. Thanks to greater population pressures on resources, blacks would have benefited more from this than any of those who left, at least for a long time. Those who left eventually became Europeans and East Asians. Let anthropologists rather than psychologists come forward with something that can really be evidenced, but for our purposes the verdict is still out.

Richard Lynn II

Richard Lynn argues that there is a genetic IQ gap between men and women that evidences itself primarily after the age of 14 (Lynn & Irving, 2004). His most impressive evidence consists of an exhaustive study of university students. Men do have an almost three – point IQ advantage at universities (ranging from America to Canada to Spain to South Africa). However, I have shown that this advantage is due to the fact that the university men are a more elite sample. These results are entirely predictable if you assume that the genders have equal IQ in the general population, with the female IQ threshold for university at about 96 and the male threshold 100. Just as the as Chinese – Americans can spot whites seven IQ points and match them for qualifying for university, women can spot men four or five points.

Why do males need a four – point IQ advantage to match females for university eligibility? This seems to be because male secondary school subculture is less educationally efficient than the female (Flynn, 2012a, pp. 141 – 157). Boys get 70 percent of the Ds and Fs and girls get 60 percent of the As. In America, about 80 percent of high – school dropouts are boys. The pattern is similar in the UK, Ireland, Scandinavia, Australia, New Zealand, and Canada. The American Nation's Report Card shows that the median for girls' reading was at the 67th percentile of the boys' curve (writing was at the 75th percentile). I had never realized how badly boys react to high school, and how many of them are discouraged from going to university, but this gap is now common knowledge.

Richard Lynn III

Lynn (2002a) asserts that the fact that black American women have a more negative attitude toward marriage is a sign of psychosis. In fact, their attitudes are not symptoms of mental illness but recognition of their social circumstances. We may see their plight as a collection of "personal problems," but that says more about us than about them. For every 100 American non – Hispanic white women of marriageable age, there are 86 promising spouses. For every 100 Hispanic women, there are 96 promising spouses, thanks to a huge influx of males from South

America. For every 100 black women, there are 57 promising spouses, which is to say that almost half of them must either go childless or have a child by a man unpromising as a permanent partner (Flynn, 2008, pp. 44 – 46). There are only 57 promising spouses because, compared to whites, there are an extra 21 black men who are dead, in jail, or missing (one million black men are so alienated that no governmental agency registers their existence). A similar number cannot find or hold a steady job (Flynn, 2008, pp.49 – 50; Wachter & Freeman, 1999), and one – third of African – American males have been, currently are, or likely will be incarcerated.

The dilemma of black women is also the product of limited racial intermarriage. In 1900, when, for example, Irish – American women found large numbers of Irish – American males dysfunctional, they could easily marry males from other white ethnic groups without much difficulty, especially if they were Eastern or Southern European Catholics. The fact that they could "marry out" of Irish – American life gave them a huge pool of promising partners. Black women are trapped by the relative rareness of interracial marriage, while black men are 2.5 times more likely to marry a woman of another race. (Flynn, 2008)

There is no ready solution. African – American women are given lectures about responsibility and castigated for bearing children out of wedlock, as if their social circumstances were identical to those of white women. They have been advised "not to lie down with any fool," as if there were enough non – fools to go around. The fact that black American women have a more negative attitude toward marriage is not a sign of psychosis. It is a realistic appraisal of the difficult marriage market they face.

Charles Murray I

In *The Bell Curve*, Charles Murray and Richard Herrnstein (1994, p. 506) claim that racial prejudice is on the wane, which poses the question: if there were no racial bias in America, would there be a case for affirmative action to redress blacks for disadvantages that seem to be increasingly historic? I believe market choices disadvantage blacks in many areas, unless people are willing to sacrifice self – interest in a deep commitment to justice

Take a widow who rents a room to supplement her pension. Two possible tenants come to her door: a young black male and a young Korean – American female. One – third of young black adult males have been convicted of a felony. He may be into drugs or crime or loud music, unemployed, and unreliable in paying rent. The Korea – American female looks a safe bet, likely to be quiet, respectable, and dependable. The key market consideration is the cost of information. The landlady has only statistical information about groups but the cost of that is nil: the black's group membership is evident from his black skin. To get personal information, she would have to hire a private detective or pay the fees of some screening or credit agency. Rather than pay a sizable cost, it is better to play the odds: why take a one in three chance of a disaster? She may bitterly regret using group membership as a criterion, but she needs the money and wants to avoid hassle.

That this is not a question of simple racial bias is signaled by the fact that black landlords prefer white tenants (Flynn, 2008, pp. 112 – 128). Additionally, black – owned or managed banks prefer to loan to whites in the belief that they are more likely to make their mortgage payments, have the know – how for small business, and possess assets that can serve as collateral. When jobs are advertised, employers see race as a reliable signal of an applicant's skills, motivation, and attitudes toward authority. Bertrand and Mullainathan (2004) sent 5,000 resumes randomly assigned to either white or black sounding names ("Emily" and "Greg" versus "Lakisha" and "Jamal") to 1,250 employers who had placed help – wanted ads. The white names received 50 percent more callbacks. Indeed, white applicants with average skills got many more callbacks than highly skilled black applicants; while high quality black resumes got no more responses than average black resumes. Human resources managers consulted beforehand were stunned. They believed that the results would reflect employers hungry for qualified minority applicants and aggressively seeking diversity. But they did not.

Location penalizes blacks. Stores in high – crime areas pass on the costs of pilfering and security measures: more in – store security, more grates over windows, more sophisticated alarm systems, and so forth. The police are more active and aggressive in such areas: at least until recently, they could search potential suspects without a warrant, and were far more likely to do so when confronting black males in inner cities than elderly white females in the suburbs. The police have their own profile of what groups are likely to be criminal: between 1941 and 1994, 23 black police working undercover were shot by their white colleagues in New York City alone (Charles & Coleman, 1995), but no undercover white policemen were shot.

Judges and juries have their own forms of profiling. Eberhardt, et. al. (2006) divided black males convicted of murder into two groups: one group of 44 murderers whose victims had been white, and a second group of 308 murderers whose victims had been black. While 41 percent of the former received death sentences, this was true for only 27 percent of the latter. When the photos of the defendants were ranked from most to least stereotypically black in appearance, records showed that appearance made no difference in cases where the victim was black. But when the victim was white, it made a big difference. Even after factors like mitigating or aggravating circumstances, the severity of the murder, and the defendant's SES were matched, the half of the distribution classed as most "black" received a death sentence 57.5 percent of the time. Black males were 2.4 – times more likely to get the death sentence if they look very black and happen to murder a white (Flynn, 2008, pp. 112 – 128).

I will not enter here into the detail of what negative consequences may attend affirmative action. But one stands out: the chance that a white from a poor background is disadvantaged in favor of a black from a high SES background. No one raised this objection about veteran's preference. After World War II, America decided to compensate over ten million veterans with preferential access to civil service jobs and targeted benefits, ranging from subsidized education and health care to pensions, special hospitals, and retirement homes. Veterans often benefited at the expense of non – veterans who were more disadvantaged: a Boston Brahmin who had a cushy job in army supply could do better than a Polish – American who spent the war in Gary, Indiana working in a dangerous mill. The cost of getting that sort of information about individual differences would include unacceptable invasions of privacy, enormous difficulties in securing testimony and assessing its reliability and relevance, and huge expenditures in time and money.

To burden affirmative action with collecting information about individual differences would sink it because the relevant information carries the highest cost imaginable. The real difference between veteran's preferences and affirmative action is that America really did want to confer a group benefit on veterans, and America is ambivalent about conferring a group benefit on groups defined by race. This ambivalence is striking when we reflect on why blacks need compensation. The very essence of racial profiling is to confer a group benefit on whites while ignoring individual differences among blacks. This amounts to nothing less than a systemic affirmative action program that gives whites special access to loans, housing, jobs, an advantageous marriage market, walking the streets without harassment, and getting a fair jury trail. Whites do not think of this as special access because it is only special compared to what blacks get.

Charles Murray II

However, the real challenge of *The Bell Curve* has rarely been addressed. What it says about class is far more disturbing than what it says about race. And the most disturbing thing it says about class is contained in "the meritocracy thesis."

The meritocracy thesis purports to demonstrate that humane – egalitarian ideals self – destruct in practice. (1) Assume we make progress toward the equalization of environments – to the degree that occurs, all remaining talent differences between people will be due to differences in genes for talent; (2) Assume we make progress toward abolition of privilege – to the degree that occurs, there will be a social mobility that brings all of the good genes to the top and allows all bad genes to sink to the bottom; (3) Therefore, the upper classes will become a genetic elite whose children inherit their status because of superior merit, while the lower classes become a self – perpetuating genetic dump, too stupid to be of use in the modern world, an underclass that is underemployed, prone to criminality, and ravaged by social problems.

The meritocracy thesis generates a prediction. If the children of the upper classes (thanks to better and better genes) are becoming more eligible for high status, and the children of the lower classes (thanks to worse and worse genes) are becoming less eligible for anything but low status, we should detect a trend. The class IQ gap, the gap between the children of the top third in occupational status and the children of the bottom third in occupational status, should widen over time. I tested this hypothesis against evidence for US children aged six to 16 and found no such trend. The class IQ gap had been remarkably stable from 1932 to 1989; indeed, it may have diminished slightly from twelve IQ points to ten or eleven.

However, this kind of evidential refutation of the meritocracy thesis leaves its core untouched. The obvious rebuttal suggests that if the genes/merit gap between the upper and lower classes has not expanded, this merely shows that there has been no trend toward the erosion of privilege and environmental inequality. The only reason that egalitarian ideals have not produced an anti – egalitarian nightmare is because efforts to promote social equality have failed. Advocates of equality must pray for eternal failure. If their idea did succeed in putting their organizing principles to work, their ideals would self – destruct in practice.

Whatever ideal the thousands that laid down their lives for social reform or the defense of the republic may have had, it was not a class system frozen into a caste system by a genetic inequality that is enhanced rather than checked by every step toward social justice.

Charles Murray III

Recently, I sought better evidence to test the meritocracy thesis. The thesis's core prediction is that if we compare societies according to the extent to which they have equalized environments, those that have done the most will show lower social mobility than those that have done the least. In other words, in the egalitarian nations, over a few generations, genes will have become closely aligned with class; and most people will be fixed from one generation to another by their inherited genetic quality – no good genes left in the lower class to give your children a chance to rise to the middle class.

Wilkinson and Pickett (2009) analysed eight developed countries and found a strong relationship between high social inequality and low social mobility. Compared to Canada, Denmark, Finland, Sweden, Norway, Germany, and the UK, the US had both the highest economic inequality and lowest economic mobility. Corak and Miles (2006) studied nine developed countries. In the US, the average son "inherited" 50 percent of his father's income advantage/disadvantage (how far his father's income was above or below the average). In Canada, Finland, Norway, and Denmark, the son inherited only 19, 18, 17, and 15 percent of his father's income advantage/disadvantage, respectively

These data raise an important question: why do equalizing environments not lift all the good genes to the top of the income scale? Assume that we have three hierarchies: (1) a genes for IQ hierarchy; (2) an income hierarchy; and (3) an autonomy hierarchy that ranks each person in terms of the extent to which he or she has the power to plan life as desired.

If you upgrade every person's environment by rendering him or her more secure, there will be an enormous gain in the autonomy hierarchy. Freed from worry about providing for children, obtaining medical care, avoiding unemployment, and enjoying a decent old age, one is free from trying to shake the last dollar out of the money tree. Without facing deprivation, one can choose to be a novelist, live off a pension or investments, or settle for a desirable part – time job that pays a lesser income but provides personal fulfimment. One can become an academic rather than a corporate lawyer or remain a schoolteacher rather than stress about becoming a school administrator. One can be a poet rather than run the family's boring hairpin factory. In other words, one can choose to do what one feels would develop one's self and contribute to society the most.

Otherwise, it is natural to choose whatever will realize a maximum income. If everyone did that, the greater autonomy argument suggests that people will use what intelligence they have to rank themselves so that the IQ and income hierarchies will coincide. But this outcome ultimate depends on social and cultural factors. A majority of Americans say they would replace rewarding work for a job that pays twice as much; a majority of Finns say no. Yet great variety can exist within a society. Many Americans are turning their society's affluence toward pursuits that give them pleasure at considerable financial sacrifice. Wanting to run a marathon under three hours may mean downgrading from a full – time job to a part – time job and spending a lot on travel to get to races. An American friend of mine wrote encyclopedia entries, a distraction from his work as a scholar, because he needed more money to get his children's teeth fixed. After he obtained adequate dental care, he devoted time writing a book that clarifies the problem of scientific realism, a more intellectually rewarding but financially dubious proposition.

There is also a causal relationship between materialism and equalizing environments that the meritocracy thesis ignores. It assumes that everyone loves money; otherwise greater autonomy would not lead to meritocracy. It assumes that money – obsessed people are so obsessed with fairness that they will transfer income (pay progressive income tax) to give everyone equality of environment. I do not believe the combination of money love and fairness love is a common trait. While there are of course exceptions, in a materialist society the affluent are usually willing to take advantage of every inequality from which they or their children benefit. Plenty of American Democrats prefer to send their children to expensive private schools and elite universities.

Scandinavian societies are often cited as models in which humane – egalitarian ideals can function without a darker side. They substitute three optimistic propositions in place of those of the meritocracy thesis: 1. When a society eliminates bad environments (poverty, no education, no medical care, no insecurity in old age) as likely fates – and 2. Subsidizes worthwhile non – profit activities (art, sport, carpentry, etc.); 3. This will give everyone an opportunity to develop talents and interests without regard to how much money they would engender and thereby weaken the correlation between SES and merit.

The real lesson is that materialism and humane ideals can be irreconcilable enemies, and that choosing one can drain the substance out of the other. It is the story Aristotle told when he contrasted Athens with

Carthage. Carthage had mercantile values and produced no great sculpture, plays, art and worst of all, little philosophy. They were, however, happy to pay to be consumers of these creative benefits. Athenians (at least leisured ones) used their autonomy to do all these things, even though they knew that philosophy did not pay.

Fate worse than death

Reading Jensen, Lynn, and Murray offers significant dividends: a plausible case that genetic differences between the major races are unlikely to confer an advantage or a handicap for desirable personal traits; a far better understanding of black America; a method that sheds light on personal development and leaves room for personal autonomy; an understanding of how differently male and female respond to formal education; a case that genetic differences between the genders seem cognitively trivial; a somewhat better understanding of the Chinese both at home and in America; a case for affirmative action that does not depend on racial bias; and, most of all, a better understanding of the dynamics of a truly humane and egalitarian society.

This is the sad fate from which the activist mob at Middlebury wanted to save themselves and their classmates. If I had not read these "discredited" scholars, I would still have a half – educated mind dominated by passions about race, gender, and class and not much else. What about the banned thinkers? Now that I have critiqued their views, why should they still be tolerated? It was once allowable for them to disagree with me, but to refuse to recant now is to promote "discredited" views. Oddly, each of these thinkers found a range of reasons to continue to disagree. The fact that they are participants in debate is all they need to be tolerated. They do not need to do what almost no one does, simply give in and admit that the search for truth is over and that Professor Flynn has had the last word.

What kind of knowledge?

The mob at Middlebury was something more than a mob. You can have (at least tentative) knowledge that something is true only if you have falsified the evidence and arguments that can be put against it. It is almost certainly the case that not one student in the mob that assaulted

Murray had even begun to perform that task. They were not only a mob but they were an *ignorant* mob, devoid of knowledge about the very opinions they wanted to declare as beyond debate.

Anyone who aspires to knowledge must conduct an interior dialogue in which they subject their opinions to every plausible thing that can be said against them. But when the passions are aroused, all of us have difficulty in putting as forcibly as possible the case for something we do not want to be true. The interior dialogue rarely substitutes for a real debate with those who believe in the arguments they offer.

When confronted by Jensen, Lynn, and Murray, I felt truly tested, and even attempted to strengthen their arguments by eliminating tangential flaws. After *Race, IQ, and Jensen* (1980) appeared, Jensen wrote me that he had thought of writing a respectable critique of his position under a pseudonym but that I had saved him the trouble. If these three thinkers had not existed, they would have to have been invented, for their data existed objectively of their analysis. Despite my argument, I do not base my case on the fact that their conclusions were interestingly mistaken. If they are correct and I am wrong, their contribution is all the more essential.

I do not mean to suggest that they were at one: Jensen never agreed with Lynn about gender. Murray has been careful to describe Jensen's case about blacks as possible rather than true. I have never detected any arbitrary bias in any of them. All of them argue that the desirable traits of groups overlap to such a great degree that ideally everyone should be judged as an individual. I do not think that is possible when market decisions are made. But that is not the fault of their books. It is the outcome of using group membership to maximize chances of a profit (recall the landlady with one room to rent). It will occur as long as any group goes on showing the behavior that any alienated group must.

What kind of right opinion?

At this point, it is time to acknowledge that it would be unrealistic to hope that university students could ascend to the status of knowledge about the issues raised by genes versus environment. Imagine them trying to duplicate what I have learned over the last 30 years. They would have to have a course devoted to the subject, which few would elect to take, and which is unlikely to be offered in most universities for political or ideological reasons.

In the current climate, it is better that they have right opinion rather than wrong opinion. Right opinion is always an imperfect copy of the truth; but it is a set of maxims about which people feel deeply and which at least predispose them to act rightly in most cases. On that level what would we prefer: a felt response that makes students suspicious of claims that there are significant genetic differences between the races; or a felt response that makes them susceptible to genetic differentiation? I would easily prefer the former to the latter. But it should be accompanied by a visceral response that favors free speech and allows for expression of the opposing view. It is easier to understand Mill's case for free speech than the race and IQ debate. Nevertheless, only some students will read *On Liberty* and attain knowledge about this issue. But the others can have right opinion: a strong feeling that it is wrong to shut someone up, an emotional response of "let him talk."

What about the academic staff at Middlebury? Some students delight in defying "authority" but many will be deterred by a united front of condemnation by their lecturers. Even among the staff, there will be few who know much about the complexity of the race and IQ debate or about Charles Murray. But the existence of those few, if they can speak up without facing opprobrium, may be crucial in staff conversation. And there is no excuse for all staff not understanding the case for free speech, so that no one is mouthing platitudes about "but free speech should not protect a speaker who is a spokesperson for a racism." Not that anyone could think of Charles Murray as such. But they should know that even the speech of a Nazi orator is privileged and should be countered by words (or silence) rather than intimidation and violence.

The staff should tell their students that knowledge is based on free discourse and that the university should set an example. The staff should accuse their students of the ultimate wickedness: perverting the quest for truth into a contest of strength. The mob showed they could use force more effectively than Charles Murray, and that is all they showed. But most important of all, how can students develop a visceral reaction against curtailing free speech, a reaction potent enough to counter their passions about race – unless they actually see that the academics do the same, rather than just defending free speech in the abstract.

At Middlebury, do they actually see staff who dare say there is a genetic component in the black – white IQ gap or in the female – male mathematics gap; and that there are certain features of black subculture that damage blacks and should be altered? If staff impose self – censorship and cannot resist their own passions about race, gender, subculture, why should the students? You may get the students to tolerate Charles Murray on campus but they are not being bathed in the atmosphere of a free speech university. The staff must demonstrate that they themselves do not take refuge in the mind – destroying maxim "anything that might please a racist cannot be true."

I must address a question I am often asked: "It is fine for you to treat the racial IQ gap as an evidential issue to be investigated. You have reached conclusions on the side of the angels: that the gap is essentially environmental. But what if you had found that there is a genetic component, perhaps one greater than that claimed by Jensen? How would you feel then?" The answer is that I would feel sad. But I do not want to seek my humane ideals in a fictitious dream world devoid of evidence. I want to know every facet of reality so that I can make my ideals relevant by designing policies that will work.

There will never be a reason for me to abandon the ideal that all people should have an opportunity to share in the good life as far as possible. Nothing I did in the American South advocating equal civil rights would seem less necessary. I would still favor wealth transfers from the rich to the poor. The case for affirmative action would still stand so long as the free market penalizes people for their group membership. I would still investigate whether the black subculture poses an environmental handicap when blacks confront IQ tests or educational tasks.

Middlebury and my mind

Middlebury has taken some steps against the student mob. It disciplined 67 students who broke its rules requiring that visiting speakers be treated with courtesy. Thus far, no student has been expelled. The worst offenders received permanent marks on their record (Saul,

2017). Eighty academic staff, including some without tenure, signed a statement in favor of free speech and condemned the notion that controversial points of view are a kind of psychological violence that must be suppressed. Professor Matthew Dickinson spoke for them when he said, "we should be looking more broadly at the institution and whether we taught these students properly" (Henninger, 2017). Clearly those who signed wanted to set an example of free speech by discussion of fundamental issues about race.

But what about educating their colleagues? How many of them share the values of the student mob? I often wonder how these people can live with themselves. How do they *know* that all races on average have equal genes for intelligence? Were they like Saint Paul, struck from their horse by God with a revelation to that effect? I have never met one who could make an evidentiary case for what they believe. Don't any of them want to *understand* how a man as brilliant as Jensen could demur? Don't any of them want to *feel confident* that they can answer his arguments logicially and with evidence? Sadly, we know what kind of staff a lot of students want: dogmatic liberals with good "feelings" about racial equality and no sophistication of intellect. I am happy not to count myself as being among their number.

Part 2
What others do to academics

3
The era of conservative oppression

From the late nineteenth century up to 1965, it was mainly conservatives that attempted to purge American universities. They held dogmas based on faith rather than reason and celebrated the status quo. Insofar as they used oppression as a weapon, they became enemies of free speech.

To defend the status quo against critics was difficult because so much of what went on was almost impossible to defend: discriminatory Jim Crow laws, massacring workers, hunting down union organizers, the excesses of the leisure class, preventable poverty, Christian fundamentalism, unjust wars, unequal treatment of women, the Horatio Alger myth, corruption, and above all, a stultifying lifestyle.

Killing union organizers continued into the 1930s and killing civil rights workers and leaders was a feature of the 1960s. When motoring in the 1950s, I encountered small town road signs that caught the mood: "Boost don't knock." There were also a few signs left telling blacks to get out of town by dark or face arrest or worse. One sign in Anna, Illinois warned: "Nigger, don't let the sun go down on you." The town's name stood reputedly stood for "Ain't No Niggers Allowed" (see Flynn, 2016c, p. 12). There were many "Speed Limit 20 mph" signs, often barely visible, so the town could profit from fines paid by "outsiders" travelling through.

No one could target all critics of the status quo without declaring war on much of urban American. But critics could target the most vulnerable, socialists, atheists, and "the disloyal," particularly during periods of wartime hysteria or intense Cold War threat. As with all crusades based on dogma, outward conformity was not enough – who knew what those with unacceptable thoughts were up to?

The concept of academic freedom

Those who tried to protect the universities slowly developed the concept of academic freedom. The concept is still contested, so I will make my own version clear, with reference both to the individual academic and the status of the university. I speak only of public universities and those private ones whose mission statement is non – sectarian (as distinct from institutions who warn students that they must abide by a particular religion or code). Two trade – offs underlie my thoughts.

First, the task of a university is to upgrade the untutored debate that exists beyond its borders without circumscribing debate too much. There is a tension here: any attempt to upgrade debate by discouraging opinions that no rational person would hold offers a temptation to discourage opinions on arbitrary grounds. What one is free to do in class and what qualifies as scholarly research is narrower than other behavior. You can preach the message that the earth is flat on campus or be advisor of a student group that does so, or invite speakers who do so, but you cannot inject it into your physics class or get much credit for publishing it. But it is up to the university to make these judgments, not outsiders who have no special expertise is assessing truth. You must treat students with courtesy and respect. This raises the whole issue of speech that might discomfit them either in or out of class. I will argue that this must always take second place to free speech.

Second, the university as a whole must practice political neutrality in order to secure non – interference. As a university, it must not advocate how to vote, what political party to belong to, or what partisan opinions one should hold. It can, of course, weigh in as a lobby group to petition governments for more money, oppose legislation limiting academic freedom, and so forth. No monies should be accepted that violate academic values in supporting research that, for example, gives a donor the power to forbid publications or misrepresent what is discovered.

When does a member of the university behave in a way that compromises political neutrality? When engaging in public debate (on campus or off, whether in speech or writing), every academic should be free to exercise the rights of a citizen. But he or she should make clear that the opinions are personal (and not, for example, use university stationery or affiliation). It may be prudent for a university's president or vice – chancellor to be more circumspect than a lecturer (did Larry Summers make a mistake when, as president of Harvard, he expressed his views on gender?). Signing petitions can be a problem but usually these are prefaced with a statement that professional titles are listed only as a means of identification and not to imply that one is a spokesperson.

Left – wing domination

What if the universities become dominated, simply because like tend to hire like, with staff that have a strong bias toward either right or left? Conservatives dominated the universities early in the century. As late as 1961, they still dominated the first university at which I taught. But the left has been overrepresented in American academia in general at least since 1955.

In that year, 67 percent of social scientists said they were more liberal than the average person in the community in which they worked (Lazarafeld & Thielens, 1958). In 1969, 46 percent of academics described themselves as liberal, 27 percent as moderates, and 28 percent as conservative. At that time, 45 percent of college students described themselves as liberal or left – wing but only 20 percent of the American public did so (Ladd & Lippset, 1975). By 1984, 57 percent of professors described themselves as liberal, 20 percent as moderate, and 24 percent as conservative, so liberals had gained a bit (Hamilton and Hargrens, 1993). In 2013, however, between 50 and 60 percent of professors were liberal. This sets them apart from the public, approximately 17 percent of whom were leftist or liberal. (Gross, 2013). In terms of party affiliation, 51 percent of university professors were Democrats, 36 percent Independents, and 14 percent Republicans. A Gallup poll of 2006, in contrast, showed that 34 percent of Americans were Democrats, 34 percent Independents, and 30 percent Republicans. (Gross and Simmons, 2014).

In Chapters 6 and 7, I conclude that a minority, consisting of radical or romantic leftist students, commit the worst sins against free speech today, and that they are tolerated by at least half of the student body and a larger percentage of the faculty and administration. A university with a staff whose politics were closer to the public might help control them. That aside, it would be better if there were more conservatives within the university so that the left, and students in general, could learn more from opposing arguments that thrive outside the campus gates.

Government to the rescue?

As we have seen, political neutrality is a trade – off against government interference. The balance in universities is unwelcome in terms of the ideal of political neutrality. But what does history show about the actions government has actually taken to purify universities? When all is said and done, it is far better to agitate for change within the university than to invite in the politicians to change the situation for them. There is a sizable constituency within the university for free speech, however intimidated at present. We ought to use public debate (as this book does) to encourage or shame them into speaking out. Government interference in the name of promoting free speech has never been that. It is sheer intimidation by those who, whatever they say, want to change the balance in their favor or simply gain popularity by appealing to popular passions. The balance of this chapter will examine the historical record.

The standard of free debate that exists in Congress today is hardly inspiring. As for the current president, he is unusual, but free speech or reverence for the truth is not known to be high on his agenda. He has banned various government departments from using the following words and phrases: "climate change," "reduce greenhouse gases," "sequester carbon", "evidence – based," "sex education" ("sexual risk avoidance" preferred), "vulnerable," "entitlement," "diversity," and "transgender" (Richardson, 2017; Sun & Eilperin, 2017). When I was persecuted for my politics in 1962, I was not so mad as to think that I would have fared better at the hands of the state legislature or the governor.

Early days

The first recorded student rebellion against administrative oppression was a Harvard riot in 1766 over the low quality of butter. Echoing those who want to allow firearms on campus today, in 1836 University of Virginia students formed a militia opposing the "tyrannical movements of the faculty" to remove all arms from campus (Wilson, 2014, p. 74). It is a pity that the faculty lost: in 1840 a professor was shot dead by a student. Prior to the Civil War, academics who argued against whatever side of the divide (North or South) believed about slavery were dismissed. Everyone was suspect if they held unorthodox religious views. During the Civil War itself (1861 – 1865), California, Nevada, and the new state of West Virginia (founded 1863) instituted teacher loyalty oaths. None of this had much to do with who was right or left.

The trend toward conservative oppression of the left really emerged after the Civil War. I will divide this era into several periods: prior to America's entry into World War I (1877 – 1917), the war years (1917 – 1918), the rise of the Communist Party (1919 – 41), the World War II interlude (1941 – 1948), and the "better dead than red" years (1948 – 1965) commonly identified with the anti – communist witch hunts led by Senator Joseph McCarthy. Ellen Schrecker, in *No Ivory Tower* (1986), and John Wilson, in *A History of Academic Freedom in America* (2014), provide excellent accounts. I will draw heavily on them, with the usual disclaimer that my departures from the originals may have introduced mistakes.

Social change

Industrialization accelerated in earnest after the Civil War and led to an ideological ferment. On the left, many academics came to believe that only trade unions, a greater role of government regulation of business, or an overthrow of capitalism could humanize industrial America. They had read Marx and Darwin. Some had become atheists and some rejected even the institution of the family. They also supported women's suffrage and the full enfranchisement of blacks. They ranged from liberal reformers to democratic socialists to anarchists to syndicalists and revolutionaries. On the right, industrialists and businessmen saw the left as their natural enemy, as did much of rural America, which felt that its beliefs and whole way of life were under siege. Many on the right cherished Christian fundamentalism and rejected the entire urban lifestyle, especially its vices of drink, weakening marriage ties, and violence (workers declaring war on the nation's tranquility).

Suspicion of change rested on a deep conviction that non – conformity was wicked. President Draper of the University of Illinois feared that students who went to Europe would come back with un – American ideas and loose habits. He advised students: "Do not stand aloof ... above all, do not get to be a freak. Keep in step with the procession. It is a pretty good crowd and it is generally moving in the right direction" (Wilson, 2014, p. 105). Academics at the University of Chicago hated President Wilson so much that the faculty club took his picture down from a conspicuous place in the main room and put it behind the door upstairs. Drury College dismissed a professor for donating a book on theosophy to the library.

Conformity to a rural ideal

That left – leaning academics could use universities to indoctrinate students with their views seemed outrageous. In 1877 Cornell refused to reappoint Felix Adler because his lectures favored rationalistic views and, in one case, he suggested that some doctrines of Christianity could be discovered in other religions. In 1878 Alexander Winchell was dismissed by Vanderbilt University for writing a pro – evolution tract on the origin of man before Adam. The following year, Yale ordered William Graham Sumner (whose politics were arch – conservative) to stop using Herbert Spencer's *Study of Sociology* as a textbook: it assumed that material elements and laws are the only forces and laws (Wilson, 2014). Within a few years, however, the scientific consensus behind the theory of evolution became so strong that campus bans became much rarer. It was in American high schools that the controversy over evolution raged as in the Scopes trial, and sadly it still rages today.

All of these cases were in the 1870s, and it was the ministers or the religiously orthodox that were getting the free – thinkers fired.

Industrialists and businessmen were sometimes fundamentalists but they saw trade unions and socialists as their real enemies. They were happy to use the religious trauma of rural American as an ally in support of political orthodoxy and continue to do so today. In 2016 no Republican who aspired to be nominated felt he could say that he believed in the theory of evolution. But with religion losing its potency to dismiss left – leaning academic staff, conservatives now needed to target them on strictly political grounds. All of the cases we are about to examine, beginning in the 1880s, introduced a new tactic: that the left is un – American and dangerous.

Conformity to a business model

On May 4, 1886, a protest rally near Chicago's Haymarket Square advocated the eight – hour workday and protested against the killing of several workers by police the previous day. Someone threw a bomb at the police, and seven policemen and four others died. The result was a national wave of xenophobia in which leaders of the labor and immigrant communities, particularly Germans and Bohemians, came under suspicion and hundreds of foreign – born radicals and labor leaders were rounded up in Chicago and elsewhere.

Henry Carter Adams, a young academic working part – time at both Cornell and Michigan, gave an address at Cornell denouncing the behavior of America's industrialists with particular reference to the aftermath of Haymarket. Cornell's Board of Trustees decided not to reappoint him. He made no protest because he knew that any publicity would endanger his chances of remaining at Michigan. He wrote a groveling letter to Michigan disavowing radicalism and calling his Cornell speech unwise. He got tenure at Michigan and never said anything controversial again (Schrecker, 1986).

In 1892, George Steele, president of Lawrence University, was fired for his views on free trade. Four years later the Trustees of Brown University told President Elisha Benjamin Andrews to cease discussing his support of free silver because his views were contrary to those held by the friends of the University. A public outcry pressured the Board to back down, but Andrews was forced to resign a year later. When Northwestern's president Henry Rogers resigned in 1900, a trustee asserted that he should not voice opinions that were antagonistic to the board of managers. People giving large endowments to its funds were nearly all opposed to the political views Rodgers expressed from time to time (Wilson, 2014).

Richard T. Ely was one of the best – known academics of his time and a member of the Christian left. In 1894 a member of the University of Wisconsin's Board of Regents charged that he had supported strikes and boycotts and entertained a union organizer in his home. The regents summoned Ely and he defended himself as really a "conservative." They reinstated him. He never again wrote for a popular audience and published only non – controversial pieces about "land economics" (Schrecker, 1986).

Edward W. Bemis (a student of Ely's) advocated public ownership of railroads and utilities. In 1894 he attacked the railways during that year's great Pullman Strike. The president of the University of Chicago (William Rainey Harper) admonished him to "exercise great caution in public utterances about questions that are agitating the minds of the people" (Wilson, 2014, p. 92). John D. Rockefeller, along with contributions from the American Baptist Education Society and land from Marshall Field, had just financed the university. Bemis was fired in 1895 and made a public issue of his dismissal. He was not reinstated and had to support himself outside the university. Harper did not set a precedent for the University of Chicago. Almost immediately afterwards its resolve began to stiffen.

Edward. A. Ross (another student of Ely's) was a progressive sociologist and gifted public speaker. Jane Stanford, the widow of Leland Stanford, was chair of Stanford University's Board of Trustees. She had already fired another left – leaning young sociologist, and when Ross gave two speeches in 1900, one denouncing the railroads and the other Chinese immigration (for undercutting the wages of native workers), he was forced to resign. The chair of History defended him (and was fired), and six faculty members resigned. Because there was a shortage of good academic jobs, a majority of Stanford's faculty signed a manifesto supporting the University. Ross was hired at Nebraska and five years later Ely brought him to Wisconsin (Schrecker, 1986).

In 1909 Jane Stanford also fired Thorsten Veblen, perhaps the most acute critic of the ethos of American capitalism (see *The Theory of the Leisure Class*, 1899). She is rumored to have done so because of his support for Chinese "coolie" workers in California (Sica, 2005). However, while Veblen moved from Chicago to Stanford to Missouri to the New School of Social Research, the underlying reason seems to have been his sexual career, which included imprudent extramarital affairs with the wives of colleagues.

In 1911, the University of Florida dismissed a professor following the publication of an article in *The Independent* in which he stated that teachers and others in positions of influence made a grievous mistake prior to the Civil War in not paving the way for a gradual removal of slavery. In 1913 the University of North Dakota forced J. L. Lewi to resign after the Dean censured him for attending a conference of leaders of former President Theodore Roosevelt's new Progressive Party (Wilson, 2014).

In 1915 the University of Utah fired a professor who had been active in the defence of Joe Hill (a member of the Industrial Workers of the World and convicted of murder). It also fired Charles W. Snow because he had read and revised a commencement address by Milton Sevy, in which Sevy attacked ultra – conservatism

The University of Colorado Law School denied James Brewster reappointment because he had appeared as a counsel for the Miners' Union and testified before the Commission on Industrial Relations (Wilson, 2014).

While lecturing at the Wharton School of Business at the University of Pennsylvania, Scott Nearing was denied promotion and then fired in 1915. The Dean had warned him: "Mr. Nearing, if I were in your place I would do a little less speaking about child labor" (Wilson, 2014, p. 150). Trustees noted that Nearing had not only antagonized industrial orthodoxy, but orthodoxy in other fields, social and religious. *The New York Times* told socialists to establish their own university and make a requisition on the padded cells of Bedlam for their teaching staff.

One university stood firm. In October 1903, Professor John Spencer Basset publicly drew attention to the racism and white supremacist behavior of the Democratic Party. He even stated that all blacks were not intellectually inferior. Many major newspapers throughout the South attacked him and demanding that Duke University fire him. Despite this, the entire faculty threatened to resign if the board asked Bassett to resign. The board voted 18 to 7 in his favor (Stephenson, 1948a, 1948b). Academics had not reached a consensus on academic freedom; at the time their instinct was to simply oppose outside interference. But this weakened if they, too, thought some of their colleagues suspect.

The World War I years

In 1917, a large proportion of the left opposed America's entry into World War I. Nearing lost his post at the University of Toledo, which had welcomed him after he was dismissed two years earlier at Wharton. The best estimate seems to be that universities fired about 120 academics because they were considered unsympathetic to the war effort. The most prominent were James McKeen Cattell and Henry Dana at Columbia (Schrecker, 1986). Many other leading universities were on the list: Michigan (seven staff), Illinois (five, three of whom had refused to buy "Liberty Bonds"), Nebraska (three), Minnesota, Wisconsin, Oregon, Wellesley, Texas, and Pennsylvania (Wilson, 2014, pp. 159 – 164).

President Wilson called Eugene Victor Debs, the leader of the American Socialist Party, a traitor. He was jailed from 1919 to 1921 for a speech urging resistance to the draft because he saw the war as a capitalist war. Debs ran for president while in jail and was allowed one press release a week. My father, in fact, drafted the petition that got Debs released. My father was not a socialist but thought America had no business fighting in a European quarrel. He was also sympathetic to Debs because, after having entered the factories to work at a very young age, he found that the boss had put up a sign over the gate: "If this county votes for William Jennings Bryan, there will be no work for two weeks." The workers voted for Bryan (a populist Democrat) and were locked out for two weeks.

The rise of the Communist Party

Rural antipathy to the urban worker remained primarily background noise. Industrialization and new transportation technology gradually decimated farmers and their economic base. They still had enough strength to force the prohibition of alcohol in 1920 but this was a last gasp to be reversed in 1933 and derided at the time.

In 1917, the Russian Revolution gave industrialists and the business community a new "danger" to attack, namely, the international communist movement and the newly founded American Communist Party, which split from the Socialist Party in 1919. Socialists recognized the USSR as an emerging tyranny while the Communists idolized the Soviet regime even under Stalin. In theory, following Marx, American Communists predicted an eventual radicalizing of the workers that would lead to violent overthrow of the government (although the time never seemed to be ripe), while the Socialists thought that their message would eventually win them victory at the polls like socialist parties in Europe. At the polls, Socialist candidates for President had far greater support. The Communists hit their peak in 1932 (the great depression began in 1929) at 103,000 and fell to 46,000 by 1940, while the Socialists recorded 882,000 and 119,000 respectively.

The Communists, however, had a far larger cadre of activists, particularly in the trade unions, and came to represent the left in the public mind. Their movement seemed to pose an ever – present danger: a faction which if presented with a choice between the interests of the USSR and the interests of America would always choose the former. This ensured that it would never become powerful enough to pose a danger as an organization. But even if it was feeble, did not the left contain those who might resort to violence in certain circumstances?

In fact, as we shall see, no individual Communist plotted an act of violence at any time. Other radical groups, like the Industrial Workers of the World, showed incredible restraint when their members were killed. Once, during a bitter dispute, the IWW did hijack a train and drove it through the capital of Colorado in an attempt to assassinate the governor, killing his chauffeur instead (Ginger, 1962).

Who they fired

Academics targeted for dismissal included none of these violent radicals. The accused professors never shot anyone or threw a bomb. As H. L. Mencken said of Scott Nearing, "he was thrown out because his efforts to get at the truth disturbed the security and equanimity of the rich ignoranti who happened to control the university … In three words, he was thrown out because he was not safe and sane and orthodox." The mood was caught by Vice President and future President Calvin Coolidge in 1921, when he published an article titled "Are the Reds Stalking our College Women." President Warren Harding's Commissioner of Education declared that "if I had it in my power I would not only imprison but would expatriate all advocates of dangerous un – American doctrines. I would even execute every one of them – and do it joyfully" (Wilson, 2014, pp. 152, 168, and 170). Fosse (1951) concludes that between the wars the atmosphere of the university was charged with fear.

There was no tolerance for gays. In 1920 Harvard created a secret court to spy on suspected homosexuals. The Court interrogated students about homosexuality and masturbation. Seven were expelled and ordered to leave the town of Cambridge. At least two subsequently committed suicide. As late as 1963, the Johns Committee in Florida was hunting down gays and lesbians. By April 1963, 71 teachers had their teaching certificates revoked and 39 professors and deans had been dismissed from universities. Hundreds were questioned and harassed, and an untold number of students expelled from college. Florida was the worst, but persecution was widespread. In 1959, at a small midwestern college, a female student told her faculty adviser that one of her friends was a homosexual. She was pressured into naming others. Within twenty – four hours, three students had been expelled; a week later, one of them hanged himself (Wilson, 2014).

As the 1920s began, a professor at Ohio State was fired for treating a coal strike favorably and pacifist leader Nevin Sayre was barred from speaking at the University of Oklahoma. In 1926, Illinois removed two students from the school paper for portraying the zinc smelting industry in an "unfavorable light." The Dean of Men saw moral danger in the car, so student automobiles were banned until 1953. The following year Illinois told a lecturer that he was not to assign James Joyce's *Ulysses* for its supposed unsuitability for undergraduates (Wilson, 2014). In 1929 Missouri dismissed Professors Max Friedrich Meyer and Harmon O. DeGraff for having advised a student who had distributed a questionnaire about divorce, "living together," and sex (Nelson, 2003).

In 1926, the Genesee New York State Normal School dismissed two teachers for "progressive" political activities. Olivet College fired John Kirkpatrick because of a book that attacked business control of higher education. In 1927 Sol Auerbach was dismissed from the University of Pennsylvania because he praised Soviet Russia. A year later Wesley Maurer was dismissed from Ohio University for publishing articles sympathetic to striking miners, as was Walter Ludwig, a student pastor who showed sympathy to the miners. In 1929 Fred Woltman was fired from Pittsburgh because he served as secretary of the local Civil Liberties Committee. In 1930 Mississippi Governor Bilbo discharged 179 faculty members, replacing them by teachers personally pleasing to him. In 1931 Herbert Miller was fired at Ohio State because he supported the Indian nationalist movement and opposed compulsory military training. Some trustees thought him too liberal on race because he hosted teas to which both white and colored people were invited (Wilson, 2014).

In 1932, students at the University of Chicago invited William Z. Foster, the Communist candidate for President, to lecture on campus. This triggered a storm of protest from critics both on and off campus. President Robert M. Hutchins responded that "our students . . . should have freedom to discuss any problem that presents itself" (and) that the "cure" for ideas we oppose "lies through open discussion rather than through inhibition" (University of Chicago, 2012). From this time on, Chicago become outstanding as a defender of free speech and its record remains strong to this day. A few years before, Harvard students were not so lucky. The Dean vetoed invitations to both Foster and Debs (Schrecker, 1986).

Colleges expelled or suspended hundreds of students for expressing liberal views. Syracuse expelled a student because she was not a "typical Syracuse girl" (the only reason given). Universities banned radicals from speaking on campus: Clarence Darrow, Arthur Hays, and Roger Baldwin (ACLU); Kirby Page (pacifist); and John Sayre (Committee on Militarism in Education). At Clark, when Scott Nearing began to speak, the president personally turned off he lights. The Liberal Club at Duke was forbidden to discuss the case of Ella May Wiggins, a textile worker killed during a strike, because it was controversial (Wilson, 2014; Schrecker, 1986).

Horace Bancroft Davis was dismissed at Bradford Junior College in 1931 and at Simmons College in 1941. He openly engaged in Communist Party activities in the community, but was scrupulous about keeping his economics lectures free of radical content. In 1936 Borrows Dunham heard that the president of Franklin Marshall was under pressure to fire him for speaking about the Spanish Civil War. The entire left backed the Spanish government against the Fascist – backed insurgents. In the late 1930s, a member of my home community in Washington DC named Sydney was killed in Spain. The left – wing families all had daughters but nonetheless they named them "Sydney" (including one of my relatives). Dunham was safe for the time being, but feared he would be fired, and Oakley Johnson managed to get him a job at Temple (Schrecker, 1986).

The City College of New York (CCNY) expelled more radical students than anyone else. The faculty advisor of its "Liberal Club" was told that no classes had been scheduled for him. The president sent police to attack students who held a rally in the sidelined man's defense. In 1931 Granville Hicks of Rensselaer Polytechnic Institute was investigated and found to have kept his English classes free of his political views. Still, He was dismissed in 1935 and, aside from a one – year lectureship at Harvard in 1938, never taught again. Public struggles led by students and sympathetic trade unions (including The Teachers Union) saved Morris Schappes at CCNY but failed to save Jerome Davis at Yale. In 1933, Columbia fired Donald Henderson (a radical economist).

By 1936, 21 American states and the District of Columbia had instituted special "teacher's oaths," usually requiring them to swear that they were not teaching or advocating communism. These in themselves did little harm in that virtually every Communist (or suspect) lecturer could attest to obeying the former and many Communists did party work that did not involve public advocacy (Schrecker, 1986).

The world intervenes

On August 23, 1939, the Soviet Union and Nazi Germany signed a non – aggression treaty that was followed by their coordinated invasion of Poland, which they divided between them. It outraged both liberals and socialists as a pact with the devil. Overnight, communist parties throughout the world switched from fighting fascism (as in Spain) to advocating pacifism, including urging America to stay out of the war against Germany. That the American Communist Party followed suit was alone proof that that it took orders from Moscow.

The American communist movement came to be seen as a conspiracy, potentially disloyal, lying whenever it suited its purposes, comprised of members who had forfeited their independence of judgment. On October 11, 1940, the Board of Regents of the University of California fired Kenneth O. May, a party member. Its rationale was that the Communist Party was loyal to a foreign government and bred suspicion and discord. Membership in it, therefore, was incompatible with faculty membership in a state university. New York State (the Rapp – Coudert Committee) began to investigate all of its lecturers holding party membership, which it regarded as sufficient grounds for dismissal. They fired Morris Schappes at CCNY and 20 others (most of them at CCNY), and got rid of another eleven who resigned while their cases were pending. Beginning in 1940, ten distinguished universities, including Harvard, banned Communist Party chairman and presidential candidate Earl Browder from speaking (Schrecker, 1986).

When Germany invaded the USSR on June 22, 1941, the Communist Party line changed overnight. Further proving that it took orders from Moscow, it now argued that America should not stay out of the war but rather plunge in as soon as possible. The change underlined a deep split between the Socialist and Communist Parties. Between 1941 and 1946, A. Philip Randolf and Bayard Rustin (both black Socialists) organized the March on Washington Movement to pressure President

Roosevelt. America was creating thousands of jobs as industry prepared for war and created more when it expanded into war production. Black workers faced discrimination in employment and some government training programs excluded them. The president of North American Aviation was quoted as saying, "It is against company policy to employ them [blacks] as aircraft workers or mechanics ... There will be some jobs as janitors" (Garfinkel, 1969, p. 17). The Communists, normally advocates of racial justice, condemned the March on Washington Movement, however, because it threatened war production that would benefit the Soviet Union. For expediency's sake, and in some cases for ideological reasons, many Americans decided that although communists might be the servants of Moscow, they were obedient to a nation that was united in a common cause and whose worst excesses might be overlooked.

The World War II years

For a brief period, other radical groups were more suspect than the Communist Party. The American Socialist Party supported the war but in the 1944 elections it ran on a platform rejecting the notion that the war could only end in the unconditional surrender of the Axis countries.

The most important issue was whether unions would take the "no strike pledge" for the duration of the war. The Communist Party became the extreme right of the trade union movement by endorsing an absolute pledge. Their overriding objective was to avoid interruption of war production. Those who followed Trotsky, who had been exiled from the USSR and was murdered in Mexico in August 1940, hated Stalin and were far more militant. Even before America's entry into the war, the government began to target Trotskyists who were trade union leaders. Their first target was Vincent Dunne of the Socialist Workers Party.

In 1941, there was a dispute between Dunne and the president of the Teamsters Union, Daniel Tobin. Prompted by Tobin, on June 27, 1941, the FBI raided the Socialist Workers headquarters. Under the Alien and Sedition Act (the Smith Act), Dunne, along with his brothers and twenty – five others, was convicted of conspiring to overthrow the government. The Communist Party endorsed the convictions. *The Daily Worker* declared that Trotskyites deserved no more support from labor than Nazis did. They themselves were persecuted under the Smith Act after the war had ended, but that was an unforeseeable future. The Communists also endorsed the incarceration of 120,000 Japanese – Americans in internment camps (Witek, 2017; Galbbermann, 1980; Lewy, 1990) after the attack on Pearl Harbor.

For at least four years, Communists were ardent patriots. Therefore, unlike World War I, World War II brought little campus repression. Only a small number of religious pacifists opposed the war and campuses were not perceived as centers of dissent. After the war ended in 1945, Communists again became suspect. Some universities refused to recognize the Communist youth group as a student club. Then with the onset of the Cold War, it turned out that the USSR was no ally after all. Its policies in Eastern Europe and the Middle East showed that it was attempting to conquer the world. In 1950, the outbreak of the Korean War turned the Cold War into a shooting war against communist nations, first North Korea and then China.

Nothing to learn from debating communists

The campus repression of World War I returned with ferocity. The universities should have fought back, but few did. Marxism was not like the flat earth society but an important perspective in the realm of ideas that deserved to be part of campus debate. This was true even of its Stalinist variant. Like all doctrines, those who believe in it, which is to say communists, would present it most vigorously. As in the past, most would probably have kept it out of their lectures but ideally they could defend it on campus, as could student communists. Both sides of the debate could invite speakers. But no one said, "We want some Communists on campus so we can debate with them."

What would students and staff have learned from such a debate? The sort of things I learned from reading scholars with whom I disagreed, such as Jensen, Lynn, and Murray. An intelligent Communist would have had knowledge and perspectives I lacked, posed problems I had not anticipated, perhaps have led me to better appreciate why this ideology had spread from Europe to the developing world and how its appeal differed from place to place, and tested my knowledge of the significance of various historical events. When I did debate a communist, he made me understand how an intelligent person could believe that it was the West that had started the Cold War (Flynn, 2012b, Chapter 2). Those who banned communists from campus were no better than the mob at Middlebury, if less violent. Thanks to their intolerance, they made it more difficult for people to learn.

The American Association of University Professors (AAUP), the main advocacy group of American university faculty members, was charged to protect academics. Yet during this period it defended no one at all. Aby (2009) suspects that a majority of the AAUP's membership and a majority of American academics in general supported firing their colleagues or at least deeply distrusted them due to communist leanings. The dominant rationalization was that by accepting the Stalinist line, they had surrendered their intellectual independence. Well, so what? This merely means that, if allowed, they would argue on campus in favor of Stalinism with fervor. What of those who have given their minds away to Freud, the Vatican, religious fundamentalism, Fox News, or mindless patriotism? Unlike communists, there was no campaign to fire any of them because of their intellectual rigidity. This argument must be among the most specious that the members of the academy have ever accepted.

America had talked itself into committing the worst sin possible: abridging freedom of thought. Hidden behind the rhetoric was a determination to punish people for thinking a certain way. Thinking revolutionary thoughts was tantamount to crime. It was irrelevant if one had committed no treasonous or violent act, or never used speech to plot such an act. There were already plenty of laws on the books to punish anyone who did these things. It was irrelevant that none of those accused was found to have been recruiting students or teaching the party line. Today, however, lecturers in minority and women's studies, and the teachers of teachers, turn their classes into political harangues in the name of social justice, and this is widely accepted practice. They openly state that they want to convert students into political activists but it is those who disagree who suffer consequences.

The menace of the Communist Party

The 1950s notion that the Communist Party was a menace and had to be eliminated was absurd. Communist spy networks were exposed and eliminated in the late 1940s, and those implicated were removed from US government service. They were expelled from the trade union movement (AFL – CIO) in 1949. By the Korean War period, its membership had declined to 5,000 and most of them were concerned with trying to stay out of jail. Never was the Communist Party so feeble as when it was most persecuted.

The FBI had infiltrated the party thoroughly. Our student group at Chicago ran all the way from liberals to a few Communists. When a new member (dressed more respectably than most of us) kept writing things down, we suspected the worst. It tuned out that he was shy and wanted to plan out what he had to say in advance. In the 1950s, Harvey Matusow joined the Ohio Communist Party as an FBI informer and even acted as an *agent provocateur* (Trahair, 2012). It may be a left – wing urban myth, but FBI agents were later said to have held the balance of power when the Central Committee voted. They had orders always to vote for the most extreme position, and only thanks to them was the Ohio Communist Party still a revolutionary party.

Better dead than Red

Targeting the Communist party was a way of targeting the entire left. One could discredit former members of the party (and members of any group in which Communists were prominent) as unrepentant if they refused to give the names of people who would then be subject to persecution. One could discredit anyone who defended Communists on civil libertarian grounds or objected to things like loyalty oaths. You could accuse any Democratic office holder of having been "soft on communism." One could encourage the public to confuse socialists with communists, something socialists found particularly irritating since they knew they would be the first ones shot in any Stalinist state. The mainstream of the Republican Party aimed at forbidding criticism of the prevailing conservative ideology in America.

Senator Joseph McCarthy of Wisconsin led the persecution from February 1950 to December 1954, when he was censured by the Senate, although the process both preceded his influence and outlasted his downfall. He and others got people fired by means of a division of labor. The House Un – American Activities Committee (HUAC) and similar state committees identified them, and universities then terminated their employment. This division of labor was not absolute. I was fired in the South for being too liberal (too pro – civil rights) and in the North ostensibly for being a Democratic Socialist, with the university playing both the role of accuser and judge.

Academics who lost their posts from 1948 to 1954 were too many to list individually: about 600 teachers at all levels, which included about 100 among university and college faculty (McCormick, 1989; Holmes, 1989). In a few cases, if a professor had tenure, taught at a less vulnerable private university, and cooperated fully with the university, he retained his job, but these cases were exceptional (Schecker, 1994). Many more academics were simply not rehired or never hired. Usually they silently accepted the decision because they did not want to be labeled publicly. Once fired, a blacklist prevented them from getting a job anywhere else for many years. For example, in 1948, when Washington University fired three of its staff, none secured a new post despite their credentials (Holmes, 1989). The blacklist began to fade in the early 1960s, and a majority of the professors fired returned to academia after a decade of disgrace (Schecter, 1994).

As case followed case, the criteria for dismissal took on substance: being a Communist Party member or a member of one of its front organizations (groups it organized to support the Spanish government and so forth); taking the Fifth Amendment to avoid self – incrimination (which happened to be a constitutional right); refusing to cooperate with either legislative or campus investigating committees, which usually meant refusing to take a loyalty oath or name people who you knew would then be investigated (Aby, 2009). Virtually every university was complicit. Only a few showed courage: Hutchins at Chicago, Harvard Law School Dean Erwin Griswold, Harry S. Rogers at Brooklyn Polytech (a conservative but a principled civil libertarian), Harold Taylor at Sarah Lawrence College, T. P. Wright and Deane W. Mallott at Cornell. The faculty at Reed College was one the few who took a correct stand: it was simply none of the government's business or the college's business what the staff thought. But they were overruled by the trustees (Schecker, 1986).

Academics in general may have distrusted communists but despite this some were left leaning. They knew they were vulnerable and censored the content of their courses and public statements (Aby, 2009). In the mid – 1950s, physics students at Chicago circulated a petition to get a soda vending machine installed in the laboratory. The fear of being labeled an agitator was so great that nobody would sign (Schrecker, 1999). Free speech on campus was crippled. Aside from Chicago, universities now banned both communists and those under indictment. As far back as 1948, Henry Wallace (Progressive Party candidate for president) was prohibited from speaking at the Cincinnati, Iowa, Missouri, California, and Michigan (Wilson, 2014). Their administrations shared the sentiments of Wayne State University's President: "I have held that even a Communist should be heard … It is now clear that the Communist is to be regarded not as an ordinary citizen … but as an enemy of our national welfare" (Schrecker, 1986, pp. 91 – 92).

In passing, newspapers fired journalists when they defied congressional committees. There were only a handful in number, but their dismissals embarrassed an industry that preached freedom of the press. *The New York Times* justified firing a copyreader in the foreign news department as a matter of national security. They emphasized that if he had worked on the sports desk he could have kept his job (Schrecker, 1994). In 1953, *The Nation* revealed that McCarthy's committee was using the contents of State Department libraries as a pretext for investigating journalists and authors who had criticized McCarthy. They took an editorial stand, asking whether big newspapers would open the gates to the barbarians.

The rest of the iceberg

It may seem that the repression of the McCarthy period was relatively mild. Only two people, Ethel and Julius Rosenberg, were executed after a court of law found that they had committed espionage. "A few hundred" went to prison (no one gives a precise figure), about 1,000 people altogether lost their jobs. However, this summary includes only those whose names became a matter of public record because they appeared before HUAC, a state equivalent, in court, or in formal dismissal proceedings. They were merely the tip of the iceberg. Thousands of others go unnamed because their stories have never been told.

To give some notion of what it was like to be a young academic during the tail end of this era, I will add a personal note with the caveat that many were affected far more than I was. I am a democratic socialist who believes America should pattern itself after Finland or Scandinavia in general: single payer medicine and education, state housing that would give the bottom third of Americans accommodation and the opportunity to own their own homes without the time – bomb of subprime mortgages, a robust welfare state, and so forth. I was always appalled by discrimination against minorities. I believed that many Cold War issues could have been settled by negotiation, and I still oppose US military intervention to nation – build. Pretty tame stuff. I am not a Marxist, never has their critique of capitalism seemed more relevant and never have they seemed more bankrupt of solutions than today.

In the early 1960s, I was fired twice. Once for being a chairman of the Congress of Racial Equality (CORE) in the South. When my CORE involvement became known, I was immediately replaced as the voluntary coach of the cross – country team. Students were paid five dollars per week to report anyone I spoke to and at least one of my telegrams was intercepted. My second firing was for being a Democratic Socialist in the North, although I suspect that the desire to replace me with a personal friend was an additional motive. I was turned down for two posts thanks to the memberships on my vita: a Southern university noted that I had been a CORE chairman, and a California institution objected to me as a member of SANE (Committee for a Sane Nuclear Policy). That university's president began the interview by telling me he thought all pacifists were cowards (I was not a pacifist by the way). He wanted to extract an oath of political non – involvement. I replied that I had no intention of getting involved in the politics of the area (labor disputes) but would exercise my rights as a citizen. My family and I moved to New Zealand in 1963 partially to find a place where my politics were acceptable or at least no barrier to employment.

It may seem that I panicked too soon in that during the 1960s the oppression of the right slowly gave way to the oppression of the left, prompted largely by outrage at the War in Vietnam. But I did not anticipate this: the Cold War atmosphere in America looked permanent. Even at that time, anyone on the left seemed at risk. The distinguished scholar Fred Warner Neal had an invitation to speak in Florida withdrawn because he argued that both America and the USSR had caused the Cold War. Samuel Shapiro had been both fired and blackballed for defending the legitimacy of Castro's government in Cuba (O'Brien, 1998).

I believe that I, and those close to me, had been classified as enemies of the people. When I left Chicago in 1957, my flat mate had a visit from the FBI. They told him that his address was on their books as my place of residence – actually they did not seem to have anything particular in mind. When I taught in the South, the FBI interviewed people I drank with at the local bar to ask them what I talked about. Sports, they were told – and didn't they have anything better to do? I was not persecuted by local police in that their treatment of me was mild for a civil rights advocate. When I was attacked on the street, with them looking on, there was no arrest, but at least I was not arrested. They did turn the day I left town into a drama. They held me for a day incommunicado, which ignited a frenzy in the black community wondering why I had "disappeared" (Flynn, 1980, pp. 115 – 130).

Local officials made complaints that I was stirring up the blacks and hoped that I might be drafted for the Vietnam War. Without a university post, I would no longer have an occupational deferment. I do not know whether they approached the draft board but suspect they did. The response would have been unsympathetic. The members were all black and very likely approved of my CORE activities. After my move to New Zealand, when I gave a critical radio talk about Kennedy (who had been assassinated), the American embassy approached my department chair with odd questions about my status.

Those close to me were harassed. My wife's family was farther left but they certainly had never conspired to commit violent or revolutionary acts. My father – in – law prudently resigned his good government job and had to over – work in a series of little shops that he owned in succession. Their home phones were tapped. This led to some comedy relief. My mother – in – law asked callers who chose to speak in Yiddish if they thought the FBI could not hire translators. Everyone else's trash went into the trash truck but theirs went into a little bag hung at the back. They burned all radical literature but tore corset advertisements into thousands of little pieces. The FBI told my mother – in – law's brothers and sisters (many of whom worked for the government or the military) that they were forbidden to speak to her, engendering a family tragedy. They tried to personally intimidate her on the street.

In 1952, at age ten, my wife got her parents called into school for a tense interview. The teacher had said that only two candidates were running for President (Eisenhower and Stevenson). She piped up that Vincent Hallinan, the Progressive Party candidate, was also running. How did she *know* – what kind of home did she come from – another entry for the FBI file. At age 12, her parents sent her to a summer camp for the children of Smith Act victims whose parents were in jail. All parents paid double so that the afflicted children could afford to attend. Some of them were among her friends.

My friend Don Anderson, also a Socialist Party member, was drafted for Vietnam. He was an honorable man. He refused to take the loyalty oath because it required him to inform on anyone he knew at university that might belong to organizations on the Attorney General's list. They sent him through basic training six times over his three years and tried to give him an "undesirable" discharge: he had fraternized with the known communists they had put in the barracks with him (he was guilty of this). The FBI tried to drive his father out of business by telling his customers that his son who was a security risk. They interviewed girls he had dated in junior high school.

A balance sheet

It is worth reminding ourselves of what things were like when the right was in control of universities. Nothing the left has done over the past 50 years, whether it be college presidents bounced, lecturers fired, students expelled, speakers banned, free speech violated, matches what the right did for almost 100 years. I hope that the hearts of conservatives burn with shame when they think of those times, just as mine burn with shame when I think of today.

Of course, during the McCarthy period, conservatives had powerful allies among Cold War "liberals." John F. Kennedy was the first to allege in the Senate that Dean Acheson had lost China to communism. His brother Robert who was a volunteer attorney for HUAC (The House Un – American Activities Committee). In 1954, the Democrats introduced legislation in the Senate to make membership in the Communist Party a crime. The vote was 81 for and only one (Estes Kefauver) against (Flynn, 2008, pp. 31 – 32). However, many conservatives were suspicious of these "allies" and suspected was that they were really communist sympathizers who were trying to dupe the public.

I do not lament my exile. When the left took control at Berkeley, I would have found myself in more trouble. I would have had to take a stand against the Romantic left, and their ignorant persecution of those they saw as their enemies and their "plans" for reforming the university, literally burning it down if necessary. As a man of the left, I would have been a particular target because of my "betrayal."

4
The transition

When America's involvement in the War in Vietnam began to escalate, I was sure that a new phase of purging the disloyal would perpetuate the era of conservative oppression. In fact, Vietnam turned out to be a war unlike any other. "Disloyalty" became a badge of honor within a new youth culture engendered by deep changes in American society.

The Vietnam War

How was Vietnam different from Korea? North Korea attacked South Korea only a few months after two shocking events: the USSR tested its first atomic bomb on August 29, 1949, and Communist China was proclaimed on October 1, 1949. After China intervened in Korea in November 1950, the Korean Conflict became a struggle against a major communist power and this made defeat seem unthinkable. America entered Vietnam in earnest 15 years later. It was not conceived as a war of self – defense but rather as a war of empire. It is always risky for a great power to use draftees in such a war rather than professional solders, but this was the unwise course the generals advocated. America was involved for ten years, and the war seemed, and indeed was, unwinnable. Military discipline broke down, and the war became immensely unpopular at home. About 210,000 men were accused of evading the draft and 30,000 fled to Canada. Others fled to Sweden, France, and the United Kingdom. Vocations to the ministry and the rabbinate soared because divinity students were exempt, as were students, many of whom pursued graduate degrees (and thus academic careers) to avoid military service. Doctors and draft board members found themselves being pressured by relatives or family friends to exempt potential draftees.

For the first time, the media showed the kind of atrocities troops can commit under the pressure of intense danger and anxiety. Students demonstrated on many campuses. At Kent State University, the Ohio National Guard killed four students and wounded nine. President Lyndon Johnson declined to run for reelection in 1968, and could only appear at carefully selected venues. Opinion leaders turned against the war, including the mainstream and consummately professional newscaster Walter Cronkite. As Johnson said to an aide, "If I've lost Cronkite, I've lost Middle America."

Equally important, by 1960, there was already a new youth counter – culture in full revolt against the conventions that made up the status quo. By 1962, the contraceptive pill had freed young people so they could have casual sex without the prospects of pregnancy, abortion, or socially pressured conventional marriage. The civil rights movement in the South had captured the imagination of young Americans, who were appalled by their countrymen who opposed it or dragged their feet in expanding civil rights. The war seemed to symbolize all that was wrong with America: coercion and sacrifice of people of color; money for war taken away from Roosevelt's New Deal and Truman's Fair Deal, which had promised so much for America's poor; and a philistine society whose disdain for the arts, the bonds of love, and ordinary human decency lurked behind an empty materialism and blind patriotism.

Soon the two came closer together: the middle class began to smoke pot and the hippies had to dress to get work in corporate jobs they never imagined having. But the universities were never the same.

The pace of transition

On campus, the transition from conservative to radical oppression was astonishingly swift. In 1949, at Peekskill, New York, a mob prevented the great African – American singer Paul Robeson from performing, lynched him in effigy, and burned a cross. In 1954, a left – wing student group at the University of Chicago, where I was studying, invited him to perform on campus. The university protected its campus community, refused to cancel the concert, and did not hide behind the possibility of violence as an excuse, as so many other institutions do today. It had recently (in 1949) defended the university's staff against the Illinois state legislature, which questioned its president about a suspect emeritus professor who still came on campus to work with mice. Asked if she might indoctrinate by example, he replied, "You mean the mice?" A bill of rights allowed students to bring speakers or performers of their choice. It is not accidental that Chicago has never disinvited a controversial speaker and recently reaffirmed its absolute commitment to free speech.

In 1954, just after the Korean War, the community ethos was overwhelmingly negative. *The Chicago Tribune* censured us and the American Legion threatened to disrupt the performance. My old friend Don Anderson and I were on the door to stop anyone who might be carrying a weapon. Fortunately, standing behind me was a huge United Electrical Worker: "If the kid says search, you are going to get searched." I was not very imposing: at age 20, I weighed 134 pounds. In 1958, we again brought Robeson to sing. The Korean War was over and no one objected. Two years later Robeson's songs were available in commercial recordings with a corporate assurance that "no one is going to find any politics in these."

The surest sign of change was the Berkeley Free speech movement, which began in the academic year of 1964 – 1965. Mass demonstrations demanded that the university administration lift its ban on off – campus political activities and acknowledge free speech and academic freedom. Sadly it did not take long for left – leaning students to go from free speech to intimidation of anyone they did not agree with. During a period of less than a decade, Tom Bouchard, an outstanding behavior geneticist, witnessed this transition. He was a Ph. D. candidate at Berkeley in 1964, and by 1973 was teaching at the University of Minnesota. As he related in a personal e – mail:

> The SDS [Students for a Democratic Society] once stormed the office of the department chairman and demanded that I be fired. He asked why, and they responded [that I was teaching about Jensen and other thinkers they did not like]. He said he agreed with me and they should go to the administration and ask that he befired. On their way out, they passed me in the hallway and threatened to kill me. I told my wife, and she reminded me that an English professor at Berkeley had had half his face shot off by a disgruntled student while

we were there ... They were entering my classroom, asking hostile questions and trying to disrupt my lectures. I solved this problem easily, as I recalled that when we took over Sproul Hall at Berkeley - during the Free Speech Movement - many students cowered and ran when the TV cameras came on. I simply brought a tape recorder to class and asked the class for permission to tape my lectures, giving them the same permission. The disrupters left and never came back.

Throughout 1968, student protests shut down or "disabled" universities all over America. From the start, Chicago refused to allow its students to coerce the university. In 1969, when Marlene Dixon was not reappointed, many speculated that it was because she was a feminist and a Marxist. Over 400 students held a sit – in at the administration building. Faculty wrote letters to *The Maroon* arguing that Dixon's reappointment decision was due to research inadequacies and over 300 students participated in a mock "anti – sit – in" to protest the original sit – in. The administration expelled 42 students and suspended another 81. Students marched to the university president's home; when they realized he was not there, a student broke the glass of the outside door. After these students were suspended, others set off stink bombs, organized a boycott of classes that 70 percent of students participated in, and carried out a hunger strike. None of these actions changed the students' sentences.

Whatever Dixon's merits, this was a sign of things to come. Chicago has never indulged student opinion about staffing and who should exercise free speech, and it has not established departments that have taken on the role of what can be said on campus about race and gender. A student can major in these areas but only through centers that draw upon staff from various university departments.

The egalitarian residue

The student protests of 1968 did not establish a real radical tradition on American campuses. The shallowness of their convictions was revealed by the precipitous decline of the left when students were no longer threatened by the draft, which has never been reintroduced to staff the American military.

Between 1972 and 1983, there was a period of political exhaustion on US campuses. The only events of note were the efforts of some universities to apologize for their actions during the McCarthy period. It took them at least 20 years to repent. In 1972 Rutgers invited M. I. Finley, whom it had fired him in 1952, to inaugurate a lecture series. In 1978 the trustees of Reed College acknowledged that they had made a mistake in firing Stanley Moore. In 1981 Temple University restored Barrows Dunham to the faculty. In 1982 the New York Board of Higher Education exonerated lecturers it had dismissed thirty years before. A year later the University of Vermont gave an honorary degree to Alex B. Novikoff, whom it had fired in 1953. (Schrecker, 1986).

Even today, there is nothing like the kind of militant radicalism among students that there was in the 1960s. They do not have the fire of an Aneurin Bevan, who once declared that nothing "can eradicate from my heart a deep burning hatred for the Tory Party. So far as I am concerned, they are lower than vermin." (Read the book, *Lower Than Vermin*, Killane, 1990). They do not have a classically socialist ideology or revolutionary strategy that governs their lives. Indeed, there is often student apathy about politics. But one thing remains: a residue of deeply held beliefs about equality. This credo is really the perfect morality for the politically quiescent. To "promote" equality, you do not have to do anything, just be pleasant, never give offense and, if you have a predilection for control, police others. Rather than eradicating how students feel about equality, the political vacuum gave the crusade for equality a monopoly of the political arena.

As usual, however, deep commitment to the indefensible cannot abide free debate or scientific inquiry. To have to defend is to bring to consciousness the alarming realization that one has no defense. The egalitarian creed has three basic principles: every group difference (sometimes virtually every individual difference) is entirely environmental in origin; anyone who disputes this should be silenced, at least within the university; all groups deserve equal treatment both in act and word. Everyone must acknowledge who has exploited whom; everyone must refrain from any speech an exploited group finds objectionable. The exploited are given an exemption from verbal abuse:

all whites are racist but blacks cannot be; all males are sexist (or, in the more radical diatribes, potential rapists) but women are not; and so forth.

Therefore, students are often more inclined use coercion over dialogue. To keep them quiet, typical universities spikes their guns in advance: they strive to create "an egalitarian campus" more egalitarian that anything the students of the 1960s ever imagined. The campus becomes "inclusive" in large part by prohibiting any speech or action that might offend any group with the exception of white males.

Codes and zones

The most important repressive measures of the new era are free speech codes and free speech zones. These were not introduced until the mid – 1980s. The problem is not in having a zone in which "soap box" debate is encouraged. The larger society does this.

When I was young, I used to enjoy going to a public park in Chicago (known as "Bughouse Square"), which was set aside for anyone who wished to speak on a soapbox. Artists, writers, political radicals, and hobos pontificated, lectured, recited poetry, ranted, and raved. My favorite occasion was watching a friend who advocated Devil worship. He had rigged up a trigger that would ignite a fast – burning fluid smeared on his hands. When he shouted, "the devil will give you great powers," he threw his hands in the air and they burst into flames. None of the Christian orators could match that. I enjoyed Lafayette Square, which served a similar purpose right in front of the White House in Washington DC.

But free speech was never confined to a few small areas. The First Amendment to the US Constitution makes all of America a free speech zone. If speech is to be prohibited, judicial rulings have concluded that it must pose a "clear and present danger." During wartime, as we know, the Supreme Court tended to interpret this to include disseminating the works of Marx or believing that it could incite Americans to overthrow the government. But by 1969, *Brandenburg v. Ohio*, limited "clear and present danger" to an "imminent lawless action" and prohibited citizens only from threatening or conspiring to do serious things like plot assassinations or other serious crimes.

5
The era of radical oppression

The Supreme Court has held that students have the same right to free speech that any citizen would have in the larger society. This introduces our consideration of the era of radical repression. Its constant theme has been the struggle between the universities and the courts. It might seem that the courts cannot help but win, but the verdict is still out.

The case of Texas Tech

In 2003 Texas Tech University banned "physical, verbal, written or electronically transmitted threats, insults, epithets, ridicule or personal attacks" that are "personally directed at one or more specific individuals based on the individual's appearance, personal characteristics or group membership, including, but not limited to, race, color, religion, national origin, gender, age, disability, citizenship, veteran status, sexual orientation, ideology, political view or political affiliation." They reserved open debate to a twenty foot – in – diameter gazebo (an area that could hold no more than 40 people) called a "Free Speech Zone." Anyone who wished to speak or distribute literature likely to be divisive outside that zone had to get approval.

Jason Roberts sought to publicize his view that "homosexuality is a sinful, immoral, and unhealthy lifestyle." When he asked for permission to do so outside the designated zone, officials turned him down his saying that it was "the expression of a personal belief and thus is something more appropriate for the free – speech area." After attorneys filed suit, the university created additional "free speech zones" but did not relax its requirements. In *Roberts v. Haraghan* (2004), the court held that the code banned speech that, no matter how offensive, is protected by the First Amendment and that the free speech zones were illegal.

In Texas Tech's 2017 handbook, the current speech code has altered little, but the university has not directly defied the court. The free speech zones are gone and, in practice, the university has become more tolerant. In 2015 local conservatives were enraged by a lecture by the radical activist Angela Davis. In 2016 a conservative student group brought Milo Yiannopoulos to speak about "lesbians faking hate crimes." In September 2017 its new president allowed a San Diego law professor named Gail Heriot to speak, despite objections that she was an outspoken affirmative action opponent and that a congresswoman had called her a "bigot" (Watkins, 2017).

The tenacity of speech codes

Texas Tech offers us an example of a positive outcome in which the rule of law prevailed following a successful court challenge. Any yet, we must ask ourselves why a university even had a restrictive speech code as late as 2003? Indeed, why does any university have one today? The courts first held that such codes were unconstitutional as far back as 1989, and there have been eleven cases since. Indeed, the universities are often determined to retain the codes even if they have to defend them in court at enormous cost. US courts have held that free speech zones are in some cases unconstitutional, but they are less frequent than speech codes: only about one university in ten has them (FIRE, 2018).

The universities want to confront students with a choice. First option: give in – confess wrongdoing, attend sensitivity training, and/or accept severe sanctions, up to and including expulsion. Second option: face years fighting through the courts at great expense and incurring the hostility of your university and possible reputational damage from having sued for an infraction that many find to be socially unacceptable even if unproved. Thousands will give in for every one who challenges the system, and universities know that. The persistence of speech codes shows that the universities want to make them binding in practice, whether or not they are legal.

The Foundation for Individual Rights in Education (FIRE) posts an annual rating of universities and classifies their speech codes (FIRE, 2018). In 2017, FIRE surveyed 461 institutions and found that 32.3 percent (color – coded red) clearly and substantially prohibited protected speech, while 58.6 percent (yellow) were ambiguous or directed at only very narrow categories of speech, while only eight percent (green) had no written prohibitions.

Only 37 of the 461 universities were green, but their number has been gradually increasing largely thanks to FIRE's efforts. The University of Chicago heads this list, with its admirable, if now unusual speech policy, which states: "Expressions that cause hurt or discomfort do not for that reason alone constitute a violation of the law or of University policy. Rather, the communications are assessed within the standards provided by ... [both] the Report on Freedom of Expression, and the University Policy on Harassment, Discrimination, and Sexual Misconduct." In other words, one cannot harass a student by shrieking racial epithets but can discuss race and IQ in his presence. Some other outstanding universities match this rating: Arizona State University, Carnegie Mellon, Duke, George Mason University, Purdue, the College of William and Mary, Oregon State, and the Universities of Florida, Maryland, North Carolina, Pennsylvania, and Virginia. Their number includes Eastern Kentucky University, which was avidly anti – leftist when I taught there in 1957 – 1961.

Prominent universities among the 149 institutions with the "red" rating are too numerous to list, but it includes Ivy League universities, including Harvard and Princeton, and many of the best liberal arts colleges: Barnard, Bryn Mawr, Carlton, Colgate, Davidson, Drexel, Grinnell, Lafayette, Middlebury, Reed, Swarthmore, Wellesley, and Williams. Reputation for academic excellence is no protection against campus censorship.

Using the same criteria, out of 42 universities in Australia, thirty – four (81 percent) were red; seven (17 percent) yellow, and only one (two percent) green (Lesh, 2017). Out of 115 universities in the United Kingdom, 73 (64 percent) were red, 35 amber (30 percent), and seven (6 percent) green (Spiked, 2017).

The tip of the iceberg

The few cases that come to public notice show what students are intimidated from doing when they obey speech codes or quietly accept penalties when charged with violations. They are the tip of a repressive iceberg. The examples I will give become more disturbing as we proceed. This is because repression becomes more visible as we go from speech codes to the newer concept of "microaggression."

I should preface our exhibit by noting that universities also censor free speech on grounds that have nothing to do with speech codes or free speech zones. On May 7, 2007, at Valdosta State University (Georgia), Hayden Barnes was told he had been expelled. He had agitated against building two parking garages as environmentally unfriendly. Barnes had written a letter to the school newspaper, politely contacted the regents, and posted a collage (showing smog, etc.) on Facebook calling the garage the "Zaccari Memorial Parking Garage." Valdosta State's president Roland Zaccari claimed that using the word "memorial" was an indirect threat against his life. In 2015, after eight years of litigation, a Federal District Court held that Barnes had been denied due process and awarded him $900,000 in damages.

In February 2006, Christian DeJohn pleaded that Temple's sexual harassment policy (which prohibited "generalized sexist remarks") inhibited discussing the role of women in the military, among other issues. Temple lost in US federal district court, appealed, and lost again. The Appellate Court held that banned behavior must be so "severe, pervasive, and objectively offensive ... that the victims are effectively denied equal access to an institution's resources and opportunities." In other words, it held that speech codes of the Temple – type are in themselves forbidden (Creeley & Harris, 2008). After more than two years of litigation, DeJohn was awarded one dollar. In October 2006, the San Francisco State University (SFSU) College Republicans held an anti – terrorism rally at which they stepped on homemade replicas of Hamas and Hezbollah flags. This offended several students who filed charges of "attempts to incite violence and create a hostile environment" and "actions of incivility." SFSU held an "investigation" that lasted five months before it was terminated under pressure (Lukianoff, 2014).

The printed word

When universities censor fliers or posters, they are legally remiss but this does not keep them from trying. In 2008 to 2009, Tarrant County College forbad students from handing out leaflets against laws that prohibit concealed weapons on campus and from wearing empty holsters to dramatize their argument. The court ruled this unconstitutional.

On November 12, 2002, Steve Hinkle, a student at California Polytechnic State University attempted to post a flier in the common area of the campus Multicultural Center. It advertised a speech by Mason Weaver, a black conservative. The flier displayed only the title of the talk, the time and place, and a picture of the speaker. Several students objected that the poster was "offensive." After a seven – hour hearing, the university found Hinkle guilty of disruptive behavior and he was ordered to write letters of apology to the offended students on pain of severe disciplinary penalties. After a suit was brought, Cal Poly agreed to settle out of court. It agreed to expunge Hinkle's disciplinary record, permit him to post fliers, and paid significant attorney's fees (FIRE, 2004).

In 2004, at the University of New Hampshire, Timothy Garneau put up posters in his dorm stating: "9 out of 10 freshman girls gain 10 – 15 pounds. But there is something you can do about it. If you live below the 6th floor, take the stairs. Not only will you feel better about yourself but you will also be saving us time and won't be sore on the eyes." The university found him guilty of discriminatory harassment because his posters targeted a specific gender. He was expelled from UNH housing and ordered to meet with a university counselor, write a 3,000 – word "reflection paper" about what he had learned, and send a written apology to the dorm. After the intervention of FIRE, the university withdrew the charge and assigned him a new room in another residence hall. He had spent three nights sleeping in his car during his dorm exile (Lehigh, 2004).

In the spring of 2007, Tufts labeled an ad in a conservative student publication as "harassment." Published during Islamic Awareness Week, the ad quoted the Koran as commanding that unbelievers be beheaded and suffer the striking "off of every fingertip." It also quoted a famous Islamic theologian who said that marriage made "the woman a man's slave" (Lukianoff, 2014, p. 49).

In 2012, at the University of Cincinnati, the Young Americans for Liberty (YAL) endorsed a statewide "right to work" ballot initiative.

They were told that if any YAL members were seen walking around campus to gather signatures, campus security would be alerted. The university's policy required that all "demonstrations, pickets, and rallies" on campus take place in an area comprising just 0.1 percent of the university's 137 – acre West Campus. Even within this free speech zone, all expressive activity had to be registered with the university at least ten working days in advance: "[a]nyone violating this policy may be charged with trespassing." In *University of Cincinnati Chapter of YAL v. Williams* (2012), the court joined other courts that had prohibited free speech zones.

In November 2016, a student at Los Angeles Pierce College passed out copies of the US Constitution outside the campus "free speech zone." He was trying to recruit for Young Americans for Liberty. He was told he would be asked to leave campus if he refused to comply with university regulations. These required him to use the free speech zone only and to fill out a permit application in advance. The free speech zone measures 616 square feet and comprises about .003 percent of the total area of the campus (CBS, 2017).

Censorship of student newspapers is another factor. At private universities, it varies all the way from those that the university censors with impunity to those that have virtually the freedom of an off – campus paper.   In 2016, at Liberty University (Lynchburg, Virginia), Joel Schmieg claimed that the President, Jerry Falwell, Jr., forbad him to publish an article critical of Donald Trump (Palfrey, 2017, p. 111). In a more positive story from 2018, Jamie Ehrlich, a retiring editor of the *University of Chicago Maroon*, asserted that despite the publication of confidential internal documents and a story on sexual assault and campus security, the university did not attempt to censor. He emphasized that the *Maroon* is financially independent. When the newspaper at Southern Methodist University turned to the university for funds, however, its editor – in – chief claimed there were repeated attempts to censor (Ehrlich, 2018).

As for public universities, state and federal courts forbad almost all censorship until 2005. In *Hosty v. Carter*, the Seventh Circuit Court held that a university subsidized newspaper at Governors State

University (Illinois) was not considered a public forum but an extracurricular activity and therefore not protected by the First Amendment. As a response, Illinois passed a law stipulating that administrators could have no editorial control or censorship abilities (eight other US states have similar laws).

In 2015, three student editors at Fairmont State University (West Virginia) resigned after their faculty advisor, Michael Kelley, was dismissed. They believed his dismissal was an administrative backlash to a toxic – mold investigation by the newspaper. On the other hand, in 2012, a University of Memphis senior, Chelsea Boozer, wrote an opinion article criticizing the director of public safety for not issuing a campus – wide safety alert after learning of reports about an on – campus rape. University officials filed police reports against Boozer, accusing her of being "rude and hostile" when conducting interviews for her article and cut funding. After a months – long battle that included attempts to cut the newspaper's funding, she was vindicated and the paper got its money back (Wheeler, 2015).

Trigger warnings and microaggressions

Trigger warnings go a step beyond speech codes. They are even more detailed and strike straight at the heart of the classroom. In 1993, at Minnesota, any student or faculty member worried that a classroom discussion might be insulting could request a "classroom climate adviser" (Kors & Silvergate, 1998). Since then, a number of universities have begun to warn against "microaggressions." For example, asking an Asian – American or Latino "Where were you born?" is suspect because this implies that he or she is not a "real" American. Assigning *The Great Gatsby* has been criticized because it contains racial diatribes and physical abuse, even though they are negatively portrayed actions of an objectionable character (Lukianoff and Haidt, 2015).

In 2013 students at the University of California, Los Angeles, staged a sit – in during a class taught by Val Rust, an education professor. The group read a letter aloud expressing their concerns, which included how Rust corrected his students' grammar and spelling. Rust had advised a student that he had wrongly capitalized the first letter of the word *indigenous*; lowercasing the capital " *I* " was an insult to the student and her ideology. In the fall of 2014, Omar Mahmood, a student at the University of Michigan, wrote a satirical column in which he poked fun at a tendency to perceive microaggressions in just about anything. A group of women vandalized Mahmood's doorway with eggs, hot dogs, gum, and notes with messages such as "Everyone hates you, you violent prick."

During the 2014 – 2015 academic year, administrators of the University of the California system presented faculty leader – training sessions to all deans and department chairs. They were presented with a list of offensive statements that were now off – limits including: "America is the land of opportunity" and "I believe the most qualified person should get the job." It was a student at Oberlin, however, who made the most absurd case for trigger warnings: "they are like ingredients lists on food ... People should have the right to know and consent to what they are putting into their minds, just as they have the right to know and consent to what they are putting into our bodies" (Barreca, 2016).

There is some resistance. In April 2015, at Brandeis, the Asian – American student association warned that it was offensive to ask an Asian, "Aren't you supposed to be good at math?" or to say "I'm colorblind! I don't see race." Asian – American students, however, complained that the association's statement was itself a microaggression. The association removed it confessing that it had been guilty of such.

As these examples show, the concept of microaggression threatens to turn, and indeed has turned, campuses into verbal minefields. Its sole function is to label words or deeds that would normally occasion a shrug of the shoulders or a gentle admonition into a serious offence worthy of punishment (Lilienfield, 2017). Chemerinsky and Gillman (2017) note some cases that we might consider ambiguous. In March 2015, at the University of Oklahoma, when fraternity members were on a bus, two students led a chant whose words included "There will never be a nigger at SAE" (their fraternity). Rather than being reprimanded and told not to be so foolish, they were expelled. The investigation allegedly involved an inquiry that suggested that students who did not reveal who started the chant would themselves be expelled.

Even more worryingly, such codes even apply off campus. In October 2016, a law professor at the University of Oregon was suspended for wearing black face at a Halloween party she hosted in her own home. She said she did it to promote a conversation about race. Whatever the truth of this, the normal response would be: take her comments as an apology; warn her that times have changed. You are certainly not safe on social media. In November 2015, Colorado College suspended Thaddeus Pryor and banned him from campus for two years, during which time he was barred taking classes for academic credit at any other institution. His offense? In reply to the comment "#blackwomenmatter," he posted, "they matter, they're just not hot" (Chemerinsky and Gillman, 2017).

Will Australia become worse?

Trigger warnings have spread to Australia. In March 2017, Monash University adopted a program involving 15 of the university's course outlines. Academics are to look for "emotionally confronting material" in their discussion of sexual assault, violence, domestic abuse, child abuse, eating disorders, self – harm, suicide, pornography, abortion, kidnapping, hate speech, animal cruelty, and animal deaths including abattoirs." The "hate speech" category caused hesitation to analyze basic issues about race. The dangerous material will not necessarily be removed from the course. The outline will simply warn students about material or texts that might be traumatic, so they can choose to miss class or not read.

The Network of Women Students Australia suggests a longer list. It includes not only racism, racist slurs, sexism, and sexist slurs, but also classism, corpses, drugs, fear of eye contact, fear of holes, fear of transgender people, food, hair pulling disorder, drugs, insects, mental illness, Nazi paraphernalia, needles, slimy things, snakes, spiders, vomit, and warfare (Palmer, 2017).

Safe spaces

Universities have begun to debate the concept of "safe spaces." Some use it to advertise campus areas in which all views are welcome. Usually it refers to spaces where everyone must be extra careful not to offend. There are already plenty of safe spaces on campus where students need not confront acrimonious debate: hostels – residential room and recreation rooms, whether the lounge or cafeteria welcomes debate is set by custom and size; the rooms or centers of various student clubs or groups (ranging from all points of the political, racial, and gender spectrum) – the members moderate debate in accord with their purpose; the library – they enforce quiet and there are discussion rooms that a group of congenial students can book. Civility forbids badgering people personally when they are on campus or playing sport.

It is when a contentious student is banned from public places, or even worse from distributing literature, that the concept can become a menace. Safe spaces also become objectionable when they inhibit class discussion including controversial topics like rape or the Holocaust. The assumption should be that lecturers will show common sense when they know that a certain topic is likely to offend and say why it must be discussed (we need to know the real causes of the Holocaust if we want to understand how a seemingly civilized nation became so brutal). When someone goes too far, a word to the head was enough without the detailed prior censorship of trigger warnings, complex speech codes, or lengthy investigations.

On September 19, 2016, there was a moment of irony. Northwestern University's president made a vigorous defense of trigger warnings and safe spaces. Some of his points were valid: students should be able to let their guard down by retreating to places like religious centers or Black House. But sadly, he called those who disagree with him "lunatics" or "idiots." Commentators noted his microaggressions against the mentally ill ("lunatics") and against people with low intelligence ("idiots"), but he was not fired (Kotecki, 2016; Jussim, 2016).

On occasion, hysteria captures the concept of a safe space. A law Professor from Cornell spoke at Vassar on October 25, 2017. His subject, that there is no constitutional protection against "hate speech," was so threatening that students put together a safety plan. The university library would be a safe place and provide coloring books, zine kits (a toy you can use to create images), markers, and construction paper. Designated

Vassar students with glow sticks would mark off even safer places. There would also be emotional support teams (Jacobson, 2017).

Disinviting speakers

An obvious way of curtailing free speech is to forbid the university or its student groups from bringing speakers to campus. Many efforts have been made to get invitations withdrawn, all of which show the low level of tolerance, but I will examine only those that have been successful.

On December 15, 2001, during a graduation speech at California State, Sacramento, Janis Besler Heaphy (publisher of the *Sacramento Bee*) said that racial profiling, secret military tribunals, and government vetting of videotapes of Osama bin Laden raised constitutional issues. The thousands who packed the Arco sports arena reacted by "silencing" her (Mohan, 2001).

In February of 2002, Laura Bush, wife of President George W. Bush, declined an invitation to speak at a graduate school commencement ceremony at UCLA. Students and faculty had protested at her shallow credentials and the "political implications" of the invitation. Previous speakers had included Annette Benning and Rob Reiner, both actors, and Kareem Abdul – Jabbar, a basketball player. As Kate Kennedy of the Independent Women's Forum said: "This is just a recurring example of the college students' inability to accept dissenting viewpoints and the inability to accept Mrs. Bush's presence on campus" (*Washington Times*, 2002).

On April 8, 2013, Robert Zoellick (President of the World Bank) withdrew as Swarthmore's commencement speaker after students called him a "war criminal" because he served in the Bush administration when Iraq was invaded in 2003. On May 5, 2014, Condoleezza Rice (former Secretary of State) withdrew from an engagement at Rutgers when she was attacked on similar grounds, this time with support from the Faculty Council (Ben – Porath, 2017).

On April 9, 2014, Brandeis reversed its decision to grant an honorary degree to Ayaan Hirsi Ali. She opposes forced marriage, honor killings, child marriage, and female genital mutilation (which she suffered). She argues that Islam contains a worldview incompatible with the Western way of life. According to the *Pittsburgh Tribune*, the local imam believes she deserves the death sentence but only after trial in an Islamic country (Acton, 2007). The president of Brandeis decided that some of her statements were "Islamophobic." This was after the Head of the Islamic Studies Department, other faculty members, and several student groups accused her of "hate speech" (Harris, 2014). Kenneth Margolin (2014), an attorney, expressed no surprise: "under many college codes of conduct, a student publicly stating on campus words identical to Ayaan Hirsi Ali's ... might find herself ... charged, sanctioned, suspended, and even expelled."

Vetoing other speakers

There is a shred of justification for withdrawing invitations to receive honorary degrees or to address graduation ceremonies. It might be argued that the first requires a university consensus that the candidate is indeed worthy, and that the second implies an innocuous address, something like praise of the graduating class plus telling them that you are sure they will make a better world. However, canceling most invited speakers cannot be defended in a democratic society.

On February 23, 2000, at the University of Texas at Austin, the Faculty Council withdrew an invitation to the former Secretary of State Henry Kissinger after campus groups called him a war criminal because of US policy during the Vietnam War, the invasion of East Timor, and the overthrow of Allende's government in Chile (Associated Press, 2000).

On November 14, 2002, Harvard barred Tom Paulin who was to be honored by giving the prestigious Morris Gray poetry reading. Protesters objected to his political views on Israel: that Israel had no right to exist; and that American – born settlers in the Occupied Territories should be shot dead (*Guardian*, 2002).

On January 30, 2003, Schenectady County Community College cancelled an appearance by Scott Ritter, a former UN weapons inspector, due to controversy about his role as an outspoken critic of President Bush's Iraq Policy – and a charge that he had attempted to meet an underaged girl. Soon after, he appeared at Washington College in Chestertown, Maryland: "We're not going to cancel the event. As an institute of higher learning, we have a duty to provide people with different points of view." (The event) is "not an endorsement of his activities ... We're just giving him a soapbox for two hours" (WND, 2003).

A student group invited John Derbyshire to speak at Williams College. On February 18, 2016, the President cancelled the talk because Derbyshire had often used "hate speech" (Wood, 2016). Derbyshire is a highly intelligent man but calls himself a realist. He cautions whites that they have much to fear from blacks and advises that one should make friends with them to escape charges of racial bias (Sorkin, 2012). A year earlier, the same group had invited Susanne Venker, a critic of feminism ("I believe a woman's attitude toward men is the single greatest predictor of whether or not she'll be happy in life"). Bombarded with "hate speech" and threats, the group cancelled. (Brown, 2017).

On February 25, 2015, two Harvard Law student groups rescinded an invitation to Robin Steinberg. She is credited with advancing feminist ideals (helping countless women) while working towards racial, ethnic, and socioeconomic justice. New York Police Department union leaders had objected to her, citing an anti – cop rap video that included appearances by two of her employees. Within hours, the two student groups asserted they "did not intend for [Steinberg's] nomination to suggest in any way that it is acceptable to harm police officers or incite others to do so." The students thus accepted the rationale for censorship: that anyone who wants to bring a speaker to campus endorses all of their views or behavior. Fortunately, the Law School extended a new invitation and she appeared in mid – April. Aside from describing her work, she accepted negligence in not checking the content of the offensive video (Duchen, 2015).

The most pathetic document about inviting speakers comes from Wellesley. Six professors who sat on the college's Commission for Ethnicity, Race, and Equity (CERE) reacted to a visit from Laura Kipnis, an outspoken critic of campus sexual harassment policing who has said that making every woman terrified of rape is the best way to disempower them. Among other things, the professors asserted:

> We are especially concerned with the impact of speakers' presentations on Wellesley students, who often

feel the injury most acutely and invest time and energy in rebutting the speakers' arguments ... When dozens of students tell us they are in distress as a result of a speaker's words, we must take these complaints at face value ... We in CERE are happy to serve as a sounding board when hosts are considering inviting controversial speakers, to help sponsors think through the various implications of extending an invitation (Morey & Harris, 2017).

In response to an inquiry from FIRE, Wellesley replied that it was dedicated to upholding free speech, but FIRE lists their speech code in the red.

Shouting down speakers

We have described the events at Middlebury on March 2, 2017, when students shouted down and attacked Charles Murray. At one time, it was a scandal for a speaker to be shouted down. Forty years ago, at Yale, protesters stopped a debate featuring William Shockley, who had won the Nobel Prize for the transistor radio and who believed that the brains of blacks were wired differently than those of whites. Yale suspended eleven students, showing, as we will see, a mettle sadly lacking today. Shouting down is now so endemic that I will confine myself only to a few recent incidents.

Milo Yiannopoulos is a conservative commentator who opposes feminism ("feminism is cancer"), Islam, and political correctness. On May 23, 2016, he went to DePaul. Two protesters rushed the stage while the crowd booed them. Campus security made no effort to remove them. Earlier, while touring the United Kingdom, he was banned from Manchester but spoke at Bristol (Krupp, Onsgard & Pars, 2016; Onsgard & Deppen, 2017; Public Affairs, 2017; Woodward B., 2017). On September 24, 2017, he appeared at Berkeley. The police canceled the event after violent clashes but later he spoke and sang *The Star Spangled Banner*. Providing him protection cost the University $800,000 (Barmann, 2017). The vice – president of the College Republicans reported that he was mocked, spat on, and punched (Fuller, 2017). Two years later, the conservative commentator Ann Coulter was invited to Berkeley for another event sponsored by the College Republicans. She was greeted by 1,000 protesters and, though able to speak, approximately a hundred tickets members of her audience were unable to access the venue where she spoke.

How to minimize the financial consequences of such events? I would call a meeting of all student groups in advance with a message: "Do you really want the university to spend a huge sum on security that could be best spent elsewhere? We will not cancel this event (either because students have a right to invite speakers of their choice or state law). Why not all agree to let this talk die from neglect, from the small audience that chooses to attend and general indifference? As we are obliged to do, those who attend and use violence or disrupt will be caught on camera and suspended." This at least would put student groups, if they mobilize, in a position to see things in different light, assuming they are open to reasoned argument. I would also approach any right – wing group that invites someone for strategic reasons. There is a tendency to invite controversial speakers precisely because they are controversial and likely to be shouted down, thus scoring the publicity coup of showing up left wing intolerance. Saying, "As you well know, this is the kind of speaker who may cost $800,000 to protect. If you really want to hear him, hire a venue just off campus, so at least the municipality will have to pay the bill" may avoid undue confrontation.

In September 2016, the University of Michigan's Political Union announced a debate: "Black Lives Matter is harmful to racial relations in the United States." This was not its position, but a claim to be disputed in a formal debate. About 100 protesters forced their way into the room, with 250 more protesters spilling into the hallway and lobby. They jeered and hurled obscenities at the debaters for an hour while chanting, "black lives are not up for debate." The campus police and university administrators present said and did nothing. Afterwards, the university did not condemn anyone and did not discipline the many protesters caught on video. In private, members of the Political Union say that since the incident it has avoided other potentially controversial debate topics for fear of shout – downs. Later, a student who had sparked condemnation of the debate received an award for social activism by the school's Women's Studies Center (Kurtz, 2017a).

On November 16, 2016, the conservative commentator Ben Shapiro appeared at the University of Wisconsin, Madison. Demonstrators arranged with university police in advance to disrupt and temporarily shut down the lecture. After half an hour, they marched out and then intimidated conservative talk – radio host Vicki McKenna in the lobby until she had to be protected by police. The university expressed "disappointment" but disciplined no one. Afterwards, some students called for members of the Young Americans for Freedom chapter, which had invited Shapiro, to be forced into "intensive diversity training" (Kurtz, 2017a).

On February 2, 2017, at New York University, the critic of political correctness Gavin McInnes was pepper – sprayed during a fight with protesters as he attempted to enter a university hall. After medical treatment on the spot, he began his talk. About 20 minutes later, antifa ("anti – fascist") protesters burst into the room and forced him to flee. Scuffles between police and protesters led to eleven arrests (Kurtz, 2017b).

On February 13, 2017, Israel's UN ambassador Danny Danon spoke at Columbia. Between 50 and 100 protesters rendered much of his talk barely audible. The audience cheered when security guards finally led the protesters out (Kurtz, 2017b). On September 27, 2017, Columbia made amends when a talk by Alan Dershowitz (who favors a two – state solution) proceeded without interruption.

On April 6, 2017, an attempt to shout down Heather MacDonald, a pro – police conservative, at Claremont McKenna actually failed. As usual, the students blockaded the lecture hall forcing the event to be moved and livestreamed from a secret location. The university was genuinely resolved to salvage what it could: "the blockade breached institutional values of freedom of expression and assembly." Far more important, unlike virtually all other universities, it levied sanctions. It suspended three students for a full year, two for a semester, and placed two more on probation (Kaufman, 2017).

On April 25, 2017, conservative radio host Rabbi Daniel Lapin was shouted down before an audience of 200 by a handful of protesters at California's Cañada Community College. He was speaking on the morality of capitalism. After 20 to 30 minutes of disruption and angry exchanges, the host YAF chapter had to sneak guests out a few at a time into a separate room to continue the lecture (Kurtz, 2007a).

On May 1, 2007, Robert Spencer, who writes on the role of Islam in jihadi terror, was shut down by close to 200 hecklers who screamed for an hour and a half as he attempted to give a talk at the University of Buffalo (Kurtz, 2007a).

On May 10, 2017, about 40 members of Students for Justice in Palestine (SJP) shouted down a panel discussion featuring Israeli military veterans at the University of California at Irvine (Kurtz, 2017a).

On September 27, 2017, Claire Gastañaga from the American Civil Liberties Union was scheduled to speak at William and Mary. Students from the Black Lives Matter chapter shouted her down chanting, "the oppressed are not impressed" and "liberalism is white supremacy." They were protesting the ACLU's defense of the right of white nationalists to assemble in Charlottesville (LA Times, 2017).

There were at least three incidents during the week beginning October 6, 2017 alone. On October 6, 2017, University of Oregon President Michael Schill was prevented from delivering his State of the University speech when about 45 chanting students took over the stage. Schill knew the disruption was coming and capitulated by prerecording his speech for later distribution. The lead demonstrator threatened, "Expect resistance to anyone who opposes us."

Three days later, Texas State Representative Briscoe Cain was shouted down at Texas Southern University Law School. After the protesters were ejected by campus police, the President called them back and cancelled Cain's talk. He said that the invitation group had not used the proper application procedures. The dean of the law school replied that they had in fact done so (Kurtz, 2017b). It appears that proper procedures are not good enough anyway. On October 16, 2017, Cain reappeared. His talk was again cancelled after protesters disrupted him with shouts of "When a racist comes to town, shut it down." Two days later, Charles Murray was met by students who turned off the lights in the room, set off the alarms on their phones, played music and chanted: "Racist, Sexist, KKK; Charles Murray go away" (LA Times, 2017).

On October 10, 2017, protesters at Columbia stopped a talk via Skype by Tommy Robinson. In 2016, he established Pegida UK, named after the German far – right political party, and he now works for The Rebel Media, a right – wing Canadian website. Students blocked entrances, shouted over Robinson, then stormed the stage and forced him to abandon his talk (Kurtz, 2017b).

On October 11, 2017, Michigan was a bit kinder to Charles Murray than Middlebury. For the first half of his talk, they interrupted by shouting, playing music, and using an overhead projector to point an arrow with the label "white supremacist" at Murray. They left, and he addressed what remained of the audience (Roll, 2017).

These incidents give a picture of the kind of thing involved in vetoing speakers and relating more would take over the book. I want to emphasize that 2017 was not a particularly "bad" year. FIRE charts trends for "disinvitations." They peaked at 43 in 2016, fell to 18 in 2018; and rose again to 30 as of this writing in late 2019, but are still below their peak (Sachs, 2019).

Finally, I want to mention one incident that occurred a few years earlier (October 29, 2013) because it was at Brown University, which has always been fairly resolute. New York City Police Commissioner Ray Kelly had to leave after 27 minutes of chanting about the sins of New York police. When Brown's vice president Marissa Quinn told the crowd, "I have never seen in my 15 years at Brown the inability to have a dialogue," they cheered (Creeley, 2013).

Israel vs. Palestine

You may get the impression that pro – Palestinian groups have a monopoly of banning pro – Israelis. But there is plenty of traffic the other way. Recall the cases discussed above: Paulin disinvited at Harvard for being anti – Israel; Hindley's claim that he was targeted for being too critical of Israel at Brandeis. In 2011, Brooklyn College fired an appointee after a state legislator accused him of pro – Palestinian views, although he was reinstated after a public outcry (Lukianoff, 2014). In 2014, Illinois cancelled a signed employment contract with Steven Salaita because he posted criticism of Israel on Twitter (Cohen, 2015). In

2015, Fordham banned the formation of a student chapter of Students for Justice in Palestine (Singal, 2017).

Tenured faculty

When tenured faculty dare to preach heresy in public, they meet with mixed results. On July 23, 1996, Edward J. Miller of the University of New Orleans published a letter in which he said he believed that racial differences in brain weight were of statistical significance. The Associate Dean for Multicultural Affairs held that a professor who holds such views must not teach African – Americans and that she hoped that black students were being steered away from Miller's classes. The university's chancellor wrote that, "the university will not tolerate anyone's use of the classroom as a forum to promote racial disharmony" (Kors & Silverglate, 1998, p.107).

Miller's views earned him death threats. Students and staff circulated petitions against him, but he was never discharged. His work leaned heavily on J. Philippe Rushton, who developed a genetic hierarchy that ranked East Asians ahead of whites and whites ahead of blacks. In 1989, after Rushton delivered a paper, Ontario's premier called on the University of Western Ontario to fire him from his tenured post. Student protesters took the streets and echoed the demand. The student council did not agree: they withdrew funding from the groups behind the protest. There was a petition signed by the many academics who supported his retention (I signed). While Western Ontario reprimanded Rushton on a number of occasions, it stood behind his right to conduct his research (Miner, 2012).

In 1989, in the Australian journal *Quadrant*, Michael Levin said that whites as a group were inherently more intelligent than blacks, that women had less occupational drive than men, and that students knew nothing. He later qualified the last statement by saying that students usually knew their own address but could not find it on a map. Having offended at least 60 percent of the residents of New York City, some for multiple reasons (such as female black students), his views were not well received. The philosophy chairman at the City College of New York forbad him to teach first – year students, and the faculty senate voted to censure him. There was an active letter writing campaign on his behalf (I wrote one). The Professorial Board ruled that teaching assignments must be assigned solely on academic grounds, and he was approved to teach his introductory course in early 1990. The dean, however, wrote a letter to Levin's students telling them that Levin held controversial views on race, feminism, and homosexuality and that the department had created another section in which they could register. Thirty of the 38 students chose to remain in his class. While it was conceded that his classes were competent and fair (it was a logic course), a committee was appointed to review whether his published views might justify his dismissal. He went to court, which decided in his favor on both counts (Kors & Silverglate, 1998).

Linda Gottfredson at Delaware has done meticulous research into the implications of ability differences in hiring. She advocates taking ability tests at face value, which would mean that the more cognitively demanding the job, the fewer blacks would qualify. She rejected using race – based norms that would ignore racial differences in test performance. Gottfredson solicited and received funds from the Pioneer Fund, which has a history of funding suspect groups like the National Policy Institute, which advocates white supremacy. I suspect Gottfredson turned to it because it is about the only source that finances basic research into racial differences. In January 1990, a staff committee on research began to investigate whether the university should accept money from the Pioneer Fund, based on complaints that it was racist and discriminatory. The committee decided, quite rightly, that the university should not but went further to dictate what use academic staff could make of whatever funds they received.

The committee held that Gottfredson could accept money from the Fund only as a recipient of a scholarship. She could not, however, use her office or any university facilities to do her research. Resulting publications would not count toward her research record, and any time spent would have to be over and above her full – time academic duties. The dean wished to read any research papers students wrote in her courses to ascertain what beliefs about race superiority they might express. Gottfredson went to court, and in April 1992 the university gave way on all counts. She received a year's leave of absence with pay. Even better, the university expressed its regret for the unnecessary disruption of her career and that of another academic whose career had been jeopardized by its actions (Kors & Silverglate, 1998).

In 1997 Chris Brand was fired at Edinburgh. His major sin was a book (that was never published) and an interview in which he described himself as a "scientific racist." The Anti – Nazi League of Edinburgh shut down his lectures. He was fired in 1997 from his 27 – year position at the University for conduct that allegedly "brought the university into disrepute." Brand sued for unfair dismissal and received £12,000 (in those days the maximum obtainable from an employment tribunal) in an out – of – court settlement. During the controversy, he was outspoken, asserting that the vice – chancellor needed a brain transplant after the latter admitted he had not read the book (Barendt, 2010).

In January 2005, Ward Churchill, a tenured academic at Colorado, published an essay in which he asserted that the September 11, 2001 attacks, while unjustified, was provoked by American foreign policy. The university fired Churchill in 2007 for research misconduct. Despite winning one dollar in damages from a jury, Churchill ultimately lost his wrongful termination lawsuit on appeal (Paulson, 2012).

In 2007, James Watson resigned his post as Chancellor of the Cold Spring Harbour Laboratory in New York. He had been awarded the Nobel Prize as co – discoverer of the structure of DNA in 1962. After moving to CSHL, he shifted his research to the study of cancer and made the Lab a world – leading research center in molecular biology. Unfortunately, he strayed outside his field to comment on other issues. He said that thin people are more ambitious than fat people, that women scientists are less effective than men scientists, and, most damaging of all, that Western policy toward African countries was based on the fallacy that blacks are as intelligent as whites, even though testing suggests the contrary. It did not help when he cited as evidence the spurious assertion that those who had to deal with black employees know that they tend to be less intelligent. He tried to apologize by saying he did not mean to characterize Africans as genetically inferior and that he was referring to geographically separated populations evolving differently (Keim, 2007).

Since then, as he says, he has become an "unperson" tainted beyond redemption. For those who think he richly deserves that fate, see the article by Rutherford (2014) entitled "James Watson deserves to be shunned." The taint is so strong that he has been refused a chance to speak even on neutral subjects. The Carl R. Woese Institute for Genomic Research at Illinois invited him to give a "narrowly focused scientific talk" about his cancer research and then cancelled after a faculty protest (Jaschick, 2017). We will never know whether the talk would have inspired other researchers. Recall that Charles Murray was considered so tainted that he was unable to give an insightful talk on America's social divisions at Middlebury. This is not to conflate the two men: Murray has never said anything about any issue that went beyond the bounds of careful scholarship.

Untenured faculty usually accept dismissal without publicity. There are a few exceptions. Thomas Klocek had been adjunct professor at DePaul for 14 years. In 2004, students complained about an out – of – class discussion about terrorism. He was suspended and asked to accept a monitor in his classes, which he refused (Grossman, 2005). In June 2017, a historically black college (Essex County College in Newark) fired a black adjunct professor for a radio broadcast in which she defended a Black Lives Matter chapter's decision to host a Memorial Day event exclusively for black people. The president denounced any program that excludes students "on the basis of their race, color, orientation or national origin" (Schmidt, 2017). To forbid the program was one thing, but to fire Durden for disagreeing was another.

Is Canada more tolerant?

I cannot find the total number of speakers cancelled or intimidated and staff fired in America and Canada, respectively. It is likely that many cases are never reported or publicized, but my limited survey makes Canada look more tolerant. Only one faculty member resigned under pressure, and Phillip Ruston survived at Western Ontario. There were only two incidents in which a speaker was intimidated. On March 22, 2010, at Ottawa University, demonstrators mobbed the venue at which the American conservative commentator Ann Coulter was to speak and police told organizers that to proceed was unsafe (Chase, 2018).

The paucity of incidents compared to the United States may be misleading: there are 96 universities in Canada, while the US boasts over three thousand. The case of Jordan Peterson may tip the balance in Canada's favor. His views, which question postmodernism and political controls on certain forms of speech, are unpalatable to the left. He is on a crusade to counter them, and has been roundly denounced around the world. Although not fired in Canada, in 2019 he lost a Cambridge fellowship because he was once photographed standing next to someone wearing a t – shirt with an anti – Islamic slogan.

As Margaret Wente (2018) has pointed out, many students are told that morality is no more than a matter of personal opinion (and therefore all moral judgments are essentially politically motivated), that Western civilization is hopelessly corrupt and evil, and that all group differences are environmental in origin. Peterson at least presents a contrary point of view, arguing that morality, order, virtue, and rules are not bad things but necessary. As a competent psychologist on the faculty of the University of Toronto, he argues that human beings are not a blank slate but are influenced by their genes, which set limits on what they can become. All hierarchies cannot be abolished, all gender differences cannot be eliminated.

An excellent example of how much people need this debate was provided when Cathy Newman interviewed him on Britain's Channel 4. She thought all she had to do was expose his reactionary biases and was stunned to find that he could cite evidence that rendered her helpless. One exchange illustrates her plight:

> **Peterson:** There's this idea that hierarchical structures are a sociological construct of the Western patriarchy. And that is so untrue that it's almost unbelievable. I use the lobster as an example: We diverged from lobsters evolutionarily history about 350 million years ago. And lobsters exist in hierarchies. And it's part of my attempt to demonstrate that the idea of hierarchy has absolutely nothing to do with sociocultural construction, which it doesn't.

Newman: "Let me get this straight. You're saying that we should organize our societies along the lines of the lobsters?" (Full interview: Friedersdorf, 2018).

The concept that genes put restrictions on human beings just as they do throughout the animal kingdom was something she simply could not comprehend. I am not endorsing Peterson without reservation, but he proves that unwelcome views do not necessarily get you fired, at least in Canada, and he is far from an unperson in the world outside academia. As of early 2018, he had 1.3 million YouTube subscribers and 9,500 fans who contribute to him to support his various projects. He has a sense of humor. When asked if he believes in God, he replied, "I think the proper response to that is No, but I'm afraid He might exist" (Blatchford, 2018).

Universities, however, are less welcoming. On March 17, 2017, protesters at McMaster University rang cowbells and sounded air horns to drown him out (they said he denies the personhood of trans and non – binary students). After 30 minutes, he took his talk outside. The protesters followed, but he continued to speak, explaining why he opposes a Canadian bill that would protect gender identity and expression in a non – discrimination human rights law. He claimed that under the new law, he could be prosecuted if he did not address transsexual students or faculty members by the individual's preferred pronoun.

Unpersons

The last two chapters have been depressing. The saddest fact is the existence of those who claim tolerance for themselves but deny it to others. On Jordan Peterson, Wikipedia noted that he "recommends that the state halt funding to faculties and courses he describes as neo – Marxist, and advises students to avoid disciplines like women's studies, ethnic studies, and racial studies." This is a distortion. He said that, "we've been publicly funding extremely radical, postmodern leftist thinkers who are hell bent on demolishing the fundamental substructure of Western civilization." In other words, he did not say that the legislature should stipulate that the university must purge these people as a prerequisite for funding.

Peterson did, however, propose to set up a website that would label courses as pernicious so students could boycott them, plans he withdrew after staff opposition (Wikipedia, 2018). Let us hope that he continues to endorse debate rather than a test of strength to determine what ideas prevail. His rhetoric comes very close to labeling postmodernists and Marxists as unpersons, and he should caution his following that they have the right to be heard without resorting to such tactics.

6
The struggle for control

If students find they can dictate who gets a hearing on campus, why not use the same tactics to control the university? Evergreen State College holds an annual "Day of Absence." Nonwhite students and faculty stay on campus and whites leave campus to participate in "anti – racism workshops and seminars." In April 2017, Professor Bret Weinstein told the multicultural office that he was going to stay on campus. When students discovered that he had done so, they forced him to hold class off campus.

President George Bridges refused to fire Weinstein on free speech grounds. He had a confrontation with students, who shrieked obscenities at him, told him that their (black) ancestors were civilized when his were coming out of their caves, and demanded that he hold his arms at his side, ostensibly because as a white he was likely to attack blacks on whim. He agreed to a set of demands: to provide sensitivity and anti – bias training of all staff; to allow staff and students (compensated for their time) to design a new equity and multicultural center; to oversee the appointment of a full – time coordinator of the Trans & Queer Center; to increase the budget of the First Peoples Multicultural Advising Services; and to create a new position to "oversee student enrollment and retention at the College" (Aaron, 2017; Huber, 2017; Piper, 2017).

Professor Weinstein appeared on Fox News and claimed that the President had allowed a mob to control the campus. On June 4, Sharon Goodman asked "community patrols" to lay down their weapons:

> We understand that these students are seeking to provide an alternative source of safety from external entities as well as those community members who they distrust. Community patrols can be a useful tool for helping people to feel safe, however the use of bats or similar

instruments is not productive. Some members of this group have been observed carrying batons and/or bats. Carrying bats is causing many to feel unsafe and intimidated. The bats must be put away immediately.

Goodman's note goes on to invite students to attend workshops with "trained restorative justice facilitators" (Kabbny, 2017).

Weinstein and his wife Heather Heying (also an academic at Evergreen) were told to lock their doors and keep their loved ones close. In September 2017, they resigned their posts after receiving a $500,000 settlement, equivalent to a year's salary for each and legal fees (Spegman, 2017). The campus atmosphere is what one would imagine: "Fear and self – censorship is pervasive among Evergreen faculty, especially under the existing budget crisis" (Paros, 2018).

Threat of mob violence was also a factor in a 2019 case at Kirkwood Community College, a public college with campuses at ten locations throughout the state of Iowa enrolling a total of about 20,000 students. Jeffrey Klinzman taught at the Santa Clara campus and was a member of a local antifa (anti – fascist) group. Antifa is a loose collection of groups spread throughout the world some of which have much to answer for, such as harassment of those it identifies as fascists, trying to deny them "platforms," and trying to get them fired. However, Klinzman left purely because he posted blogs: a recent post responded angrily to Trump's angry denunciation of the movement; a 2012 post quoted two lines from a poem written by Ilya Ehrenburg (a Russian anti – fascist of the World War II era) as part of his expression of disapproval of the Christian Right. Kirkwood College does not claim that either post was made or quoted in the classroom or that either had any connection to Klinzman's duties at Kirkwood. On August 22, 2019, however, the president told Klinzman that he could not continue to teach at Kirkwood and offered the choice of resignation or forced termination. Confronted with this choice, he resigned (Smith, 2019).

The intimidation that prompted these decisions was intense. In the 24 hours between Klinzman's comments coming to light and the decision to remove him, a right – wing outrage mob descended on Kirkwood. Some vowed to burn the school to the ground. Klinzman received a barrage of death threats, and his wife was forced to flee their home. Police patrolled their neighborhood and continued to do so into the next academic year (Sachs, 2009).

Intimidation is sometimes used to try to dictate more than who is fired. In May 2017, at the University of California Santa Cruz, the Afrikan (*sic*) Black Student Alliance occupied Kerr Hall for three days. Chancellor George Blumenthal agreed to give all black students a four – year housing guarantee to live in the Rosa Parks African American Theme House, and to paint its exterior the "Pan – Afrikan colors" of red, green, and black. He also agreed to *force* (italics mine) all incoming students to go through diversity competency training. The group then made new demands and warned UC Santa Cruz that it had four months to comply or "more reclamations" will result. All of them made serious financial demands on the university (in passing, blacks are two percent of the student population), but the most important was to establish a Black Studies department (Stein, 2017).

There is already a BA in Critical Race and Ethnic Studies (CRES) taught by a core faculty drawn from various departments. Its blog identifies its mission: "Against the nativism, xenophobia, jingoism, homophobia, and reactionary rage of these troubled times when white supremacy garbs itself in the language of multiculturalism and identity politics, we renew the commitment to politically engaged scholarship, structural analysis, and social justice activism that galvanized the creation of CRES in the first place. We recognize that the cooptation of liberal discourses of diversity points to their exhaustion and insufficiency in the face of structural inequality." This, of course, is the manifesto of a political party not an academic department. The university would do well to take a stand. It is clear that a Department of Black Studies would strengthen the hand of those dedicated to a takeover of the university.

The students at Santa Cruz do not spare their fellow students. In the same month, they responded to a Facebook blog urging them to "reject the 'right of assembly' or 'right of free speech' for fascists." Demonstrators shut down a College Republicans meeting by forcing the doors and chanting at the group, calling them fascists, racists, and white supremacists. The group offered a dialogue, but the disruptors continued to chant, demanding that the campus Republicans end their meeting (Kurtz, 2017a).

Physical invasion

We have seen how trigger warnings can impede free discussion in class through censorship in advance. Physical invasion is an even more direct test of who really controls what goes on is class. On May 16, 2017, students drove a representative of the Immigration and Customs Enforcement (ICE) office out of a Northwestern University sociology class where he had been invited to give a presentation. They had been allowed to enter by the administrator on condition that they not disrupt the presentation (Kurtz, 2017a). Other invasions target ordinary classes. On October 5, 2017, students at Columbia stormed into a class on sexuality and gender law. An attack on the cultural left, they were specifically protesting Columbia's handling of Title IX sexual assault claims. They targeted the instructor, Suzanne Goldberg, a pioneer of Lesbian, gay, bisexual, and transgender law. They left after they had read out their statement (Kurtz, 2017b).

At Reed College in Oregon, Humanities 110 is a required first – year course in which students learn how to discuss, debate, and defend their readings. On September 16, 2016, Reedies Against Racism (RAR) began in – class protests that continued throughout the academic year. RAR says that the course perpetuates white supremacy: its beginning texts are about the ancient Mediterranean, Mesopotamia, Persia, and Egypt and are thus, in RAR's curious opinion, "Eurocentric." RAR supporters stood beside the professor and quietly held signs reading "We demand space for students of color," "We cannot be erased," and "Fuck Hum 110." On one occasion they confronted the professor after class: "(I am) scared to teach courses on race, gender, or sexuality, or even texts that bring these issues up in any way – and I am a gay mixed – race woman." She said that some of her colleagues – "including people of color, immigrants, and those without tenure" – now avoid lecturing altogether.

At the start of the new academic year, RAR ran into trouble from freshmen of color taking the class. In the first session, when Elizabeth Drumm introduced a panel presentation, three RAR leaders took the stage and ignored her objections. When the professors got into a heated exchange with RAR leaders, an African – American student stood up and protested: "This is not the place! Right now we are trying to learn! We're the freshman students!" The room erupted with applause. Drumm canceled the lecture.

Kambiz Ghanea Bassiri refused to teach the *Epic of Gilgamesh* in front of signs tying him to white supremacy. Shortly into a lecture on *The Iliad*, a RAR "noise parade" shut it down. An RAR leader read a statement about how Reed is complicit in "modern – day slavery" because its bank has ties to private prisons. She faltered as she watched the freshmen walk out. Most followed the professor into another classroom, where the lecture continued. After the university barred upperclassmen who had participated in the noise parade from lectures, protests ceased (Bodenner, 2017). It took Reed an awfully long time to take corrective action – and the penalty was awfully mild.

The plight of untenured faculty

In America, the delusion that the classroom is a safe space has led to the firing of untenured staff and adjunct professors upon student demand. Universities hire adjunct professors to save money. Typically, they are paid low wages and have no access to tenure or job security. They and other part – timers now comprise two – thirds of those who teach at US colleges and universities.

In 2005, Roosevelt College in Chicago fired Douglas Giles because he had allowed a discussion of Israel and Palestine in his world religion class. In 2007, Emmanuel College in Virginia fired Nicholas Winsett for saying that the media had overhyped the killings at Virginia State only because so many victims were white women (Schneider, 2010). On September 21, 2007, Southwestern Community College in Iowa fired Steve Bitterman because he had said in his Western Civilization course that the Biblical story of Adam and Eve should not be interpreted literally (Brayton, 2007; CHE, 2008).

In October 2007, Brandeis found Donald Hindley guilty of racial harassment for using the word "wetbacks" in class. He alleges he did so in order to explain the origin of the term and criticize its use. Hindley has claimed that the provost never gave him an opportunity to defend himself. He also claimed that the real motive behind his troubles was that many at Brandeis (a Jewish university) targeted him as pro – Palestinian. The provost placed a monitor in his class to determine whether he could conduct himself appropriately and ordered him to attend racial sensitivity training to educate him in words he should not say. She threatened him with termination if he did not "correct" his supposed conduct. The Committee on Faculty Rights and Responsibilities at Brandeis University issued several scathing reports but terminated its hearings after almost two years, on the grounds that it was being ignored (Watson, 2007).

For every person fired or not hired, thousands more are intimidated. Edward Schlosser (2015) teaches at an unnamed middle – size state university. By 2015, he felt that he could no longer defend a classroom remark by appealing to its rightness or wrongness or even acceptability. The criteria centered solely on whether the remark had affected the student's emotional state. If one responded in any way other than apologizing and changing the materials used in class, professional consequences would likely follow. He had seen graduate students removed from classes after a single student complaint. One adjunct professor did not get his contract renewed after students complained that he exposed them to "offensive" texts written by Edward Said and Mark Twain. He responded that the texts were meant to be a little upsetting. This only fueled the students' ire and sealed his fate. "That was enough to get me to comb through my syllabi and cut out … texts ranging from Upton Sinclair to Maureen Tkacik – and I wasn't the only one."

Douglas Belkin (2017) claims that lecturers across America believe a word or turn of phrase has the power to end a career. Frank Tomasulo has taught film studies at universities since 1977. In 2016, he eliminated D. W. Griffith's *The Birth of a Nation* and the W. C. Fields comedy *It's a Gift* from his syllabus for fear of giving offense to blacks and to blind people, respectively.

I have no comprehensive data on the insecurity of untenured staff in the UK, but there is no doubt that students want to intimidate them. Some months ago, I received an email from Noah Carl, a postdoctoral research fellow at Cambridge. His sins: he attended a series of the London Conferences on intelligence and has also published articles that raise problems about the screening of immigrants and Muslims. Student activists successfully demanded that he be fired as a racist and pseudo – scientist. The attendees at the London Conferences include many scholars I respect. His critics have offered replies to this articles. Why was this not enough?

I hope that UK universities are immune to the US tendency to fire people purely because of the content or purported content of their views. American academics are trying to influence UK academic practices: Kourany (2016) urged them to set up an Advisory Board for Social Research that would impose "tighter restrictions" on race – and gender – related cognitive differences research.

Tenured faculty

Even tenured faculty are subject to "one – mistake" intimidation. I have another email from an academic of outstanding distinction at a great Midwestern University: "About 20 percent of our undergrads have bought into the worst stances of the thought police. You have to watch everything you say around them." A few tenured faculty members have begun to go public. Kelly Oliver of Vanderbilt stated, "I harbor a fear of expressing views that will offend other progressives, scholars, and teachers … I fear being subject to public shaming on social media, and receiving private hate mail. In short, I find myself in an educational environment in which outrage, censoring and public shaming has begun to replace critique, disagreement, and debate" (Oliver, 2016).

A case from Canada: on November 16, Henry Parada left his position as director of the School of Social Work at Ryerson University. This was 20 days after he (quietly) walked out during a black instructor's anti – racism presentation. The next day, the Black Liberation Collective (BLC) sent him a letter in which they demanded he resign: he had walked out "at a time when black folks were giving praise to a young black woman professor at a critical and vulnerable time" (Zubairi, 2016). Some Schools of Social work ask incredible things of their students, fortified by what they "know" to be the values any decent person would accept. In 2007, Rhode Island College told students they could not complete their degrees unless they helped lobby the state government in favor of gay marriage. At Mississippi State, a class assignment required the student to go out in public, display homosexual behavior, and write an essay about it (Lukianoff, 2014).

Guns and intimidation

As of August 2006, the Texas state legislature ruled that students may carry concealed guns into all classes in the Texas University system. Three professors at the University of Texas at Austin argued that guns in the classroom would inevitably narrow the scope of discussion. The US district court held against them. Anne Marie Mackin, an assistant attorney general representing the university, said the idea that the law would impinge academic expression was "rooted in assumptions and prejudices" (Benning, 2016). Perhaps the professors should use the concept of a trigger warning: knowing that guns are present might disturb students who are sensitive to violence, suicide, or the cruelty of hunting animals. Indeed, in November 2019 Cambridge University removed from a student dining hall a painting that included dead animals and thereby offended vegans.

The Water Buffalo case

My last example does not show speech of any political import being forbidden, but does illustrate the lengths to which a distinguished university will privilege student opinion over common sense, at least until the facts attract public attention. On January 13, 1993, at the University of Pennsylvania, Eden Jacobowitz was trying to study in his dormitory room late at night. For over 20 minutes, members of a black sorority had been "serenading" the dormitory with loud singing. He put op his window and shouted, "Shut up, you water buffalo."

The university ordered him to apologize, attend a racial sensitivity seminar, agree to dormitory probation, and accept a temporary mark on his record, which would brand him as guilty of racial harassment. He was told the term "water buffalo" could be interpreted as racist because a water buffalo is a dark primitive animal that lives in Africa, which is untrue. He refused and sought legal advice. A university panel weighed the charges. It later came under fire when it was revealed that it charged him with using racial epithets despite knowing that he had been absolved by a university police investigation (Kors & Silverglate, 1998).

After much hostile press, the university offered Jacobowitz a deal: he could apologize for rudeness and the university and the plaintiffs would drop the charges. The aggrieved women agreed, stating that the media coverage made it unlikely they would get a fair hearing (Lukianoff, 2014). In February 1996, after graduation, Jacobowitz sued the university, alleging that it had inflicted emotional distress and violated its contract with him. The suit was settled out of court (Lanman, 1997).

This case had a certain irony. The equivalent of "water buffalo" in Hebrew is "*behema*," which is slang for a thoughtless or rowdy person and has no racial connotation. Jacobowitz claimed that when he attended yeshiva, the students used "*behema*" all the time and "the teachers and rabbi would call us that if we misbehaved." In other words, for a non – Jewish student to use "water buffalo'" might be a racial epithet, but to forbid a Jewish student from using it might imply that Pennsylvania lacked respect for his religious heritage. Oh, the dilemma of it all!

Comedy dissipates when we understand why Pennsylvania pursued the Water Buffalo case with such fanaticism. By 1993, it had forfeited any claim to equity in its treatment of white and black. In 1990, some fraternity students decided to teach a lesson to a white student named Sheffield, whom they believed to be a bigot. By mistake they kidnapped a different student. They drove him to a secluded area, handcuffed him to a tree, barefoot and minimally clothed. They conducted a mock trial, talked about lynching, whispered "Sheffield Deathfield," and shouted obscenities ("You're a neo – Nazi fuck"). Handcuffed and blindfolded they finally left him on a street corner that he believed to be the middle of a highway.

The university suspended the fraternity for five years, meaning only that its frat house would remain vacant: no individuals punished, no entry on a student's transcript, no sensitivity seminars. The state indicted nine members of the fraternity. None did jail time. All accepted places in a rehabilitation program, with the proviso that upon successful termination, the charges would be erased from their records (Kors & Silverglate, 1998; Jung, 1990).

At the time of the Water Buffalo case, another incident illustrated just how intimidated the university was. A group of black students "confiscated" the entire press run of the school newspaper. When its staff protested, they were threatened and abused. The university did not censure any of the black students. The president commented that the theft had been "precipitated by the pain and anger many members of the minority community have felt (when the paper) exercised its First Amendment Rights to freedom of the press." The only person penalized was a museum employee who had tried to stop black students from running away with their confiscated copies. He was suspended for having overreacted to a political protest (Kors & Silverglate, 1998).

Pennsylvania was so ridiculed in the press that its trustees announced that they expected students to enjoy the protection of the Bill of Rights. In February 1994, a commission called for the immediate abolition of speech codes. The new president asserted, "the content of student speech is no longer a basis for disciplinary action" (Kors & Sliverglate, 1998, p. 365). Valarie Cade became vice provost for university life and asserted her belief in free speech. When a student wrote a letter to the *Philadelphia Inquirer* critical of the moral principles of affirmative action, an administrator told him he was unfit to hold his post as a tutor. Cade cautioned the administrator and sent the student a letter of apology (Kors and Silverglate, 1998). After the Water Buffalo case, so many students told Kors and Silverglate about punishment under speech codes that they decided to set up FIRE.

In 2012, FIRE listed Pennsylvania as one of its seven best colleges and universities for free speech. However, it is clear that while the new provost may have protected students in the 1990s, her university does not now protect lecturers from their colleagues. In 2018, 33 academics (including a majority of the Law School faculty) signed an open letter urging students to monitor Amy Wax's law classes. She had co – authored an article critical of what she believes are counter – productive traits in the subcultures of Native American, blacks, and lower – class whites. Students were to report on any "stereotyping and bias" that they might perceive (Loury, 2018). Wax later made claims about the failure rates of black law students, which were essentially correct. In response the dean forbad her to teach first – year courses (MacDonald, 2018).

Unequal treatment of students

I doubt that any university wants to treat some of its students as above the law. Nonetheless, confiscation of campus papers without penalty has been widespread: such incidents at the University of Maryland at College Park (1993), Duke (1993), Berkeley (1996), and the City College of New York (1996) were all well publicized cases. At the University of Massachusetts at Amherst, confiscation included destroying property and attacking a staff member with a baseball bat. The local court sentenced the assailant to counseling, but the university took no action. The student editor asserted that after the incident, his paper altered its content so that no minority could find it objectionable (Kors & Silverglate, 1998). The peak year for destroying newspapers was 1996 – 1997, with at least 30 other cases reported. Perhaps self – censorship accounts for the drop since then (Hollingsworth, 2000), but I did find a case as recently as 2014 at the University of Minnesota at Morris (Hacker & Theriot, 2014).

As for speech codes, they are rarely if ever enforced in an even – handed way. When a federal court examined all cases at the University of Wisconsin at Madison, every complaint referred to nonwhites or women. You can call a white a "racist" or a dissident black an "oreo" (black on the outside white on the inside, like the popular cookie) with impunity. Christian groups are not privileged. A fundamentalist must be very careful not to offend gays (no posters that say gays can be "cured"). But anyone can post caricatures of the Pope or slogans that invite you "to spread your legs for Christ" (Kors & Silverglate, 1998). If speech codes were universally enforced, and everyone on campus reduced to abnormal speech, they would disappear overnight.

How militant are the students?

When I ask faculty members to take a stand against student oppression, I do not underestimate how resolute America's students are in their contempt for free speech. John Vellasenor (2017) conducted a nationwide survey of 1,500 undergraduate students at four – year colleges and found that 51 percent think it is "acceptable" for a student group to shout down a speaker with whom they disagree, while 19 percent think it acceptable to use violence to prevent a speaker from speaking. Results by political allegiance show how non – partisan the egalitarian ideology has become: 20 percent of Democrats endorse violence, 22 percent of Republicans, and 16 percent of independents. Women endorse violence less than men: 10 percent as compared to 30 percent. This seems to be more a matter of distaste for violence than weaker ideology: "acceptable to shout down" drew the support of 47 percent of women and 57 percent of men.

Democrats, however, are nearly twice as likely to endorse shouting down than the Republicans: 62 percent to 35 percent. This difference may actually have something to do with rejecting egalitarian ideology in favor of more free speech. The students were asked to choose between two options: 1) create a positive learning environment for all students by prohibiting certain speech or expression of viewpoints that are offensive or biased against certain groups of people, or 2) create an open learning environment where students are exposed to all types of speech and viewpoints, even if it means allowing speech that is offensive or biased against certain groups of people. The first option (repress speech) got 53 percent support overall – 61 percent from the Democrats, and 47 percent from the Republicans. Note how relatively close these "repress speech" option percentages are to the "endorse shouting down" percentages (51 – 62 – 35). There are just as many violent Republicans as Democrats, but fewer Republicans prefer the repress speech university to the free speech university.

These results do not show that there will be campus chaos if the president and senior staff take a stand. Only 19 percent of students are at present incorrigible. What the survey shows is that staff must confront their students and reeducate them about the purpose of a university and the rules of public discourse. Recall that Pennsylvania suffered no disruption. Students pause when they find that virtually all their lecturers think their behavior utterly vile.

Despite the effort to make everyone feel at home on campus, there is one area in which many do not feel safe. In 2010, Dey, et. al.

surveyed 24,000 students and asked the question, "It is safe to have unpopular views on campus?" The results across all institutions whether public, secular private, religious private, research universities, or liberal arts colleges were much the same: 80.6 percent "agreed somewhat" that the unpopular were safe, and of these 35.6 percent "strongly agreed." Interestingly, those who "strongly agreed" fell off from 40.3 percent as freshmen to 30.0 percent as seniors. But we do not know whether they thought free speech codes enhanced safety or undermined it. We do not know whether something else was uppermost in their minds, such as the perennial student fear that disagreeing with a lecturer's opinions will get you a lower grade. We do not know how many students believed that expressing an unpopular view (as distinct from merely holding one) was safe, or how many students thought that they personally held any unpopular views.

The academic staff was not equivocal. Only 37.8 percent "agreed somewhat" that unpopular opinions were safe and of these, only 16.7 percent "strongly agreed." That does not bode well for what they felt free to discuss in class or on campus. As to what they feared, it could only be either the students, the administration, or *other professors*. The last opens up a whole new dimension concerning what circumscribes free speech on campus: what academics do to themselves. That will be the theme of Chapters 9 to 11.

7
Chicago and Yale and Harvard

Chicago is the preeminent free speech university. I have commented on how I profited from being at Chicago during the conservative era (when we were allowed to invite Paul Robeson to sing) and how it expelled students who were trying to usher in the radical era. As a morality tale, I will compare Chicago to Yale and Harvard.

Chicago standing firm

The 1967 Kalven Committee stated: "The mission of the university is the discovery, improvement, and dissemination of knowledge. Its domain and scrutiny include all aspects and all values of society. A university faithful to its mission will provide enduring challenges to social values, policies, practices, and institutions. By design and by effect, it is *the institution* (italics mine) that creates discontent with the existing social arrangements and proposes new ones. In brief, a good university, like Socrates, will be upsetting."

In 2014, the university restated its position. It quoted the former president, Hanna Holborn Gray: "Education should not be intended to make people comfortable, it is made to make them think. Universities should be expected to provide the conditions within which hard thought, and therefore strong disagreement, independent judgment, and the questioning of stubborn assumptions, can flourish in an environment of the greatest freedom." The statement goes on to say that: "In a word, the University's fundamental commitment is to the principle that debate or deliberation may not be suppressed because the ideas put forth are thought by some or even by most members of the University community to be offensive, unwise, immoral, or wrong – headed."

In July 2017, President Robert J. Zimmer was asked if Chicago did not risk discouraging the "inclusion" of students who might be alienated by unwelcome speech. He replied, "Inclusion into what? An inferior and less challenging education? One that fails to prepare students for the challenge of different ideas and the evaluation of their own assumptions? A world in which their feelings take precedence over other matters that need to be confronted?" (Stephens, 2017).

In 2016 Chicago's dean of students sent all students about to enroll the following: "Our commitment to academic freedom means that we do not support so – called trigger warnings, we do not cancel invited speakers because their topics might prove controversial, and we do not condone the creation of intellectual 'safe spaces' where individuals can retreat from ideas and perspectives at odds with their own."

As of September 22, 2017, twelve other universities had officially adopted the statement Chicago made in 2014: Princeton, Johns Hopkins, Chapman University, Columbia, Franklin and Marshall, Southern Indiana, the University of Missouri system, the Citadel, Kansas State, Claremont – McKenna, Michigan State, and New York State at Buffalo. The Board of Regents at the University of the Wisconsin system passed it. It has been affirmed by Faculty Senates at 16 other institutions. The only student government that has adopted it was Purdue (FIRE, 2017). How well these universities live up to the statement remains to be seen.

Yale and what lies within

At one time, nothing seemed much amiss. In 1986 Yale gave a Christian student a two – year probation because of a handout that satirized Yale's Gay and Lesbian Awareness Day. In 2009 the administration began to get upset about slogans on t – shirts. They banned the word "sissies" as insensitive to gays even though the word was explicitly directed at Harvard students without reference to sexual orientation.

Yale's president later apologized for intervening, but in 2000, there was a more serious issue. The university abolished the Yale Initiative for the Interdisciplinary Study of Anti – Semitism and replaced it with a new body with much the same name. Accusations were made that this was done because the study had addressed anti – Semitism within Islam, which offended lucrative donors from the Middle East (Lukianoff, 2014). I believe Yale should get the benefit of the doubt. The university claimed that the study did not meet academic expectations. More compelling were similar opinions from those in the field. Anthony Lerman argued that those who "genuinely support the principle of the objective, dispassionate study of contemporary anti – Semitism" should welcome the closure (Treiman, 2011). Robert Winch of Hebrew University said that there was "no way that Yale could have come to a different decision" given the study program's perceived lack of academic rigor (Ahren, 2011).

All in all, Yale's public record signaled that the university welcomed free debate. In addition, Yale endorsed the Chicago statement on free speech in all but name. But statements are one thing and campus culture is another. I will analyze events that show where power truly lies – beginning with the Halloween debate and culminating in the question of renaming Calhoun College. Some of what is quoted or summarized is based on emails a Yale graduate forwarded to me.

The Halloween debate

Halloween has become a fraught time at American universities. For example, the University of Florida invites "bias" reports from those offended by costumes that perpetuate stereotypes. It has a Bias Education and Response Team (BERT) that will not only offer counseling to victims but also might "reach out to the person who was listed as wearing the costume and see what support or resources they might need as well" (Owens, 2016).

Yale has an Intercultural Affairs Committee composed of 13 people ranging from administrative officials, to members of various culture centers, to representatives of the university chaplain's office and athletics department. On October 28, 2015, it sent a letter to all students whose message is captured by the following: Halloween is also unfortunately a time when … poor decisions can be made including wearing feathered headdresses, turbans, wearing 'war paint' or modifying skin tone or wearing blackface or redface. These same issues and examples of cultural appropriation and/or misrepresentation are increasingly surfacing with representations of Asians and Latinos … So, if you are planning to dress – up for Halloween, or will be attending any social gatherings planned for the weekend, please ask yourself these questions before deciding upon your costume choice:

- **Wearing a funny costume?** Is the humor based on "making fun" of real people, human traits or cultures?
- **Wearing a historical costume?** If this costume is meant to be historical, does it further misinformation or historical and cultural inaccuracies?
- **Wearing a 'cultural' costume?** Does this costume reduce cultural differences to jokes or stereotypes?
- **Wearing a 'religious' costume?** Does this costume mock or belittle someone's deeply held faith tradition? Could someone take offense with your costume and why?

At that time, Erika Christakis was associate master of a Yale residential college and her husband, Professor Nicholas Christakis, was the master. On October 30, 2015 she sent a letter to the residents as follows:

> Nicholas and I have heard from a number of students who were frustrated by the mass email sent to the student body about appropriate Halloween – wear … Even if we could agree on how to avoid offense – and I'll note that no one around campus seems overly concerned about the offense taken by religiously conservative folks to skin – revealing costumes – I wonder, and I am not trying to be provocative: Is there no room anymore for a child or young person to be a little bit obnoxious, a little bit inappropriate or provocative or, yes, offensive? … Nicholas says, if you don't like a costume someone is wearing, look away, or tell them you are offended. Talk to each other. Free speech and the ability to tolerate offence are the hallmarks of a free and open society … In other words: Whose business is it to control the forms of costumes of young people? It's not mine, I know that.

The reaction to this email was extraordinary. Students called for the resignation of both Christakises, even though the husband had said nothing. Over 740 Yale undergraduates, graduate students, alumni, faculty, and even students from other universities sent an open letter to

Christakis telling her that her "offensive" email invalidated the voices of minority students on campus. The following week her email was castigated at a meeting of 350 people in the Afro – American Cultural Center. A student complained that the possibility of insulting costumes in her college had rendered her unable to eat, sleep, or do her homework. The next day 100 students confronted Nicholas Christakis in the courtyard of his college. After several hours, he said that he was sorry that he had caused pain but stood behind his wife's statement as an exercise of free speech. A student told him that it was his job to create a place of comfort and home, and when he demurred, shouted, "Who the fuck hired you?!" (Hudler, 2015; Bromwich, 2016).

An incident occurred during that week that showed how hostile students were to reasoned debate. On November 6, 2015, Yale's William F. Buckley Program held a forum on "Free speech on university campuses." At 4pm, Greg Lukianoff said: "Looking at the reaction to Erika Christakis' email, you would have thought someone wiped out an entire Indian village." His words were posted online and at 5:45pm, as the participants left, a crowd of 100 student had gathered chanting, "genocide is not a joke." Several attendees were spat on as they left and one was told he was a racist (Adler, 2015).

The President's email

On November 6, 2015, Yale's president sent the following email to all members of the Yale College community:

> Last night ... I met about 50 students, primarily students of color, for four hours of listening. We heard deeply personal accounts from a number of students who are in great distress ... I want to reiterate our community expectations of inclusion and diversity. As Dean Holloway wrote this morning, Yale belongs to all of you. Yale must be a place where each person is valued automatically, without having to demand or labor for that recognition. I do not want anyone in our community to feel alone, disrespected, or unsafe. We must all work together to assure that no one does.
>
> Our community also shares a commitment to free expression and an open exchange of ideas free from

intimidation. We have had that important conversation before, and we will continue it in the future ... We can be better – and we will take actions that will make us better – in all these respects. I hope you will join me in this effort. We must all hold ourselves accountable – I most of all – for making Yale a better place.

There was not a word of censure about how people should reply to Christakis in debate rather than want to fire her and her husband. The president's point about "a commitment to free expression" is empty without noting that it is the students who are a threat to free expression and that they would do well to examine their consciences. The body of the email actually reinforces the rationale of those who feel that Christakis has committed some great sin: Do or say nothing that might make us "feel alone, disrespected, or unsafe" (by, for example, seeing someone wearing an Indian head dress). His last two sentences are essentially a plea for forgiveness ("Let us all promise to do better..."). This is the email of a frightened man on the defensive.

If the Yale's president is panicked by a dispute about ethnicity, if students are brought to a "boiling point" by Halloween garb, we can only wonder about the state of free speech below the level of public emails. How many Yale professors can safely debate about the role of genes between racial, gender, and ethnic groups either in class or in a campus speech with fear of censure or dismissal? Can they publish articles or books on the subject? What prospects would you have for being hired, promoted, or tenured if you took a controversial stance on any current issue? Perhaps tolerance is absolute below the public façade, but it is hard to imagine that any seriously controversial subject can be discussed without risk of hysteria.

Over the next ten days, the president sent messages that were more balanced: "Yale ... has shown a steadfast devotion to full freedom of expression. No one has been silenced or punished for speaking their minds, nor will they be. This freedom, which is the bedrock of education, equips us with the fullness of mind to pursue our shared goal of creating a more inclusive community." Then there was an assertion that raised my hopes: "To continue conversation outside the classroom, throughout the university, Yale will launch a five – year series of conferences on issues of race, gender, inequality, and inclusion." Was I mistaken about their resolve, were they really going to educate their students in tolerance by an open discussion of forbidden issues with speakers representative of the full range of scholarly opinion?

To sponsor its new series of conferences and other events, Yale opened a centre for "The Study of Race, Indigeneity, and Transnational Migration." Here is its program for the last four months of 2017:

Fictions: Black children wearing strange headdresses

Interview: Musa Syeed (directed films about Kashmir and the experiences of a Muslim refugee in Minneapolis)

Lunch: The Expansion of Native Arts at the Metropolitan Museum

Lunch: Migration, Race, and the Nation in the Dominican Republic

Workshop: Ethnography and Oral History Initiative at Yale

Symposium: The Incarceration of Japanese Americans during World War II

Film: The Untold Story of Baseball's Desegregation

Panel: Chinese in Mexico from the Revolution to the Cold War

YGSNA: The Yale Indian Papers Project

     Pueblo pottery

     Invasive Species in Indian Country

     The Unpredictability of Violence

     Native American Bondage as a Preamble to African Slavery

     The Henry Roe Cloud Conference to celebrate Native excellence at Yale

     Interview: Why Slave Societies Existed in Pre – contact Tropical America

     Tea: Kao Kalia Yang (a Hmong American who writes about her family as they went from a refugee camp in Thailand to Minnesota – worth reading by the way)

     Talk: An Asian American Mental Health Intervention

     Join: Tarot Card Reading Workshop with Mimi Khúc

Talk: Researching Immigration in an Era of
Alternative Facts

This is a rare case in which we can look behind appearances at the mores that really govern behavior. Yale has no more intention to debate genuinely controversial issues than it has to change its name to "Next Best to Harvard."

It is the kind of agenda that inspired Professor Samuel Abrams to write an op – ed for *The New York Times* about the liberal bias of university administrators at Sarah Lawrence College. He accused its Office of Student Affairs of "organizing many overtly progressive events … without offering any programming that offered a meaningful ideological alternative." He concluded that this was a threat to "the free and open exchange of ideas, which is precisely what we need to protect in higher education in these politically polarized times" (Harris, 2018). Immediately, his door was plastered with threatening signs and the Student Senate held an "emergency meeting" and called on the administration to condemn him and give additional funding to the Office of Diversity and Inclusion so that students would feel affirmed. Three weeks later, the college's president wrote a strong letter in his defense. Why did it take so long (Abrams continually lamented his lack of support)? Faced with this kind of student pressure, a president has to tread very carefully.

The fate of Nicholas and Erika Christakis shows how much the students need to be educated. Neither of them taught in the semester following the Halloween controversy. During that semester, students marched on their house, scrawled angry messages in chalk beneath their bedroom window, and shouted insults and epithets. On May 23, 2016, at the college's graduation ceremony, some students refused to accept their diplomas from Christakis. Two days later, he and his wife resigned from their posts (Hartocollis, 2016). He continued to hold his post as a tenured professor, and in August 2018 was appointed to the prestigious Sterling professorship.

Despite this partial redemption, Connor Freiedersdorf (2016) drew the obvious moral of the story: "(This) outcome will prompt other educators at Yale to reflect on their own positions and what they might do or say to trigger or avoid calls for their own resignations. If they feel less inclined toward intellectual engagement at Yale, I wouldn't blame them." Direct evidence of the faculty's state of mind confirmed this fear: when Professor Douglas Stone drafted a letter of support, he was warned that he was putting himself at risk. Relatively few humanities professors signed it. Journalists who interviewed academics found that they were unwilling to be identified whatever their opinions. They were at least as intimidated as the administration, and perhaps more so.

Students share this dilemma. In April 2017, a survey asked 872 undergraduates, "How comfortable do you feel about voicing your opinions on issues such as politics, race, religion, and gender?" Responses were divided into "comfortable" and "not comfortable (*Economist*, 2017). Only 29 percent of conservatives felt "comfortable" as compared to 74 percent of liberals. Taking all students together, the "comfortable" percentage fell by more than half as they progressed through university: between freshman and the senior year, from 61 to 30 percent. Fully 72 percent opposed codes that circumscribe speech, compared with just 16 percent in favor.

The saga of Calhoun College

Yale's decision on another matter shows a university struggling with an increasingly dubious campus culture. In 2016 the Yale community considered whether the name of Calhoun College should be changed. John C. Calhoun, a Southerner and vigorously defended slavery, was a Yale graduate class of 1804 who rose to be Vice President of the United States. Yale's president declared in an e – mail of April 28, 2016 that "the name of Calhoun College will remain." The rationale for retaining his name was that "ours is a nation that continues to refuse to face its own history of slavery and racism. Yale is part of this history, as exemplified by the decision to recognize an ardent defender of slavery by naming a college for him. Erasing Calhoun's name from a much – beloved residential college risks masking this past, downplaying the lasting effects of slavery, and substituting a false and misleading narrative." He did, however, announce that Yale's colleges would no longer be led by "masters" – a term associated with slavery – but by "heads of college."

The president later became less confident. Now he felt a need for a set of principles about renaming and appointed a committee. In 2017 he reversed his earlier decision. The name was changed because of Calhoun's potency: he ensured "that slavery not only survived but expanded across North America." Calhoun College is now Grace Hopper College, named after a woman computer scientist who received her Ph.D. from Yale and reached the rank of admiral in the US Navy.

It is absurd to make Calhoun's role a sufficient condition for the existence of slavery. In private, he acknowledged that the tariff issue was more fundamental in dividing North and South. However, he was the leading spokesman defending slavery prior to his death in 1850 and lived in a society where it inconceivable that his name would be removed from an educational institution 167 years later. He made Southerners feel better about their "peculiar institution" but with or without him, the South was committed to slavery and the Civil War was inevitable.

Is this not the kind of education that the president hoped, in an e – mail to the entire campus community, would occur thanks to keeping the name Calhoun College? It is certainly better than what he identified as a "false and misleading narrative" that Yale used to defend the renaming. Why not put a plaque under his name that acknowledges his pro – slavery views and adds, "Those who wish to know more about the antebellum South should take American history courses."

One could argue that the name "Yale" itself is tainted beyond redemption because of its history of discrimination against Jews, Catholics, and women. In 1986, Dan A. Oren published a book with Yale University Press that lays bare its record. In 1922, for example, the admissions chairman placed limits on "the alien and unwashed element." A discriminatory quota limiting the number of Jews remained in place until 1960. Women were not admitted until 1969. John A. Wilkinson (Yale University Secretary, 1986) acknowledged, "There were vicious, ugly forms of discrimination," a fact "we've all suspected and some have known for a long time." Following the logic in the Calhoun College case, Yale could renamed to break with its legacy, which some may find troubling.

Renaming

My position on renaming often attracts this reply: "If you were a Jewish student how would you like to walk around campus and see a building named Adolf Hitler?" Not much: this would be a calculated and gross insult. But the analogy is inappropriate. The case in question is analogous to a Jewish student seeing a building named after Werner Heisenberg. The latter was a great physicist who compromised himself by becoming a principal scientist in the Nazi German nuclear weapons project during World War II. Thanks to Hitler's anti – Jewish policies, he had no help from many of the top minds in nuclear physics and got nowhere (most do not accept his plea that he was not really trying). Sadly, few Jewish students would know anything about him. But for those who do, a plaque would suffice: the bare facts plus "Those who wish to know more about the position of Jews in Germany should read Amos Alon, *The Pity of it All*."

Yale's president's email revisited

The President's initial email should have said something like:

> The debate between Erika Christakis and the Intercultural Affairs Committee is moderate in content and language and exactly the sort of debate Yale wants. I would no more dream of taking sanctions against her than firing the Committee. Those who are outraged should ask themselves what a university is all about. I intend to seek faculty approval of my position. Those who wish to debate whether this debate was tolerable can, of course, argue the contrary, just as a democracy should tolerate those who endorse some alternative. On another matter, I met 50 students who had personal concerns about their campus experiences and will weigh these and see what remedies are appropriate.

In other words, rather than "soothing" the student mob, he should have educated it. He needed the support of his faculty. If he had received less than 80 percent support for statement such as the one suggested above, he should have resigned and left Yale to be run as a parody of a university. It is easy for an outsider to say this of course, but it would have been a more principled response.

The hubris of the radical student

Yale's recent record, and those of other universities, feeds the hubris of radical students: when we push, they surrender. Students are moving toward altering the curriculum. In early 2016, the university received a petition calling for Yale to "decolonize" the English department: "Where the literary contributions of women, people of color, and queer folk are absent actively harms all students, regardless of their identity … We write to you today inspired by student activism across the university, and to make sure that you know that the English department is not immune from the collective call to action" (Damron, 2017).

The English department now allows students to choose three out of four required courses: Readings in English Poetry 1; Readings in English Poetry 2; Readings in American Literature; and a new course, Readings in Comparative World English Literature. Because Chaucer and Shakespeare are both studied in English Poetry 1, this means that an English major can graduate without ever reading either. They must read some of the usual great authors: Readings in English Poetry 2 includes Milton through Eliot. They can also take options beyond the required courses. English 128 features white male writers such as Daniel Defoe, John Millington Synge, and James Joyce. As for the new course, Professor Stephanie Newell describes it as the opposite of "close reading." She says the course spends a great deal of time discussing cultural, linguistic, and historical contexts, and classic works of postcolonial theory, in conjunction with the primary texts. Her research focuses on issues of gender, sexuality, and power as articulated through popular print cultures.

Adding such a course does no great harm on its merits, though it is a pity to see Shakespeare deemed optional. However, let us hope that the balance of power has not shifted too far. The relationship between Yale and its campus community looks akin to that Plato describes between the sophist and the great beast: "Suppose a man was in charge of a large and powerful animal, and made a study of its moods and wants; he would learn to approach and handle it, when and why it was especially savage or gentle, what the different noises it made meant, and what tone of voice to use to soothe or annoy it" (Plato, *Republic*, VI, 493).

Does Yale's president approve of the coercive campus environment to which he gave in? He may regret the compromises he was forced to make during the Halloween controversy or his backtracking on Calhoun College. Even at the time, he took the proposal that Professor Christakis should be fired off the table. And in 2018, three years after the controversy, Christakis was awarded the university's highest faculty honor, the Sterling Professorship, which must be proposed by the President and approved by the Board of Trustees (Wang, 2018). Here we have a university that wants to honor its tradition of free debate and an activist subgroup of students who want nothing of the sort.

Harvard one of the worst?

In 2017, FIRE listed Harvard as one of the ten worst American colleges for free speech. I have no data on what goes on beneath the surface at Harvard in terms of discussion of the usual banned topics and cannot certify that rating. But Harvard does have a history of cases that have come to public view that make it plausible.

Harvard and race

The worst incident occurred 15 years ago. Jason Steorts (2002), a columnist in the campus newspaper *The Harvard Crimson*, discussed an incident that made him wonder whether or not "objective discourse is possible at all when race is involved."

A law student (Kiwi Camara) posted a course outline on a website, referring to a case involving restrictive racial covenants: "Nigs buy land w/ no nig covenant; Q: enforceable?" When another student filed a complaint, she replied "We are at the Harvard Law School, a free, private community where any member wishing to use the word 'nigger' in any form should not be prevented from doing so … I have actually began [*sic*] using the 'nigger' word more often than before the incident." I presume she stops short of shouting the word at fellow students on campus. Her case was complicated by an anti – Semitic pamphlet some

80 students received a few days later. The student (Matthias Scholl) claimed it was distributed as a test of free speech.

Harvard did not sanction either student. So that hard questions could be asked and deliberated, Professor Charles Nesson suggested a mock trial in which he would defend Scholl. The Harvard Black Law Students Association demanded that for this alone he be publicly censured and banned from teaching first – year students. Incredibly, after discussions with the dean, Nesson "agreed" to step down for the rest of the semester.

We have commented on Yale's lack of intent to educate students about the forbidden issue of race and IQ. I hoped that Harvard might do better but can find no evidence that it has. In 2017, Vivian Chou published a piece courtesy of The Graduate School of Arts and Sciences. It is an apology for evading the whole issue, arguing that there are no true races and that we are sophisticated enough to know this but sadly the public is too ignorant. Nevertheless, in 2019 Harvard vigorously challenged a lawsuit following from the perception that Asian – American students were in practice discriminated against in admissions. Harvard won the case in district court, but was compelled to release its previously secret admissions records, and the case will likely continue on appeal.

Harvard and the press

Harvard certainly does not unambiguously endorse freedom for its own student press. In 2002, the Harvard Business School computer system made a mess of interviews that were supposed to match students with jobs. Its student newspaper published a cartoon spoofing excuses (one read "incompetent morons"). The director of the MBA (Master of Business Administration) program threatened the editor and cartoonist with punishment for violating Harvard's community standards. The sanctions range from admonition to expulsion. Fearing for his career, the editor resigned. After much public pressure, the School apologized but still, a message had been sent: criticizing Harvard is unwise for one's career prospects (Lukianoff, 2014).

In 2011, Subramanian Swamy, a professor in Harvard's summer school, published a column in India after a series of terrorist bombings in

Mumbai killed 26 people and injured 130. He proposed disenfranchising Muslims and prohibiting conversion from Hinduism to any other religion. Harvard students signed a petition calling for the university should repudiate his remarks and terminate his association with the university. It cancelled all of his classes, citing his column as part of the indictment. Aside from this rejection of his right to free speech, it is noteworthy that his courses had nothing to do with Indian politics but economics (Lukianoff, 2014).

Harvard and loyalty oaths

In 2016 the University of Chicago told incoming students that it put education ahead of making people feel comfortable. When Harvard freshmen arrived in 2011, they were asked by their resident advisers to sign a pledge "to sustain a community characterized by inclusiveness and civility" and to affirm that "the exercise of kindness holds a place on a par with intellectual attainment." They could refuse but then their names would be missing from a list of signatories posted on dormitory entryways. After objections, the freshman dean decided to forbid the postings, and I can find no evidence that the pledge was continued thereafter (Lukianoff, 2014). But it signaled a state of mind ready to sacrifice freedom of expression to student sensibilities.

Harvard began in 1989 to offer a whole week of sessions for incoming students called AWARE (Actively Working Against Racism and Ethnocentrism). The first program's keynote speech asserted that 15 percent of whites were total racists and the remaining 85 percent subtle racists. The speaker exulted that "during the discussion period ... no one rose to challenge his contention that we are all guilty of racism" (Kors & Silverglate, 1998, p. 222). After a week of this stuff, it is difficult to see how any Harvard student could participate in any intellectually respectable discussion of thinkers like Jensen, Lynn, or Murray.

There is one bright spot: most students simply did not attend anything after the keynote speech (*Harvard Crimson*, 1989). However, they did not escape. Timur Kuran (1995, p. 226) notes that AWARE appoints "race relations tutors" for every Harvard house to monitor the racial atmosphere, "raise consciousness," and report violations. He cites students who claim that no one is ever reported for demeaning comments about whites. I should add that Harvard University Press published Kuran's book.

Harvard is not unique. Other universities give AWARE – type programs, some of which are mandatory. Georgetown, Washington State, Michigan State, Ohio State, Clemson, North Carolina, and Florida Sate give entrants "Tunnel of Oppression" courses. There are local variants. At Illinois State, students can witness images of atrocities against underrepresented groups. The University of Delaware wins the prize for indoctrination thanks to a mandatory four – year program that, until recently, it administered through resident assistants (RAs) in the dormitories. Students were asked to fill out questionnaires on whether they would be comfortable dating a heterosexual woman or an openly gay or bisexual man. Any who refused were reported as among the "worst examples" of those resisting the program. The RAs aimed at getting every student to recognize that systematic oppression exists and to learn how to be a "change agent." Training sessions have classified all whites as "racists" because they had purportedly benefited from a white supremacist system, while no person of color could be a racist because they lacked the power to back up their prejudices and hostilities.

A brief digression on racism

Individual racism is a certain state of mind (judging people by their color). Competitive systems exist that have differential consequences for races even when actors are not racist and the rules are not racist. Call these systems **institutionalized racism** if you wish, but it adds no clarity to the analysis. Sometimes an ethical person should try to "reform" the system and sometimes not. The hundred – meter dash appears to hold advantages for black athletes over white ones. Reforming it would be easy: give every white competitor a head start. But who would ever entertain such a suggestion? As Chapter 3 showed, the market posits rational actors, and it is sometimes true that rational actors will penalize blacks even though they have no racist psychology: recall the landlady who rented to a Korean female over a black male for economic reasons based on experience rather than prejudice.

I believe that an ethical person will endorse governmental affirmative action to benefit blacks in order to balance out some of the harm the market does. Chapter 9 will expose you to black conservatives who think this a humiliating concession with counterproductive consequences for blacks themselves. Their position is not presented in "tunnel of oppression" programs that place indoctrination and even intimidation ahead of free debate. Only social science analysis will clarify who is right. Rhetoric will not.

Back on track

Some college personnel (not at Harvard or Yale) have been trained to do something even worse: intervene in any spontaneous discussion of politics or religion. They would give each student one chance to state her position and then command them all to disperse without debate or resolution. When one such program came to public attention in 2007, it was abolished (Lukianoff, 2014).

More loyalty oaths

Harvard has off – campus single – sex clubs (male) that are informal (they are not registered student organizations). In 2016 the university proposed another pledge: "I affirm my awareness of the College's policy regarding the principle of non – discrimination, particularly with regard to membership in unrecognized single – gender social organizations. In taking a leadership position in a student organization/applying for a sponsored grant or fellowship/becoming a varsity athletic team captain, I affirm my compliance with that policy." Aside from barring students from office in campus organizations and sports teams, this disqualifies them from recommendations by the dean for prestigious Rhodes or Marshall scholarships. Some donors and members of the Harvard community, and FIRE, objected that the policy interferes with the students' rights of free association (Fernandes, 2017). In December 2018 students filed a lawsuit further claiming that the policy discriminated against them on the basis of sex. In August 2019 a federal judge ruled against Harvard's motion to dismiss the lawsuit, which is now proceeding.

Harvard and Larry Summers

In 2005, Larry Summers, then Harvard's president, was foolish enough to give what he called a thought – provoking speech on the dearth of women in science and engineering. He suggested that small differences in IQ in certain areas (having to do with mathematical aptitude) might be a factor and that some research argued that these differences were innate. He added that he would like to be proved wrong, but the question should be addressed.

He did use an example, which, while relevant, was hardly going to pacify the audience. He said that one of his daughters, who as a child was given two trucks in an effort at gender – neutral parenting, treated them almost like dolls, naming one of them "daddy truck," and one "baby truck." Nancy Hopkins of MIT, sitting close to Summers, closed her computer, put on her coat, and walked out. "It is so upsetting that all these brilliant young women [at Harvard] are being led by a man who views them this way," she said later in an interview. What Summers said was true, however, particularly with the qualification that at least *some* research supports genetic differences between the genders (see my discussion in Chapter 3).

Over 100 Harvard faculty members attacked Summers in a public letter. He issued a series of groveling apologies. The Arts and Sciences Faculty passed a vote of no confidence in his leadership (he had had some earlier confrontations with faculty). They then passed a second motion, by a vote of 252 to 137, stating: "The faculty regrets the president's mid – January statements about women in science and the adverse consequences of those statements for individuals and for Harvard (Fogg, 2005)." He resigned about a year later.

I think Larry Summers was foolish. One of his students (Pollak, 2016) says he covered gender imbalances in his classes without inhibition (the level at which free debate is most important). They discussed an interesting hypothesis: women may be better than men at everything but not as much better in science; therefore, the rational strategy is to go into non – scientific careers to maximize their advantages. When he became president, Summers should have vowed (out of prudence) never to make a public speech about issues that divided his university, except to explain how he was running it. If one wants to encourage the expression of all views, one should avoid taking sides on divisive issues. The danger is that academics will take the president's public stance as an indication of what views are tolerated within the university and which ones are not.

Charles Murray again

On the plus side of the ledger, on September 6, 2017, Charles Murray appeared at Harvard without incident. Harvard has an explicit policy of ejecting disrupters but so does practically every other institution. Unlike others, however, it appears that Harvard is actually willing to eject them. Members of the Harvard Police Department, including the chief, stood quietly at the back of the hall during Murray's appearance, looking at once benevolent and completely willing to do whatever was necessary to enforce the rules.

Harvard students' willingness to tolerate Charles Murray does not show that they themselves expect to be tolerated. Jonathan Zimmerman (2017), Professor of Education at Harvard, reports a 2016 survey of over 3,000 undergraduates. More than half agreed that the climate on campus prevents some people from "saying things that might offend others." Perhaps they do not mind very much. More than two — thirds favored restrictions on racist and offensive speech.

Chicago and disinvestment

Whether the University of Chicago's record is unblemished has been debated.

In 2006, it was under pressure to review its investments to ensure that it was not supporting entities that do evil. Here we must remind ourselves of Mill's distinction between thought, speech, and actions. I have the right to think what I want, the right to speak as I want (within very broad limits), but limited rights to act as I may want. As a morally responsible agent, and someone with humane ideals, I must take the consequences of my actions into account. Chicago stated that it had done this in clear cases: those in which the evil was evident to virtually the entire community (investment in apartheid South Africa), but that it did not want to compromise the political neutrality of the university.

If the university were a private individual, it should ignore the public and try to maximize the morality of its investments. And yet, I approve of the university's stand. This brings us back to prudence. Throughout its history, Chicago has had to fight off a state legislature only too willing to interfere. Its position has always been political neutrality: we should not force us to stifle voices others find obnoxious or even dangerous (communists and so forth). Anything that compromises that principle in the minds of the legislators would be taken as hypocrisy, as proof that Chicago was really an agent of the left, and as an excuse for the legislature to abandon self – restraint in policing it with undesirable attention and consequences. This consideration requires Chicago to truncate what humane principles would ideally dictate. It really should make sure that disinvestment is confined to things the general public would consider beyond politics.

This puts Chicago in an impossible debating position with its students. One group (the legislature) sees the status quo as morally acceptable, the other group (the students) see it as morally deficient. This lack of consensus means that there is no such thing as a politically neutral position, and to use that phrase to defend the status quo is simply bad logic. It is a phase to disguise what the university is really thinking and cannot say publicly: that the status quo may be morally indefensible but it is as good as the university can get away with. Chicago students are bright enough to see behind the talk about political neutrality and see it as no more than an admission that the university is settling for what is morally second best. They should comfort themselves by reading Aristotle on prudence and be happy that they are where they are rather than at Yale or Harvard. They are at a free speech university, and that is too valuable to be endangered.

This does not mean that an atmosphere of tolerance prevails at Chicago that embraces all of its academics. Two of them (they had allies at Pennsylvania State) actually got a published paper erased from the online research journal, the *New York Journal of Mathematics*. It presented a mathematical model in favor of a hypothesis supported by Darwin that, although there are many exceptions for specific traits and species, there is generally more variability in males than in females of the same species throughout the animal kingdom. As its principal author says, the phenomenon has been reported in species ranging from adders and sockeye salmon to wasps and orangutans, as well as humans. Multiple studies have found that boys and men are overrepresented at both the high and low ends of the distributions in categories ranging from birth weight and brain structures and 60 – meter dash times to reading and mathematics test scores. There are significantly more men than women, for example, among Nobel laureates, music composers, and chess champions – and also among homeless people, suicide victims, and federal prison inmates (Hill, 2008).

In other words, the article trespassed on the debate that got Larry Summers fired at Harvard. Critics claimed that its mathematical content was poor and that it should never have been accepted, at least in a mathematics journal. We would have all profited had the article been retained and criticized by published rebuttals, perhaps even rebuttals that shed fresh insight on the comparative data. Rather than pursing that path, the journal decided to try to erase the controversy from the collective memory of humankind. I have expressed agnosticism about whether there is a genetic basis for fewer women at the top in mathematics (Flynn, 2017), but if scholars had to meet the criterion of a case that could not be rebutted, no debate would be possible.

Hill knew of the reputation of Chicago's President, Robert Zimmer, and therefore wrote him to complain about the conduct of the two Chicago professors. Hill found his reply unsatisfactory: that they had exercised their academic freedom in advocating against the publication of the paper and that their behavior had not been either unethical or unprofessional. It seems to me that Zimmer had to take that stand. Even if Hill's suspicions are accurate, the university cannot single out for censure those on campus who put political rectitude ahead of free speech. They have a right to argue for their positions, so long as they do not require that their students toe the line or persecute colleagues up for promotion, and so forth.

Disclaimer

I do not claim that Chicago is the only free – speech campus. In fact, there are ten institutions that free speech advocates have identified as committed to serious and diverse debate (Maschek & Haidt, 2019). The rest of the list: Arizona State University, Chapman University (California), Claremont McKenna College (California), Kansas State University, Kenyon College (Ohio), Linn – Benton Community College (Oregon), Purdue University (Indiana), St. John's College (Maryland), and the University of Richmond. I am sure others exist and that even on less friendly campuses, there is a lot of civilized discourse on important and controversial topics, and that many teachers open the minds of students to new ideas. It is a pity that they are so often at risk.

Part 3
What academics do to themselves

8
Black studies

We have detailed how the combination of militant students and a quiescent administration coerce academics. But I have not explored the dimension of what academics do to themselves. Setting aside other factors, some departments have an internal dynamic that cripples freedom of speech and inquiry. The most obvious candidates are Black Studies and Women's Studies.

Black Studies

The discipline of Black Studies has had many difficulties to overcome. The first department was founded at San Francisco State University in 1969 and the number grew to 100 within a few years. Initially, there were simply not enough blacks with Ph.D.s to staff them adequately, and the idea that whites might staff them was out of the question. Due to lack of student interest, their numbers fell to 50 by 1988 (Sowell, 1993, pp. 148 – 151). The collapse winnowed out some unsustainable programs, but the need to retain students encouraged lenient grading. As of 2013, the number stands at 126 (Alkalimat, et. al. 2013). In recent years, thanks to rampant grade inflation, they would not have as much to gain from lenient grading as they did in the past. However, there is some evidence that coaches still advise athletes to take Black Studies as an "easy" option. I do not have the data to assess their academic standards and will therefore focus on the extent to which they encourage free debate.

A good indication of how open debate would be within the university is the tone academics strike when issues are debated in public. I will begin with Leonard Jeffries as a worst – case scenario. His image of debate is pure vituperation and his tolerance is nil. I will then record an incident that was far more important: a case in which many mainstream Black Studies scholars simply shut down a public debate about their discipline. Finally, I will endorse McWhorter's critique of Black Studies: how these departments might alter to encourage a real debate about American blacks and their future by exposing students to the full range of intelligent opinion.

Throughout there will be a persistent theme: thinkers are divided between the "assimilation" camp and "bi – cultural" camp, the latter of whom reject the notion that blacks can (or should) disappear into the American melting pot.

Schlesinger and Jeffries

In 1991, the prominent historian Arthur M. Schlesinger, Jr. published *The Disuniting of America: Reflections on a Multicultural Society*. He argued against "politically correct" education that puts too much emphasis on America as a collection of angry and self – conscious groups. He decried treating American history as simply an extension of European racism and rejected those who advised blacks to redeem themselves by infusions from African culture. The danger, as he saw it, was that assimilation would be replaced by fragmentation and integration by separatism, and that the historic idea of a unifying American identity would be set aside. He believed that African – Americans have less interest in separatism and more faith in the melting pot than do the militants who dominate the debate (Schlesinger, 1991).

Leonard Jeffries (1991), Chairman of Black Studies at the City College of New York, was offended. In a public talk on July 20, 1991, he called Schlesinger "devilish and dirty and dastardly" and characterized those who read and talked about his book as "pimps and prostitutes parading." The notion that Jeffries would be more tolerant of colleagues or students who agreed with Schlesinger is unlikely given the content of his lectures. Blacks, he said, are "sun people" and whites "ice people." The sun people, the African family of warm communal hope, meets an antithesis, in the ice people – Europeans, colonizers, oppressors, the cold, rigid element in world history. Melanin, the dark skin pigment, gave blacks intellectual and physical superiority over whites (Benjamin, 1993 – 1994).

The Journal of Blacks in Higher Education describes Jeffries as bizarre. In November 1994 *The New York Daily News* reported a speech in which he compared Jews to "skunks" who "stink up" everything. City College replaced him as head of department but was overruled by the courts. There are others like Jeffires. By 1993, Anthony Martin, a professor of African Studies at Wellesley, had taught for 21 years. During that time, they had hired him, promoted him, granted him tenure, and given him frequent positive assessment and merit raises, despite full knowledge of his views, which included assertions that Jews were particular enemies of Africans and African – Americans. When he assigned a notoriously anti – Semitic book to his classes, his department chairman described it and him as absurd, and he was denied a merit raise. Why the department challenged his scholarship then, and not earlier, is unclear (Kors & Silverglate, 1998).

I want to reiterate that Schlesinger endorsed "assimilation" as the best option for blacks. As we will see, those who wish to abolish or radically reform Black Studies departments often use that word.

Riley and The Chronicle of Higher Education

The Chronicle of Higher Education published a report on the first generation of students completing their Ph.D.s in Black Studies with particular reference to those at Northwestern. They were cited as examples of a discipline attaining academic maturity. The Chronicle has a debate page, called "Brainstorm," which presumably is meant to attract vigorous debates between their readers about important subjects. On April 30, 2012, Naomi Schaefer Riley wrote a one – page opinion piece. It was entitled: "The most persuasive case for eliminating Black Studies? Just read the dissertations" (Riley, 2012).

Riley had read abstracts of the dissertations and commented on three. She called these "a collection of left – wing victimization claptrap" whose main virtue was that "they're so irrelevant no one will ever look at them." She identified themes including the overlooked nonwhite experience in the "natural birth literature" (midwifery); the role of racism in the subprime mortgage lending crisis of 2009; and the purported roles that black conservatives like Thomas Sowell, Clarence Thomas, and John McWhorter played in assaulting "civil rights" that benefited them. Riley defends these three thinkers as targeting not "civil rights" but rather affirmative action and rightly identifying problems in black culture that cannot be blamed on white people.

In a genuine debate, people provoke controversy with a hard – hitting comment, which is designed to provoke others who may disagree. They reply with rebuttals and as the debate widens, the issue may be clarified. Riley is a white woman married to a black conservative. She is bathed in a consensus that Black Studies is artificial and counterproductive. She clearly wanted to write a hard – hitting contribution that would provoke its friends into debating the merits of the discipline. Those who answered her did not welcome the invitation. Their main tactic was to substitute a debate about whether she should be fired from her post, hardly a step toward encouraging those who might have the courage to defend an unpopular position.

Riley's sin was that she had not read the full texts of the three dissertations (only the abstracts). In fact, the texts were not available for anyone to read because they were not in final form. I believe that she may been guilty of not attempting to get copies. If she had, she would have discovered this and would certainly have used it to fortify her case. Here were people defending Black Studies on the basis of dissertations that no one could evaluate except the students and their supervisors. As far as I can tell from the public record, I was the first person to write the department to request copies. In late 2017, five years after the controversy, one was still in the writing stage, and the authors of the other two had used their right to keep them confidential for seven years to protect their research while they seek publication.

Should Riley have been fired for not doing what no one else bothered to do, neither the original reporters of the piece nor anyone else? Again, I assume that if her critics had done so, some would have contrasted her harsh assessment based on the abstracts with praise for what the dissertations actually said. The reaction was varied but dominated by a social media backlash.

Chronicle editor Liz McMillen initially stood by Riley defending her piece as an invitation to debate and allowing her to respond to critics. A few days later, faced with a deluge of angry mail and an anti – Riley petition with over 6,500 signatures, she reversed herself. AN "Editor's

Note" stated that Riley's post "did not meet *The Chronicle's* basic editorial standards for reporting and fairness in opinion articles" and that Riley had been asked to leave Brainstorm. McMillen apologized for initially treating Riley's post as "informed opinion" and "for the distress these incidents have caused." Sixteen Back Studies faculty at Northwestern joined a guest post on Brainstorm calling Riley's comments "cowardly, uninformed, irresponsible, repugnant, and contrary to the mission of higher education" (Young, 2012).

A potentially fruitful debate was thus closed down rather than being conducted in a way that might have educated all concerned. As the *Chronicle* editor initially said, Riley's piece was an invitation to *begin* a debate. It was treated as if it were a fully argued and documented case against Black Studies. Ideally Riley should have moderated her language. She should have argued that a case for the "maturity" of Black Studies could not be based on fragmentary evidence, no matter how good the dissertations were. She should have detailed her doubts: that Black Studies eschewed hard analysis of black subculture in favor of victimization, and that it oversimplified complex issues like the lessons of black history and the value of affirmative action.

What about the reaction? Fire her, intimidate the *Chronicle*, shut down the debate. It is a "black mark" against Black Studies departments that some did not fly to Riley's defense. They might have said: "We know that there are those who hold us suspect, and we welcome the fact that the debate is out in the open and we have a chance to defend the credentials and publications of our staff, the content and conduct of our courses, and the dissertations of our students." However much they might disapprove of Riley's opinions, they could have overwhelmed them with their own contributions rather than invite suspicion that they had no rebuttal to offer. Riley had one great virtue that should not have been squandered: this "coward" had the courage to debate something that every department must be willing to face – its value to the university. The response to Riley recalls the reaction of a Nazi stormtrooper reading extracts from a Jewish communist author at a book burning. It will hardly encourage free debate.

I want to address in particular a response by Ta – Nehisi Coates (2013), a national correspondent for *The Atlantic*, as indicative of how those who think they value free speech manage to talk themselves into shutting it down. Coates was initially appalled because he did not believe that writing something stupid about race should be a fire – able offense. However, he did believe "that proudly defending one's ignorance in a publication dedicated to higher education should always be fire – able." Riley admitted that she had read only the précis of the dissertations. She thus admitted ignorance of the very evidence she used to condemn Black Studies. Coates concluded: "to defend her doesn't simply mean accepting the right to criticize Black Studies. We're all in agreement there. It means accepting the right to criticize Black Studies without doing any substantive research into the field. It means accepting the right to speak out of ignorance. How is this even an issue? Why would anyone defend the right to be stupid? I'm serious here. This looks really open and shut to me."

Coates should make up his mind: does he want to encourage free debate or discourage it? Punishing will discourage it, even if it is reserved for someone who is proud and stupid. Does he think that firing Riley will encourage people to make negative comments about Black Studies, or make them feel that this is a minefield too dangerous to enter? Unless they work for the Ku Klux Klan, there are thousands of people out there at the mercy of someone who might punish them for being too outspoken about Black Studies. To endorse firing them because of their participation in a public debate is the professional equivalent of "shouting fire in a crowded theater." I once asked a lecturer about the quality of Black Studies at his university while drinking in his faculty club. He drew back in horror, looked to see who was at near – by tables, and said "For God's sake shut up – let's go outside," like we part of some kind of revolutionary underground.

There would be few debates left if we did not let those who hold "offensive" positions go unpunished. This is true of academics as well as journalists. Hans Eysenck, the most cited author in twentieth – century psychology at the time of his death, and who is sometimes compared with Freud, Piaget, and Plato, publicly defended these positions: that cigarettes were not harmful (long after scientific opinion was unanimous); that American blacks were on average genetically inferior for intelligence compared to whites but *not* African blacks; that the Irish in Ireland were genetically inferior for intelligence to those who had emigrated; and that cognitive behavior therapy could prevent cancer and extend the lives of those with advanced cancer. We would all be far worse off if we took Eysenck at his worst and shut him up.

We would be equally impoverished if we labeled Riley an unperson and unworthy of a hearing. She has, by the way, written sympathetically about disadvantaged black girls and a passionate book about Native Americans titled, *The New Trail of Tears: How Washington is Destroying American Indians* (2016). Her seven books and their publishers amply attest to her ability and to her sympathies to issues of racial justice. We might actually have learned something from her if she had been encouraged to continue this debate, but her critics preferred the sterility of silence.

A few came to Riley's defense. They imagine that someone advocated the abolition of the Classics Department on specious grounds (don't we have enough translations of Horace?) or suggested that we should cut by half the number of academics studying Virginia Wolff (without having read all their books). They speculated that she might have faced well founded criticism, but that no one would have been fired. What stands out is that no one had the stomach for such a debate; they preferred to vent their outrage at the fact that someone had started one. The only punishment the offensive deserve is to be punished by powerful contrary arguments. Coates thinks that was done in the case of Riley. Why was that not enough?

McWhorter and indoctrination

John McWhorter acknowledges that the story of African – Americans is to a considerable extent the story of America. American history and society would have been very different without slavery, the civil rights revolution, and the black contribution to American music and culture. He does not want to abolish Black Studies. The majority of black conservatives, however, do want to abolish it. They see no reason why these topics should be pursued in a separate department, rather than at appropriate places in the curriculum. I suspect that many of them would be won over to McWhorter's position if they thought that there were any chance for his recommendations to reform Black Studies to be adopted.

McWhorter wants to make Black Studies into a medium of discussion rather than indoctrination. He cites the 1969 mission statement at San Francisco State, which was to expose the roles played by "liberal – fascist" ideology, capitalism, and "white supremacy." He hopes that today's departments do not still march to this tune, and teach their students that they are oppressed by factors far beyond their awareness, ones so deeply rooted that only a revolution can alter them. He does not deny that this point of view should be taught but suggests that it be balanced by less apocalyptic analyses that acknowledge black progress and prospects (McWhorter, 2009a).

American history can and should be taught with full acknowledgment of what blacks suffered but this can degenerate into consciousness – raising as in end in itself. Students should not take the past as a sign that meaningful advancement is impossible. The best departments advise them as to how they can hope for a better future for themselves and blacks in general. Black students should also know mundane facts such as that before racial preferences were banned in admissions at the University of California at San Diego, only one in 3268 black students made freshman honors, while the year after the ban, one in five did, the same percentage as white students. As for world history, they should know that the "fact" that the Greeks stole their learning from a "black" Egypt is absurd, and reject assertions that Ancient Egyptians were in any way ancestors of black Americans. The best departments would not, of course, present such a view as "real" history (McWhorter, 2009a).

In a word, McWhorter wants a balanced rather than an ideologically skewed reading list. Few blacks have identified with radical politics and its advocates have had only marginal impact on the lives of most blacks. With this in mind, McWhorter suggests a reading list that would not prejudge the debate. Academics may be surprised by the wealth of the literature and how little of it most students get to read. His first suggestion is that students take a course on black conservative thought (McWhorter, 2009b). They should also recognize that whites often do contribute to Black Studies:

Black conservative thought – a reading list

Stanley Crouch and Playthell Benjamin (2003) reassess the great African – American intellectual W. E. B. DuBois. They argue that his message of black self – improvement is relevant today and deserves sympathetic treatment by Black Studies departments.

George Schuyle, as far back as the 1920s, said that "your American Negro is just plain American." He provocatively labeled the artists of the "Harlem Renaissance" as provincials without significant merit.

Lawrence Mead (1989), a white sociologist, advocated "workfare" as a substitute for welfare. Government aid becomes contingent on all able – bodied family heads and single adults accepting work in some legal job, however menial it is, in preference to crime or dependency. An American must be a functioning citizen before he or she can claim economic rights. Work must be guaranteed, if necessary through government jobs, as well as childcare and other support. Welfare alone means that people can choose to remain idle rather than accept jobs that fall below middle – class norms, such as jobs they see as dirty or low – paid. They should not be allowed that option.

Shelby Steele (1999) argued that "assimilation is not a self – hating mimicry of things white but a mastery by Negro individuals of the modern and cosmopolitan world." He believes that Richard Wright (*The Outsider*), Ralph Ellison (*The Invisible Man*), and Zora Neale Hurston (*How It Feels To Be Colored Me*) wrote works of lasting value precisely because no one valued them as "black writers."

Thomas Sowell (2004) has challenged us to test our views against the evidence of history. He argued powerfully against all forms of affirmative action and asserted that an ethnic group progresses faster when uncorrupted by either preferment or the welfare state. He is perhaps the best spokesman for the conservative point of view.

Dan Subotnik (2005) endorsed the use of standardized achievement tests despite the fact that they produce ratios that favor whites over blacks in academia and employment. Blacks must dispel the suspicion that they are unable to perform at a high level and thus avoid the stigma of owing their jobs or university places to the helping hand of affirmative action. They can do this only by hard work. Racial quotas are pernicious in that they generate ill will, resentment, and social division, particularly when they place people in positions for which they are ill prepared.

Peter H. Wood (2003) rejects diversity as a slogan. When you "diversify" the university (or society) ethnically, you assume that people are, above all, members of social groups and products of the historical experiences of those groups. This assumption is profoundly anti – individualist and at odds with America's ideals of liberty and equality.

Walter E. Williams (2016) says that, "for decades, colleges have purchased peace by creating whole departments of ethnic, diversity, and multicultural studies. All too often, these 'studies' are about propaganda and not serious education. Plus, they provide students with an opportunity to get an easy A."

Stephen and Abigail Thernstrom (1999) endorsed "racelessness" for blacks (and whites) and castigated expressions of racial solidarity, whether in music, on t – shirts, or in Black Studies departments, insofar as they are divisive, and particularly if they declare that whites are the enemy.

Debra Dickerson (2005) challenged African – Americans to stop obsessing about racism, take a good, hard look in the mirror, and start focusing on problems they can fix.

Implications for other courses

McWhorter (2009b) also offers suggestions for other areas of the curriculum:

Black history. This should be told as it really happened. The standard works by William Julius Wilson, Elijah Anderson, and Douglas Massey must be included. Whites who have written excellent black history should be recognized, including books such Massey's, Allan Keiler's *Marian Anderson* (2000), and Kevin Boyle's *Arc of Justice* (2004). The last book details how (during the 1920s) racism in Detroit persecuted Ossian Sweet through the legal system, leading to the deaths of members of his family and the destruction of his career as a physician.

Thomas Sugrue's *Sweet Land of Liberty* (2009) will please those who welcome confrontation with whites but his tactical advice must not be ignored: that the freedom struggle in Northern cities was most effective when civil rights groups formed alliances with one another and reached across racial and class lines to work with other activists, such as labor leaders. The benefits of welfare reform since 1996 should be covered: Jason DeParle's *American Dream* has been called honest and readable. George Galster's work (2012) should also be assigned: he argues that efforts to disperse housing project residents to suburbs have not born fruit.

Black education. Prudence Carter (2003) argued that blacks in high school have a special problem that celebrating black culture cannot solve. They must do a balancing act between black and white cultures so that they can adapt dress, speech, and manner to be successful in things like job interviews. John Ogbu (2003) generalized the problem when he says that African – Americans' own cultural attitudes pose a serious problem too often neglected. The kids are looking at rappers in ghettos as their role models although their parents work at two jobs to attain middle class status. The middle – class parents "want" their children to do well at school and yet generally spend no more time on homework or tracking their children's schooling than poor white parents.

As for university, students should hear both sides on whether affirmative action benefits or damages blacks who go on to university. Derek Bowen and William Bok *The Shape of the River* (1998) argue the pro side, but in addition McWhorter recommends Faye Crosby's *Affirmative Action Is Dead, Long Live Affirmative Action* (2004). The anti side should include Larry Purdy's *Getting Under the Skin of Diversity* (2008), Peter Wood's *Diversity* (2003), and Thomas Sowell's older but still potent *Black Education: Myths and Tragedies* (1972). The last makes the powerful argument that blacks are being systematically mismatched to their universities: those who could pass at Michigan are creamed off by Harvard, those who could pass at Southern Illinois are creamed off by Michigan, and so forth, and many blacks who could qualify for a profession (if dropped down the ladder) are forced to take Black Studies to survive. McWhorter recommends Chapter 8 of his

Winning the Race (2005), which is anti – affirmative action, so I will recommend Chapter 4 of my *Where Have all the Liberals Gone* (2008) which favors it except for strong reservations about how universities implement it in practice.

Black Music. This should be presented for its own sake without portraying it primarily as a coping mechanism against racism and injustice. African – Americans have not made music only to thumb their noses at white people. A complete curriculum should include black classical music by early figures like William Grant Still (his *Afro – American Symphony*), the classical/ragtime fusion of Will Marion Cook, jazz in all of its endless majesty (and not just black performers), with Coleman Hawkins (Body and Soul) balanced by the white contribution of Richard Sudhalter (Lost Chords). The emergence of Rhythm & Blues in the forties should be covered despite the fact that Louis Jourdan was not thinking much about Jim Crow while he was forging the foundations for rock and roll. Hip – hop should be covered in all of its messy essence as just the new thing, not as a historically crucial "political" program.

Black theatre and film. The goal should be to show how black artists achieved with how they did so in opposition to racism as a sideshow. Ethel Waters, Dorothy Dandridge, Sidney Poitier, Pearl Bailey, Brock Peters, Roscoe Lee Browne, Diana Sands, Cicely Tyson, and Diahann Carroll, and today Tisha Campbell, Wesley Snipes, Taraji Henson, Halle Berry, Tyler Perry, Will Smith, and Jennifer Lewis. These "black" performers are reduced to plastic figurines if they are treated as interesting only because they "speak truth to power."

The struggle for survival

The dominant theme of the conservatives, only sometimes acknowledged, is that blacks can hope to be assimilated into the mainstream of American society just as other ethnic groups have been. Of course, for a long time at least, they will have the kind of self – identity characteristic of other groups such as Irish – Americans. My grandfather was a revolutionary in Ireland who came to America in the 1870s and remembered the great famine of the 1840s with bitterness. My father was fully aware of Ireland's unhappy history and believed he faced an Anglo – Saxon elite hostile to his ethnicity. He lived in an

America where Catholics faced all manner of discrimination. Born in 1934, I was also aware of Irish history and the difficulties he faced, but my Irish identity is confined to a sense of pride that Ireland became independent and to rooting for Irish athletic teams that play England. My children and my brother's children are not Catholics and, perhaps thanks to the fact we both married out, they never seem to think about being "Irish" at all. It took four generations, but we have come to the end of the line. Conservative thinkers believe American blacks may walk the same road.

Now we see why the debate about Black Studies is a tense struggle. It is between blacks who believe in assimilation and blacks who see this as a racial suicide that cheats blacks (and the world) of some special merit that only black culture or black genes (recall Leonard Jeffries) can provide. The problem seems intractable.

Remedy for Black Studies

There may be a solution. A relatively conservative university like George Mason could offer an inclusive curriculum in Black Studies. Holding up an ideal that others could copy (a pattern laid up in heaven) would itself be laudable. This solution poses a second problem, namely, one of tolerance among colleagues. George A. Levesque (2009) complains that he was persecuted because he refused to take the "all blacks are victims" line. During his twenty – eight – year career at the University Center at Albany (as a tenured member of the Department of African Studies), he had to fight no fewer than four determined attempts by four different chairpersons to get him fired. No one wants a department so divided over curriculum, appointments, tenure, and promotion that staff will find it unlivable.

The University of Sydney's Philosophy Department was so split between Marxist and more traditional philosophers that the university created two departments. Each was self – governing and students could choose. Universities could follow suit and include both a Department of Black Studies (conservative) and a Department of Afro – centric Studies (more "radical") and let students choose, piecing together a major from one or the other or both. Over time, staff from the two departments might find they had enough in common to team – teach a few courses and cooperation might begin to replace hostile camps. History may be a solvent. By 2100, African – Americans may both feel American enough to remember their origins in Africa as a mere detail of their backgrounds and not an essential part of their identity that determines all others.

9
Women's Studies

Daphne Patai and Noretta Koertge (2003) have written the most interesting critique of Women's Studies. There are parallels with Black Studies in the sense of restricted content in the curriculum dictated by the academic community that controls it. But there are differences. The hierarchy of people whose views matter more than the views of others is no longer simply a hierarchy of radical versus conservative or black versus white. It is complicated by a criterion based on gender and sexual preference as well. The discipline has also developed its own set of dogmas that circumscribe the search for truth and cripple the thinking of its students. Worst of all is the claim that it has some alternative method to orthodox science.

Patai and Koertge allow for exceptions. But they also hold that flaws are widespread and have become even more endemic as universities entered the present century. The first edition provoked both denial and a tacit admission of veracity in the sense of saying that "we may be biased but so are all university departments." The prevalent sop to conscience was an ideological assertion that "we must counterbalance the fact that patriarchal ideology infects young women from everywhere else." Patai and Koertge note how many of those who fought for a place for Women's Studies in the university are now alienated.

The authors are both self – described feminists. Both were enthusiastic about Women's Studies at its inception. They first met in 1988. Patai was on leave from Women's Studies at the University of Massachusetts and gave a lecture at Indiana in one of Koertge's courses (concepts of gender and sexuality). They remained in contact and realized they were coming to a common conclusion: that the central tenets and favored practices of Women's studies were seriously flawed.

They compile a long list. I have added my own analysis of the fallacies involved.

Knowledge on trial

Every step towards truth is described as irrelevant or dangerous. Lecturers mock logic, quantitative reasoning, objective evaluation of evidence, and fair – minded consideration of opposing views, all as the creations of Dead White Males. In fact, these things are the steps that take us from crude empiricism to the scientific method. Even on the level of crude empiricism most have their place. Among pre – scientific peoples logic prevails: "Don't eat that. Why? It is a kumquat. Why not eat a kumquat? All kumquats are poisonous." Statistics counts because people want to know whether something is prevalent or simply a chance event: "We should cast out our nets at dawn as well as at dusk. Why? Yesterday at dawn I saw lots of fish close to shore. Was that just yesterday or is that true most days?"

Logic is so fundamental that every article a feminist writes uses it. Otherwise we could not follow them: "Is she saying both that women are shorter than men on average and that women are taller than men on average?" We are told what traits are rare among women/men or which are widespread or which are universal. The attack on these "male inventions" is brought into play only when feminists wish to ignore evidence against their dogmas. But logic aside, they can do very bad research based on ignorance of the scientific method.

All who reject astrology, magic, and the infallibility of scripture accept that evidence is the only truth – test for both scientific theories and hypotheses that posit facts about the universe (light bends as it passes mass). The latter include hypotheses about human behavior (a person raised in an orphanage is more likely to become a prostitute). The soul of the method is finding a fecund theory that generates a multiplicity of hypotheses that can be tested. However, when the social sciences study human behavior, there are a host of new problems that must be solved.

You must be careful to define the population to be sampled and try to get a random or representative sample of sufficient size so that your hypothesis can be said to be evidenced rather than due to random error. You will never get a response from all those you sample. You must use mathematical techniques to dictate sample size and allow for nonresponse bias. You must watch for a placebo effect, the possibility that any remedy, particularly one that seems endorsed by an expert, may have a psychological effect and that the treatment you use adds nothing. If you want to see whether an educational intervention raises IQ in infancy, you must have not just an experimental group but control groups – say a group of siblings who are measured only at the end of the regime rather than throughout (the experimental group may be merely be learning how to do IQ tests better). And another group who are tested throughout but do not get the intervention. We use path analysis to discriminate between cause and effect, and factor analysis to determine whether the causes are one or many. We use algorithms to make problems susceptible to computer analysis.

We know how natural science has shaped the modern world but often neglect the role of social science. Here are a few recent contributions from the UK alone:

Predicting the future: Social scientists estimated how many part – time jobs would be eliminated if a minimum wage were imposed (economics).

Ethnic analysis of costs: They also demonstrated that the charges for using ATMs disproportionately affected minorities and got the charges eliminated.

Developed strategies to reduce crime: There was a serious problem of lead being stolen from community building roofs. They recommended that dealers in the scrap metal market should keep meticulous records. It became too risky to sell what might be stolen lead.

Detecting secondary consequences: a study showed that laws that provided opportunities for some women to become wage earners not only enhanced family income but also reduced hazardous work.

Analyzing personal behavior: They found that choosing unhealthy foods was sometimes rational. If the person doing the shopping knows that others will simply not eat the healthy option and it will just go to waste, they will not buy it. They also showed parents how crucial their role is: many parents, particularly parents of younger children, are more concerned that their children enjoy school, than that they are academic stars.

Does any academic really want social science to go away? Every large institution in the modern world including universities uses it to predict (e.g. how large will the entering class be next year), budget, audit accounts, do surveys, and estimate the quality of its product (how many graduates distinguished themselves). Every Women's Studies department does all these things. To turn your back on science is to pretend that the modern world does not exist.

However, let me propose a thesis less extreme than abandoning science: that women are more likely to have personal traits that make them better at using the scientific method, once they have mastered it. Recall Elsie Moore from Chapter 3. She was careful to select infant adoptees that had at least one black parent. She was careful to select two groups of adoptive parents one of which was black and the other white, but both of which were matched for high SES. She was careful to give the children the same IQ tests normed at the same time at about age 8.5; and measure the difference between black and white adoptees. She at least attempted to get a sample size that would rule out chance as clouding the results.

But she did more. She made an intuitive leap a man might not have made, that the root cause of the IQ difference of the children might be the mother – child relationship when doing problem solving. So she called the mother and child in to do a problem – solving task. As a woman, she might have had greater rapport with the mothers in general. As a black woman, she might have had greater rapport with black mothers. And as a professional woman, she might have won the respect of both. In others words, her intuitions may have led her to propose a more interesting hypothesis and her empathy and femininity may have allowed her to access the kind of evidence that would test it.

Even in the hard sciences these things count. Maxwell's equations were such a leap beyond what was thought at the time, we are amazed that he could formulate them. But his intuition had to be given the precision to be tested and had to pass the truth – test of verification. The Greek obsession with circular motion impeded the hypotheses they posed about planetary motion, and it is good that non – Greeks eventually discarded that bias. Later astronomers also had the advantage of the telescope that gave them access to far improved data. If women really are better at science than men, it is tragic that Women's Studies departments tend to regard it with such suspicion.

Women's special road to truth

Belenky, Clinchy, Goldberger, and Tarule (*Women's Ways of Knowing*, 1986) has become a standard text. The book's first two sentences are deceptive. They say that its purpose is to describe both "the ways of knowing women have cultivated" and "the multitude of obstacles women must overcome in developing the power of their minds." Actually, the book says nothing whatsoever about ways of knowing that are alternative to the scientific method. It does not even show why women might do science better. It is entirely devoted to its secondary purpose, the obstacles women must overcome to get a clear notion of what knowledge is all about. It is a sad indictment that Women's Studies scholars do not see *Women's Ways of Knowing* for what it is. They tend to think it that is shows that women have not only a different but also a superior way of knowing. On the dust jacket, Carol Gilligan of Harvard University tells us that it "encourages one to think in new ways about what constitutes knowledge," as if it presented an alternative to our usual way of thinking about what constitutes knowledge.

Women's Way of Knowing is pure pedagogy. It may be sound in the sense that the psychology of a group is relevant to how to teach or address them. If I am giving a talk on the benefits of progressive taxation, I had better know my audience. If it is a wealthy one, I should be prepared for the objection that the market benefits the poor the greater the investment capital of the rich. If this book is correct about women, its real message is this: a women's studies lecturer faces many obstacles in convincing students to respect the scientific method. Its analysis of women's psychology begins with those who have the most naïve notions about truth and ends with those who are only somewhat less naïve.

From one level of naïveté to another

According to *Women's Way of Knowing*, women begin with silence. Next they are passive in the face of what experts call received knowledge. Then they feel they know, thanks to an inner voice (gut feelings, instinct, intuition), but quickly realize that this is fallible. Next comes procedural knowing. On its lowest level, one is reluctant to separate thought from the thinker (because you do not want to hurt someone's feelings by rebutting them). At the next level, this turns into connected knowing, occasions when people interact with one another to attain consensus through empathy, trust, and forbearance. The final level is constructed knowing, which integrates everything valid from all levels: it integrates reason, intuition, and expertise. It is not an "objective" procedure. But it does incline one to work for improvement in the quality of life of others.

I wish to underline the conclusion that neither intuition nor empathy alone provides a new way of knowing. A woman over breakfast may believe she sees telltale signs that her husband is sad and believe that he would miss those signs in the reverse case. But the truth of this hypothesis must still pass the test of verification: if he gives all the signs of being merry throughout the day rather than depressed, she was wrong. Maybe he was merely pensive.

It is a pity that *Women's Ways of Knowing* stops at the point it does. Given its emphasis on connected knowing, the next logical step should be recognizing that there is a whole community of scholars, thousands of people mainly seeking the truth, people one can meet at conferences, contact by email, and engage with by reading their books and articles. The next step after that would be ascertaining why these people think their methodology works and, if one is very good, detecting flaws and offering correctives.

One can read the literature with a critical eye trying to detect bias of any sort and be careful not to confuse methodological defect with anti – woman bias. Richard Lynn (Chapter 3) is not biased against women; he just used bad sampling. One may not be impressed with the authority of the expert or appeals to intuition. However, really immersing one's self in the literature would give the game away, for it would concede that women would have no special "ways of knowing" but only special "ways of learning" or at best, special traits that lead to new hypotheses and collecting a wider range of data.

If a woman chooses to isolate herself from the literature and communicate only with people with whom she has empathy, this is not good. It is pathetic. Those in Women's Studies generate their own literature but to the degree that it deviates from the methodological rigor of all the relevant disciplines, it is inferior. *Women's Way of Knowing* attributes virtues to women that are morally elevating: modesty, willingness to listen to others, and benevolence, but this ultimately presumes that no men have these virtues and that no women are without them.

Some may defend the notion that there are different ways of knowing by appealing to the postmodernist argument that all scientific or epistemological theories are relative and that rationality itself is a tainted concept invented by oppressive (white) males. It bases this conclusion on the fact that all concepts occur in a social setting (where else would they occur?). This assertion has never stopped anyone from jettisoning Ptolemy's astronomy (a product of Greece) for Newton's astronomy (the product of a seventeenth – century Englishman) for Einstein's astronomy (a product of a twentieth – century German – American). When science reveals what the real world is like, it transcends time and place. It is noteworthy that this kind of postmodernism is endemic in women's studies departments and not, for what should be obvious reasons, in physics departments. Even if it were true, epistemological relativism would not validate a women's road to truth: it would merely suggest that it might be an option among an infinite number of other options. If anyone ever gives a coherent account of this other option, we can assess it. At present, there is no more a women's epistemology than there was a Jewish physics.

Creating a better world

Women's Studies has a special antipathy toward traditional social science in general and economics in particular. These describe what happens and what is possible in the real world. Women's Studies largely posits an ideal world whose practicality rests on a simplistic assumption – that men are villains who are responsible for every evil – and tries to justify that ideal as in every way superior to what exists. Vulgar Marxism influenced the content of Women's Studies. At one time it was focused on consciousness raising and recruitment. Sophisticated Marxists balanced their analysis with a vigorous attempt to educate students in alternative schools of thought. They were not imitated. Patai and Noretta Koertge (2003, p. 6) believe that the National Women's Studies Association's conferences advertise the discipline's inherent anti – intellectualism. Next to publishers' displays of academic books stand booths featuring crystals, drums, and massage oils, things that are supposed to be the paraphernalia of "women's culture."

Effects on classroom practice

If Women's Studies focuses on consciousness raising and recruitment, its classes will tend to be skewed toward making students realize that the way in which society disadvantages women is acute and pervasive. Therefore, women should speak about their experiences; the most insightful contributions will come from those women who suffer most as determined by identity group(s). This establishes a pecking order of black lesbian women, white lesbian women, and white straight women, each of whom must defer to those surpassing them in degradation to diagnose the worst disadvantages women suffer. If men are present, however acute their appreciation of structural rather than personal disadvantage, they are there to learn rather than to enlighten. In some cases, they are bade not to speak.

Patai and Koertge (2003, pp. 14 – 16, 23) give examples, describing behaviors that range from outrageous to merely objectionable. Three accomplished academics who abandoned Women's Studies (a historian, a social scientist, a humanities professor) relate how militant students are sometimes encouraged to create an environment hostile to open discussion: planned disruption of the classes of "errant" lecturers, stomping their feet and hooting at what they dislike, shouting down a paper on anti – Semitism if it conflicts with anti – oppression narratives. Patai and Koertge add detail to the pecking order that ranks those most likely to be gagged. They begin with the most vulnerable. All page citations in the following paragraphs are from their book.

Men in general might say: "You know, sometimes I have a hard time sitting here because I feel you are blaming men for all the problems in the world." In reply, the Women's Studies adherent would reply: "You obviously have no understanding. You are a man. You can only try to empathize" (p.90). "I brought up an experience with my brother in class and it was like, Ugh! You were hanging out with a man" (p.90). "If a man is going to speak, he'd better have a *damn* good thing to say, and it had better be right!" (p. 86).

Straight women: "People are always declaring themselves, what her sexual orientation is … within a week you *know* what everyone in your class is." And "if you are heterosexual, strictly heterosexual, or conservative, you don't have a right to say much in Women's Studies. You're classified with men." (p. 87)

Women with intellectual integrity: A woman objected to the thesis that rape is simply something men to do to women to assert dominance. The lecturer humiliated her: "Are you saying that rapists are just poor misunderstood people who should be patted on the back and sent out?" (p. 84).

Women with a sense of humor: "The class made me think of a Monty Python skit … where the answer to every question is 'pork' (what's the capital of Pennsylvania – the answer is 'pork'). In the class I took, the answer was always 'men.' The question could be 'What style of architecture is that?' and the answer is, 'Men's architecture.'" (p. 83).

Women with conventional aspirations: "I should have been free to walk into a feminist theory class and say, regardless of what anyone else believes, I want to be a housewife." (p. 89).

Women of conventional appearance: A woman said I happen to like men. She was completely cut to pieces. "She was completely at a disadvantage, because here she is sitting in full makeup, a skirt, heels, well – done hair." (p. 89). "Why should anyone care whether you shave your legs or not." (p. 88)

White and black: When white women preach the dogma that a women who alleges rape is always to be believed without further investigation, they are a bit stunned when black women confront them with all the times black men have been lynched simply because a white woman accused them of rape. Usually, however, the practice of accepting what black women say at face value just means educating them badly: "What could be more racist and/or condescending than ... to allow an individual to present positions (and even praise them) that are riddled with inconsistencies." (p. 63).

Effects on scholarship

Wherever these dogmas and practices exist, orthodoxy is likely to overshadow scholarly credentials in recruitment of staff. This fact, plus antipathy to statistics and social science (including social psychology), clouds analysis. Take the vexed question of the income gap between men and women. To address this phenomenon at all, we must begin with a statistical analysis: are women concentrated in highly paid occupations to the same degree as men. This is not the end of the story. Certain occupations may be underpaid precisely because women are dominant. But is that discrimination or a market result? Given that women are often looking for part time and undemanding work (while burdened with child – rearing), they may flood certain labor markets and thus drive wages down. Their role of second earner may result from agreements with their husbands as to who puts career advancement ahead of household duties. Fortunately, rising numbers of men are exchanging the role of breadwinner for that of caregiver.

Every staff and student member of a Women's Studies department must answer Thomas Sowell (2009, 226):

> As early as 1971, women in their thirties who had never married and had worked continuously since school earned slightly *higher* incomes than men of the same description. In Canada, women who had never married earned more than 99 percent of the income of men who had never married. Among college faculty members, American women who had never married earned slightly *higher* incomes than men who had never married, as far back as 1969 ... While married men tend to earn more than single men and married men with children still more, the exact opposite is the case for women.

Why is this last phenomenon true? The obvious answer is that when women have children, they assume a greater burden of childcare than men do. When men have children, they tend to be spurred to work harder to increase family income. Many universities confirm this in their parental leave policies, which traditionally grant maternity leave to women professors but not paternity leave to male professors. The ideal solution would be women negotiating more equitable arrangements with their spouses, but there might be an unpleasant trade – off. Where such a treaty exists, there should be no presumption that women have a *prima facie* case for custody of children after marriage breakdown.

This analysis does not imply that ideal solutions are impossible. The civil service can set aside whole blocks of jobs that are shared by a couple working half – time. Or they can just make half – time work more attractive by giving a full year's credit toward seniority and permanent tenure for each year of service, with the ever – present option of switching to fulltime when convenient.

Would such measures entirely eliminate the income gap? Perhaps women may be less willing to sacrifice rewarding leisure and socialization to the work ethic and less willing to work for firms that require you to come to the office on weekends and holidays. When women have salaries on par with men, they may be less interested in shaking the last dollar out of the money tree. Sub – cultural differences exist between ethnicities; perhaps they also exist between genders.

The dogmatic view that there are no genetic differences between the genders can veto intelligent analysis. To analyze why fewer women are near the very top in pure mathematics, one must discuss the possibility that genetic differences affect mathematical ability. If true, it is possible that these differences affect character rather than cognitive ability: perhaps more women are temperamentally less drawn to mathematics unless it has human significance, though this tendency could also be environmental (Flynn, 2017). Professor John Loehlin reports an incident at the University of Texas at Austin in which a colleague gave a talk to a group consisting of mostly humanities professors and mentioned that some sex differences might be genetic. When a woman professor objected, he said, "Look, men are on average taller than women, do you suppose that is because of how they are raised?" She responded, "I wouldn't be surprised."

Such dogmatic reactions cripple research in areas other than Women's Studies. Would any sociologist want to be labeled as anti – woman, regardless of what the data show? Charlotta Stern (2018) made the point in an interview:

> Gender sociologists are so wedded to the idea that there shouldn't be any difference or very slim differences between women and men. So when they see differences, they think that there has to be something wrong. You know, either discrimination or wrongful socialization of boys and girls or what have you … differences cannot just be differences. They're somehow always a sign of inequality … I think that is impoverishing our science … Since people don't really theorize about potential differences playing a role in how we live our lives, we end up perhaps creating problems where there are no problems, and we definitely end up not asking questions about the potential impact of these other types of mechanisms and I think that is – that's not good for a science.

A word about some feminist journals

The standards that some journals use to screen articles for publication reflects the degree to which Women's Studies replaces methodological rigor with ideology. In 2017 – 2018, three self – identified leftist academics – Helen Pluckrose, James A. Lindsay, and Peter Boghossian – perpetrated a hoax. They summited 20 papers that were deliberately absurd to leading journals: 17 of these were reviewed before the hoax was disclosed, and seven – 35 percent of the total – were accepted for publication while an additional four were invited to for resubmission after revision. To appreciate how absurd the papers were can be captured in a few excerpts.

First citation: Wilson, Helen (2018). "Human Reactions to Rape Culture and Queer Performativity at Urban Dog Parks in Portland, Oregon," *Gender, Place & Culture*:

> (1) The phrase 'dog rape/humping incident' documents only those incidents in which … the humped dog [had] given no encouragement and apparently [was] not enjoying the activity.

(2) When a male dog was humping another male dog, humans attempted to intervene 97% of the time. When a male dog was humping a female dog, humans only attempted to intervene 32% of the time.

(3) No female dogs initiated humping ... since we generally do not consider the sniffing of one dog's anus by another dog to be a sexual behavior amongst dogs.

(4) Males also referred to female dogs as 'girl' (e.g. 'come here, girl,' 'good girl.')

(5) The obvious parallel can be made from yelling at female dogs ... to yelling at human females in domestic abuse situations.

(6) It is also not politically feasible to leash men, yank their leashes when they 'misbehave,' or strike men with leashes (or other objects) in an attempt to help them desist from sexual aggression and other predatory behaviors.

All the so – called observations described were, of course, invented. This paper gained special recognition for excellence from *Gender, Place, and Culture* as one of twelve leading pieces in "feminist geography" as a part of the journal's 25th anniversary celebration.

Second citation: Smith, M. (2018). "Going in Through the Back Door: Challenging Straight Male Homohysteria, Transhysteria, and Transphobia Through Receptive Penetrative Sex Toy Use. *Sexuality & Culture*:

(1) Do men who report greater comfort with receptive penetrative anal eroticism also report less transphobia, less obedience to masculine gender norms, greater partner sensitivity, and greater awareness about rape? ... This analysis recognizes potential socially remedial value for encouraging male anal eroticism with sex toys.

(2) It ... explores the questions: 'Why don't straight men (tend to) use penetrative sex toys on themselves to experience (anal) sexual pleasure?' and 'What might change if they did?'

(3) Ultimately, there are few, if any, non – transphobic/hysteric reasons for straight men to exclude trans women from their dating and sexual interests. Still, the most common fixates upon the trans woman's genitals, especially when she has a penis ... Ultimately, this concern for the transhysteric male includes the performance of sex acts deemed demasculinizing only because

they involve another penis, even when that penis is part of a woman's body.

Third citation: Gonzalez, M., & Jones, L. A. Our struggle is my struggle: Solidarity Feminism as an Intersectional Reply to Neoliberal and Choice Feminism," *Affilia: Journal of Women and Social Work*.

The quality of this paper can be judged by the fact that it is a chapter from Adolf Hitler's *Mein Kampf* with textual alterations, including replacing "Nazism" with "feminism."

The flagship feminist philosophy journal, *Hypatia*, invited resubmission of a paper arguing that "privileged students shouldn't be allowed to speak in class at all and should just listen and learn in silence," and that they would benefit from "experiential reparations" that include "sitting on the floor, wearing chains, or intentionally being spoken over." The reviewers complained that this hoax paper took an overly compassionate stance toward the "privileged" students who would be subjected to this humiliation, and recommended that they be subjected to *harsher* treatment (Cofnas, 2018).

These hoaxes attracted much adverse criticism. Some argued that matching hoaxes were not perpetrated on non – feminist journals, and that they would have garnered the same results if they were. Peter Boghossian, one of the authors, was placed under an ethics investigation by his university for allegedly having conducted unauthorized research on human subjects and for having used "falsified data" in writing the articles. He was defended by heavy – hitting public intellectuals, including Steven Pinker (who defended this book), Richard Dawkins, and Jordan Peterson, but a disturbing number of his more rank – and – file colleagues excoriated the hoax.

Gloom and doom

The focus on the specter of an unyielding patriarchy encourages students to underestimate how much things have in fact improved. Women have made enormous progress over the last 50 years – see Chapter 3. The fact that their mean IQ on Raven's Progressive Matrices has risen to at least equal that of men is a sure sign that their minds have full access to modernity, and that they have the sort of educated minds that can perform the full range of jobs our societies have to offer.

Some studies suggest that women benefit from a temperament that allows them to adapt to formal education better than men. Remember that in America and elsewhere, the average 17 – year old girl is at the 67th percentile of the boy's curve for language and at the 75th percentile in writing skills. More women graduate from university in most Western societies and in many non – Western ones. They are flooding into verbal professions (journalism and law), including the therapeutic professions (counseling, clinical psychology, and the general practice of medicine). Women who do not major in Black Studies or Women's Studies may be short on outrage, but tend to get the cognitive skills they need to compete with men in many professions.

Less fortuitously, the group psychology that dominates Women's Studies stifles individual autonomy to the degree that it makes women believe that they can rise no higher than to be spokespeople for the groups to which they happen to belong. They lose autonomy if they feel they cannot rebel against the dogmas that all groups (from communists to women) try to put above rational critique. Every step I took toward autonomy meant freeing my mind from a group identity that tried to blind me to what science says about the real world and the causes of its injustices. Sometimes this tension is called group loyalty versus individualism.

If I had not transcended my Catholic identity and faith by the age of twelve, I would likely have prepared for the priesthood. If I had not transcended the Irish nationalism of my heritage, I would still be huffing and puffing about the English rather than doing other things. If I had not risen above the sentiment of patriotism, I would not be able to critique American foreign policy since 1960. If I had not transcended the dogmas characteristic of the left, I would still be defending the blanket nationalization of industry – and never have read Jensen, Lynn, and Murray. If I had not risen above the racism of my parents and the white guilt of some fellow academics, I would not have offered a sympathetic and intelligent analysis of the black marriage market. If I had not risen above male chauvinism and male self – guilt, I could not take a realistic view of Women's Studies.

Activists produced by Women's Studies take seriously all of its dogmas, particularly dogmas about the corruption of "male science" and the sin of taking the evidence of the social sciences seriously. This does not mean a properly educated woman cannot be an activist. To be effective, everyone must compromise to the degree of biting his or her tongue and participating in groups that deserve a better deal. But the mind should see the world clearly and empirically. If Patai and Koertge are correct, graduates of Women's Studies departments must be very strong – minded to attain the dignity of intellectual autonomy.

Remedy for Women's Studies

The best remedy assumes that academics give students an option to choose social analysis over emotion. Institutions could frame course regulations so that a Women's Studies degree can be earned by taking relevant courses from either the traditional departments (history of women in America, a cross – cultural analysis of the role of women in various societies, the position of women in the American economy) or from Women's Studies proper or both. Let students punish or reward the lecturers who offer analysis rather than therapy and recruitment and who assess the contributions of all students based on content rather than hierarchies of privilege or oppression. If a Women's Studies department wants to elevate consciousness, why not confine it to a weekly tutorial? The practice of giving extra credit for political activism is a disgrace. As for the recruitment of pre – and post – graduation activists, this should be left to a student club.

10
The Walden Codes

In his utopian novel, *Walden Two*, the famed behaviorist B. F. Skinner (1948) restricted free speech to a tiny elite and forbad the masses from discussing with one another the performance of their rulers. Anyone with a personal grievance can go to someone higher up and state it. The instrument he uses to enforce this stipulation is the "Walden Code," which set out rules that if broken, automatically classify the offender as mentally ill and to be sequestered for treatment until "cured." It also contains a speech code. Everyone is forbidden to say "thank you" or gossip. Both of these are forbidden because they violate the system's basic philosophical tenets: they imply that it is sensible to rank people into a hierarchy of better (singling them out for thanks) or worse (disparaging them by gossip). Skinner (1971) believes that we are all products of our genes and environment (neither of which we choose) and, therefore, no one is deserving of praise or blame. Words that imply the contrary show that one has not embraced science and is a source of primitive irrationality likely to make others feel uncomfortable.

We have seen how Black Studies and Women's Studies tend to adopt modern – day "Walden Codes" that restrict free speech using institutional sanctions: penalizing those who hold certain views, most effective of all, ensuring that students never hear those views expressed. It would be wrong to assume that they are the only culprits.

I will argue that other disciplines, like Anthropology, Sociology, Education, Psychology, Political Science, and Philosophy also tend to have Walden Codes. Note the word "tend." I have given no questionnaire to the universities of the Western World. I will simply report my impressions based on 60 years at seven universities and as a reader for three scholarly journals, whose content collectively embraces the fields listed (referees' reports from other readers are very revealing). I know that a lot of departments have Walden Codes. I leave it to academic readers to assess whether or not their particular department is guilty.

Anthropology

There is a strong tendency toward cultural relativism or the rejection of cross – cultural assessments about truth or worth. Those who rank societies in terms of scientific versus pre – scientific, or beneficial versus vicious, are often censured. In fact, everyone or everyone who thinks clearly does these things quite naturally and without making an extreme judgment.

Anthropologists do not deny that societies are different; indeed, the subject is all about describing or accounting for these differences. One of these differences is the extent to which a society has mastered the scientific method, that is, the best method of discovering truths about the universe and human behavior. Whatever they may say, anthropologists all privilege that method over alternative methods of truth – seeking such as magic, appeals to legend, prayer, astrology, and so forth. Which of these other methods prevails in a society is important for understanding it, but anthropologists never adopt any of them in plying their craft. They do not take at face value the legends of any society but use carbon dating and careful excavation of artifacts to map its history. They do not immerse themselves into Dobu society to learn how to do magic but to experience how Dobu magic satisfies (and defines) basic human needs. They do not sit up all night hoping to see yams activated by magic march from one man's plot to another, but note how the concept of magic embitters personal relations in that every poor crop is taken as evidence of theft.

In other words, when anthropologists compare cultures, they do not replace science with magic *as a method* but use science to study the role of magic *as a subject*. They can, of course, study the rise of science in our society as a subject but they use science to do it. The only exception is found among anthropologists who espouse deconstructionism or postmodernism to deny that anyone's interpretation of the universe or human behavior is worthier of regard than another. Plato refuted this nonsense 2,000 years ago in *The Theaetetus* (182c, line 1 – 183a, line 5). When confronted by Heraclitus, who claimed that the universe was in such flux that no one could find anything stable enough to make sense of, Plato replied that flux did not necessarily mean chaos. It could mean orderly change with fixed points of reference over time. For example, the words he and Heraclitus were using had to have a constant meaning that endured for the length of their conversation. Otherwise, Heraclius could not even communicate his view that nothing was comprehensible. He would need to invent a new language.

Postmodernism is seductive because it gives one the illusion of having a deep philosophy when actually it is an excuse for having none at all. Its absurdity is exemplified by the fact that practitioners expect us to read their articles and comprehend what they mean and dismiss us if we do not. Jacques Derrida would not brook an interpretation of his words if it said that, rather than being about truth, they were really a description of the trip of the Bobbsey Twins to the seashore. If we can discern the difference between plausible and implausible interpretations of his text, there seems no reason why we cannot distinguish between plausible and implausible interpretations of the "text" of the universe or human behavior. Presumably, he would assign plausible interpretations of his text cross – cultural validity: they would be equally defensible when translated from French into English.

Reading Derrida's prose, it is possible that he did not intend to communicate anything. In his lecture on universities, every page shows how little he desired to be reader – friendly (Derrida, 1999). In the first two pages we find the terms "adequation," "theoretico – constative discourse," "poetico – performative events" – and the more familiar but nebulous *Aufklärung, Lumières, Illuminismo, mondialisation*. He took 30 pages to make one substantive, if banal, point: that thanks to the internet, the locus of learning now extends far beyond the physical confines of the university.

The extent to which a society has developed the scientific method ranks them epistemologically, that is, according to the degree to which they know how to test assertions about the universe external to man or the complexities of human behavior. When we examined the postmodernist pretentions of some of those in Women's Studies, we saw that all societies find a place for the crude empiricism that preceded the scientific method, if only to stay alive. That does not coerce anyone to assess human societies as better or worse in terms of the degree to which they have mastered science. You may far prefer some pre – industrial culture in which life was simpler and its consequences less lethal than our own, and the fact we are more epistemologically advanced is not nearly enough to tip the scales. If so, that is scarcely evidence that one cannot make cross – cultural value judgments. Given the variety of ideals held by human beings, it is hard to imagine anyone who ascribed equal worth to Hitler's and post – Hitler Germany, Stalin and Putin's Russia, America before and America after she developed an imperial animus (see Sumner, 1899: "The conquest of the United States by Spain"), or Dobu society (contentious) and Zuni society (harmonious).

Anthropology has only one legitimate contention in warning its practitioners to be careful about ranking societies. It is reasonable to contend that anyone obsessed by such a hierarchy will be a bad anthropologist. It has a *vocational* ethics that one should adopt to practice the discipline effectively. Anyone who finds a human society too disgusting, and cannot put that assessment aside when studying it, is likely to do a bad or at least a biased job. All professions have rules suited to their practice: a doctor should take every patient seriously; an auditor should be honest enough to audit the books impersonally; and an entomologist should study a wasp as carefully as she would a bee. But the professional code of anthropology should not be elevated to the status of some kind of "ethical truth." If that is done, it has a Walden Code hostile to the pursuit and expression of truth.

For example, the continental followers of Piaget, particularly George W. Oesterdiekhoff (2012), have attempted to link psychology to anthropology. Oesterdiekhoff argues that the worldview of children in advanced societies recapitulates the worldview of adults in preindustrial societies. Pre – industrial cultures assign "personhood" to the forces of nature and animals, believe in magic and prayer and charms, and believe that thoughts and dreams have real – world consequences. Children in our society accept all of these things until a certain age, when thanks to formal schooling, more and more of them begin to believe in impersonal causality, and master both logic and the scientific perspective.

Oesterdiekhoff offers a fascinating explanation of why average
IQs in pre – industrial societies are so low when measured by the tests
we have invented within a scientific society: just as children have low
IQs if measured versus our adult norms, so pre – industrial peoples score
accordingly when measured versus our adult norms. The tests do not
measure the "intelligence" of pre – scientific societies but how far they
have progressed toward our worldview. He charts the moral progress that
has accompanied cognitive progress (Flynn, 2013b). We no longer try
animals in court (a horse that killed its rider), do not think that every
lethal thought makes us guilty of murder, or use logic to universalize our
moral principles (ask if we would be worthy of ill – treatment if we woke
up with a black skin). He believes that thanks to Piaget we can appreciate
how science and secularism and humanism interacted to create the
modern world

Oesterdiekhoff rightly believes that he is often ignored in the
English – speaking world because of its aversion to anything that seems
to imply a hierarchy of human societies. He has been accused of saying
that we can rank societies from childish to adult. This is absurd. In every
society people play an adult role as defined by that society. Whether their
cognitive and moral perspective resembles our own children should be
tested on its merits, not as if the honor of anthropology is at stake.

Anthropology has an obligation not to allow its Walden Code to
spawn similar codes in area studies. Respect for the integrity of every
culture does not mean it makes sense to talk about fictitious disciplines.
There is no women's epistemology in the sense that women have some
kind of avenue toward truth valid for them alone, or black psychology, as
if blacks can understand blacks without applying the usual scientific
method, or Maori history, as if Maori legends about their past have the
status of real history. There is only the history *of Maori*, with their
legends to be studied as essential to their psychology. There is only the
psychology *of blacks*, although like any other group they may well have
special features in their worldview.

Every science needs to shed prejudices that limit how creative
we are in inventing scientific theories, that make us think we know all of
the relevant data when we do not, and that make us arbitrarily ignore

certain facets of human behavior. When astronomy was dominated by the prejudices of Greeks, who were obsessed with circular motion, it could not see that the planets moved around the sun in ellipses. Good that non – Greeks started to do astronomy, but there is no such thing such as Greek astronomy any more than there is Jewish physics. Blacks may well have greater empathy with other blacks than most whites do, and without their insights whites might think they understand blacks when they do not. When women did not do medicine, the results may well have neglected female health in favor of male health problems. The scientific method pays the most dividends when its practitioners are inclusive. But no one has invented an alternative to observation, theory, and prediction to constitute a women's medicine.

Sociology

Sociologists tend to marginalize those who explain group differences in behavior by reference to ethnic differences rather than differences in SES (socio – economic status). This struck me when I was a Fellow at the Sage Foundation in New York in 2009.

I gave a paper that explained different patterns in reaction times (RT) between Chinese and English children by hypothesizing cultural differences (Flynn, 1993). The RT task begins with your finger on a home button. There are three target buttons. Sometimes two of them light up and sometimes one of them lights up. You must identify the "odd man out." When the light or lights go on, you *release* the home button and *move* your finger toward hitting the correct target button. The task takes milliseconds and the fact that the Chinese were faster overall was taken as evidence that their brains possessed more efficient neural speed. I divided the overall time into release time and movement time. The Chinese were faster on release time (which had little correlation with their IQs) but slower on movement time (which had significant correlation with their IQs). The English children were the reverse.

I drew the obvious inference: Chinese children were risk takers who immediately released the home button and "thought" their way to the target button as they moved toward it. English children were more cautious: they would not release the home button until they knew where they were going, and then moved toward the target button quickly and without reflection. I thought this would be welcome evidence for the 30 distinguished social scientists sitting in front of me. It showed that this behavioral difference was due not to genes but to environment. The temperamental differences between Chinese and English Children were very likely to be the result of socialization in different cultures.

Most of those present, however, attacked me for "stereotyping" Chinese and English children. This despite repeated assurances that I was *not* saying that *all* English and Chinese children were different but simply asserting that cultural differences produced *average* behavioral differences. They wanted to know what SES differences existed between the two groups (difficult to say in that the Chinese were schoolchildren in Hong Kong and the English schoolchildren in Britain). It was quite clear that SES differences would be a respectable explanation while cultural differences were not. Bill Dickens (the economist) was an exception: afterwards he said, "Welcome to America" in a sarcastic admission of how thoroughly the politics of equality neutralizes academic discourse.

Conversation with others over lunch suggested the thinking behind the preference: that groups were different in SES was society's fault because some groups were less affluent because of their unfortunate history and society's failure to give them equal opportunities (home, school, jobs), often because of overt discrimination. SES was an *innocent* causal factor in explaining behavioral differences, such as IQ differences, differences in school and occupational achievement, crime rates, and so forth. Ethnic differences always verged on *indicting* the group's subculture. The Elsie Moore (1986) study is a case in point. White couples and black couples adopted black babies. When she had mother and child work on cognitive problems together, the white mothers were positive and encouraging (that's good, but let's try this); the black mothers negative and censorious ("you know better than that"). The result was a 13.5 IQ – point gap.

Note the danger in explaining the black – white IQ gap in terms of differences peculiar to black subculture. Are you saying that black mothers lack a constructive approach to problem solving and have more punitive relations with their children, with more corporal punishment in the wings? Ranking white and black parents as better and worse seems to follow; indeed, you seem to be blaming the victims for their misfortunes. Ranking subcultures in a hierarchy of merit raises its head.

But to deny sub – cultural differences is to forbid adequate explanation. There is no doubt that alcoholism was part of Irish – American subculture and that it had crippling effects in 1900, and this contrasted with its relative absence in Jewish – American subculture at that time – even when the groups were equated for SES. Indicting individuals for their subculture makes no more sense than indicting them for their group's history or SES, but this line of argument will not appease those who extend cultural relativism beyond societies to ethnic groups within a society. The next week after my presentation at Sage, an eminent black sociologist with Ivy League credentials addressed the seminar. He told them not to neglect ethnicity in favor of overreliance on SES. Coming from him, the same audience accepted the message without a murmur.

A prejudice in favor of SES over ethnicity should not be part of the Walden Code of Sociology. I have spent 40 years defending the proposition that the racial IQ gap is more likely to be environmental than genetic. Without reference to black subculture my case would fall to the ground. Equating for SES simply does not eliminate the difference. See Box 3.

Box 3. Black subculture and the IQ debate.

Recently I have heard from colleagues who are totally opposed to my use of black subculture in the race and IQ debate. To my mind, this leaves Jensen's "respectable opponents" with the following dilemma: they have no real rebuttal, therefore they are left only with appeals to the legacy of slavery, and black history, and black SES disadvantage. How could any of these things be potent unless they handicapped the minds of blacks *right now* taking IQ tests or performing in schools?

This means that there is a real difference in black/white cognitive skills, which demands an examination of cultural differences, just as I did in explaining the RT difference between Chinese and British. There is only one way out: stereotype threat. But even this grants that there is at least one cultural difference that separates races. Blacks can have lower cognitive skills because they sometimes feel intimidated when competing with whites. At one time, Black gangs physically intimidated Jewish – Americans; they did not physically intimidate Irish – American gangs. That is certainly a difference in subcultural traits. Hermann Göring is thought to have said, "Whenever I hear the word culture, I reach for my revolver." When American social scientists hear black subculture, they run for the hills.

Education

Education takes the refusal to rank people as "better" or "worse" on the basis of group differences and applies the prohibition to individuals. Thus, it entertains a powerful hostility to conventional IQ tests. I get a steady stream of students in my office who major in education or go to teachers' college whose first words are, "IQ tests are just crap, how can you rank people with a few silly questions." See if you can find an education department with a faculty member who takes IQ as seriously as it deserves to be taken. In schools, the recognition that any pupil is better than another is now anathema; American schools are eliminating the practice of naming and celebrating valedictorians or keeping score at basketball games.

The notion that there are no real individual differences cannot be sustained. Therefore, when Howard Gardner (1983, 1993, 1999) developed his theory of multiple intelligences and devised scales of measurement for each, his popularity among educationalists was guaranteed. Each child gets a score for eight intelligences: Linguistic, Logical – mathematical, Musical, Spatial, Bodily – kinesthetic (sport, dance, mime, acting), Self – oriented personal intelligence, Other – directed personal intelligence, and Naturalistic intelligence (discerning the flora and fauna of their environment). Assuming that these abilities were uncorrelated (not entirely true of course – Wechsler Vocabulary and Arithmetic have a robust correlation), the odds in favor of each child having an above – average score for some kind of intelligence would be 255 out of 256. Almost everyone gets recognition for some kind of cognitive ability. Despite doing badly at reading and arithmetic, a child above average at softball is not labeled "dumb" (Gardner, 1983, p. xi; 1993, pp. xx).

I have no objection to diagnosing the strengths and weaknesses of each child, and I wish society valued everyone more whatever their abilities. However, at present, society does not value different capabilities to the same degree. Being good at reading and writing and mathematics opens up a world of educational and vocational opportunities for a child inept at sport. Being above average at baseball may brighten one's leisure but will not make him a viable earner unless he is among that tiny elite who can earn a living at professional sport. By emphasizing mainly Linguistic and Logical – Mathematical intelligences, conventional IQ tests tell a parent much about their child's prospects. Parents are not fooled by "multiple intelligences" even if the academy is. Contrast their joy when their child does well in the relevant school subjects with their dismay at a bad report card, sport notwithstanding. Children do not really need a musical IQ score – either a child who takes piano lessons performs well or she does not. Ignoring conventional IQ tests in favor of multiple intelligences simply miseducates students about the significance of their school performance and allows teachers to live in an egalitarian dream world.

Gardner and I have had a very civilized exchange about the theory of intelligence (Flynn, 2009; Gardner 2009). I do not in any way dispute Gardner's scholarly integrity. On purely theoretical grounds, there is a good case for recognizing that a composer like Mozart reduces complexity to simplicity in a way analogous to Einstein's reduction of the complexity of the universe to the simplicity of his elegant equations. It is true that these talents are not highly correlated and should be recognized as distinct and equally admirable skills.

We agree on the need to build a more inclusive society. But enforcing a Walden Code on educationalists that omits sense in favor of egalitarian rhetoric will do nothing to achieve that goal. If anything, the code distracts from the real problems of how education must adapt to new economic realities, such as the fact that industrial progress is now replacing cognitively demanding jobs with undemanding service work. Middle – class parents are going to demand even more elite performance in conventional subjects, as the competition for professional jobs gets tougher. On the other hand, we may move toward a universal basic "wage" for all rather than see many sink into poverty. Cultivating talents that brighten "leisure" may gain traction. The hyper – egalitarian values of educators may be politically beneficial. They will at least use their vote to overwhelm the Calvinist ethic at the ballot box.

Psychology

Psychology has the misfortune to be the discipline in which the race and IQ debate is most likely to be fought out. There are desperate attempts to define the question of whether blacks on average have worse genes for IQ as a non – scientific issue, one that need not be addressed. There are four arguments in question:

1) That we cannot define intelligence. We have an excellent working concept of intelligence that is sufficient for scientific inquiry: who learns to solve better or faster certain cognitive problems, namely, those prioritized as important at a particular place and time. It must be recognized that all do not have an environment that affords them a reasonable opportunity to develop the requisite cognitive skills. This rough concept is just as satisfactory as SES, which after all does not perfectly define economic status. Every science begins as broadly heuristic and refines it as it proceeds, as astronomy does with the concept of gravity (Flynn, 2016a).

2) That IQ tests are not culture – free. Quite true and quite relevant but no impediment. It is foolish to think a conventional IQ test can cross cultures and measure Australian aborigines against Americans. The traditional Aboriginal culture emphasized map – reading (find water before you die in the desert) and rote memory (to master a huge oral history) more than ours. We emphasize the verbal and analytic skills required by formal education and cognitively demanding jobs. At one time, Raven's Progressive Matrices was supposed to be a culturally reduced IQ test but I have shown it to be flawed (Flynn, 2016a, cha. 7). The point is that no one lives in a culture – free zone, and if conventional tests measure what cognitive abilities will progress a child in our culture, then that is what we want to know. It is no solace to tell a black parent that however badly his child does on the Wechsler, it does not measure how well his child would do as a Kalahari Bushman. He wants her to do well on the SAT (Scholastic Aptitude Test).

3) That race is not a scientific concept. This is irrelevant because American blacks are not defined by race. Race is a social construct, and the members of socially constructed communities can have different average potential. If the Irish are divided into those who live on the right side of the tracks ("lace curtain Irish") and the wrong side ("shanty Irish"), they are not divided by race but may have different genes for IQ because of history. After they arrived in American, those with better genes for IQ tended to do better in school, tended to earn enough to live in a better neighborhood, and tended to marry one another.

4) Genetic commonalities imply that there are no differences for intelligence genes. This is false. Humans and bonobos, their closest genetic relatives, have 99 percent of their genes in common, so one percent is enough to dictate a huge difference in cognitive potential. A tiny fraction of one percent could account for the racial IQ gap.

These threadbare evasions compelled me to accept a conclusion as inescapable. Many US academics simply do not want to know the truth about race and IQ because even the suggestion of a racial component is deeply disturbing to them. Some years ago, I gave a prestigious lecture at one of the best universities in America. Afterwards, there was a meeting between myself and about 30 people, not only psychologists but also other social scientists, administrative personnel, and students. I asked why the Psychology Department had never funded any research on the role of environment and genes in the racial IQ gap (I had some proposals in case they were interested: Flynn 2007, pp. 75 – 76, 80 – 81,94 – 97). I accused them of being afraid to know the truth: they were afraid to take the chance that the study would come out on the side of genes and they would then be in the impossible position of either suppressing the results or reaping the whirlwind.

They said I was mistaken. It was a matter of resources and it was just that everything else they had funded over the past ten years was more important. As a guest, I refrained from reading out the more trivial of the studies they had financed. I felt I was not really being fair. Some of them might well agree with me but could hardly say so in that setting.

Psychological research

I often read the advice eminent psychologists give to the discipline about methodology. Concerning individual differences within groups, no journal should accept a correlational study as evidence that parenting is causal *without* performing the necessary controls for genetic relatedness and hence heritability. To do so is actively deceptive. For example, in 1997, one scholar cited a paper that hypothesized a high correlation between the actual vocabulary to which a preschool child is exposed and the child's IQ. An obvious solution: we can elevate a child's low IQ simply by exposing him or her to an enriched preschoool vocabulary. The flaw in this was pointed out by Galton over 150 years ago and it continues to be discussed right up to the present, with critics arguing that substandard parental genes for intelligence both restrict the parent's vocabulary and handicap the child with substandard genes for IQ. No doubt preschool intervention will do some good. But to expect it to eliminate inherited genes as a causal influence on IQ is absurd. Only a discipline afflicted by egalitarian dogma could persist in this foolishness (Bouchard, 1998).

And yet, when between – group differences in desirable traits are investigated, how rare the same advice: "no journal should accept evidence that culture is explanatory between groups *without* acknowledging the possibility that genetic differences are potent." Sometimes, the rule is obeyed regarding gender differences, but racial differences are taboo. Even the best scholars at the best universities fear the egalitarian steamroller.

I challenge each US university to say whether it has financed a study on the role of genes and environment in racial differences in cognitive performance. I challenge them to say how they would treat an applicant for appointment or tenure who listed race and genes on his or her vita as a research area. Even tenured faculty work with a sword looming over their heads. At the Sage Foundation, there were three of us (all tenured at our respective universities) who actually publish on race and IQ. One asked whether, if we did a study that clearly showed there was a significant genetic component in the racial IQ gap, would we publish it. I said, "yes." The other, a scholar whose reputation far exceeds my own, said, "yes, but I would have to leave town as soon as my colleagues read the paper."

If one wants to know the truth, he will use science to illuminate the issue. Otherwise, he makes genetic equality an article of faith. Anyone who questions it is a heretic who must be silenced. Everyone saw how Jensen was treated after his 1969 article. It was as if a heretic had fallen into the hands of the Spanish Inquisition. His classes were disrupted, and he received death threats directed at himself and his family (Flynn, 1980, 2013a). As far as I know, Berkeley took no academic sanctions against Jensen. Animosity abated somewhat, but until he died in 2012, his public talks were often disrupted not only in America but also in England and Australia. Plenty of psychology staff and students were in the mob.

Teaching psychology

The veto on free discussion of race and IQ intimidates American psychology departments from offering undergraduate courses on intelligence. Fewer than ten percent do so (Norcross et al., 2016; Stoloff et al., 2010). The fear is that some student is sure to raise a hand, and ask, "why do you think blacks have a lower average IQ?" The instructor is then in the uncomfortable position of saying that genes play a role (and violating a speech code), or that SES explains the difference (which he knows to be false, if he is sophisticated), or that black subculture has facets which need to be altered (inviting actionable accusations of racism and victim blaming). Intelligence is usually consigned to a topic in an introductory course. Even here there is a subtle influence. Wayne Russell (2017) surveyed the 29 bestselling texts and found a skew toward thinkers like Gardner, who are associated with egalitarianism.

These results confirm my impressions from a tour of twelve leading US universities in 2007. Everyone found my talks interesting and novel. This was hardly surprising, for only one of these universities offered an undergraduate course on intelligence. I can add that according to Charles Murray, there are courses on this book *The Bell Curve* in which the book itself is not assigned.

Politics departments

Politics is always vulnerable because by definition it is likely to involve contentious political issues. At present, a major issue that students and staff do not find discussible is Palestine versus Israel. This spills over into history departments and area studies programs and affects anyone else who takes a strong position either way. New York City shows the split: Columbia students shouting down "pro – Israeli" speakers, while "pro – Palestinians" find other institutions hostile.

That the hostility is nation – wide was evidenced in 2007, when John J. Mearsheimer (Chicago) and Stephen M. Walt (Harvard) published *The Israel Lobby and US Foreign Policy* and faced a massive scandal. I had eagerly anticipated their book because certain things seemed clear to me. First, the dispute is a zero – sum game. What is minimally acceptable to Israel is not minimally acceptable to even moderate Arab opinion. Therefore, we have the charade of trying to negotiate the non – negotiable. Second, American support of Israel (with arms and money) alienates opinion throughout the Islamic world. It makes a mockery of America's stated policy for a nuclear – free Middle East, which translates into endorsing an Israeli nuclear monopoly in the Middle East.

In addition, America is identified with a nation whose fundamental policy must be to welcome disaster for any Middle Eastern state that, if it progressed, could challenge Israel. Hence Israel's frustration that America did not attack Iran after Iranian provocations in Israel and Syria.

I think all of the above is true no matter whether you favor Israel or the Palestinians. But if I am mistaken, it is still a debatable position. And if I am not mistaken, it poses a problem that goes to the core of political science. Client states do not normally dictate the foreign policy of their patron so that the latter acts against its interests. Jewish – Americans make up only 1.40 percent of America's population. So what in the world is going on?

Mearsheimer and Walt (2007) argue that the United States has a special relationship with Israel that has no parallel in modern history. What makes Israel's relationship with the United States extraordinary is not simply that Israel has received more foreign aid than any other country or that Washington almost always backs Israel diplomatically. What makes it truly special is that the aid is given unconditionally. In other words, Israel gets aid even when it does things that the United States opposes, like building settlements in the West Bank. The authors note that while many ethnic and special interest groups promote their cause, none are as effective as pro – Israel groups in influencing the mainstream media. They claim that the American Israel Public Affairs Committee AIPAC) has a stranglehold on the US Congress, due to its ability to reward those who support its agenda and punish those who challenge it.

I felt the authors neglected (later they rectified this) that although the Holocaust occurred over 70 years ago, many American intellectuals remain silent about Israel out of respect for their Jewish associates. The latter, understandably, have a nationalistic attachment to Israel, though polls show an age divide, with younger Jewish – Americans expressing sympathy for a more even – handed policy. Mearsheimer and Walt also recommend policy changes that would give Israel a better chance of long – term survival. I think that they are correct in this but can understand the feelings of Jews who, thanks to their history, assume that the Arabs will never accept Israel anyway, and that she might as well take advantage of her military superiority as long as it lasts.

But the point is that the book is moderate in tone and evidential in argument. The authors should be congratulated for having the courage to discuss an issue that had been taboo – both were distinguished and looked soon to retire. Naturally the book can be critiqued. However, a large number of academics simply tried to close down the debate with accusations of anti – Semitism. The debate is so bitter that many American academics are censoring themselves into silence, lest Israel vs. Palestine tear their department apart.

There have been efforts to recruit troops to shut down the debate. Daniel Pipes runs a website called Campus Watch, which asks students to report comments that might be considered hostile to Israel. It used to post dossiers on suspect academics. After harassment and death threats, Pipes removed the dossiers, but the website still invites students to report alleged anti – Israeli behavior at US institutions. Jewish lobbies have asked Congress to deny funding to universities judged to have an anti – Israel bias (McNeil, 2002; Kurtz, 2003; Kampeas, 2005;). This split the Jewish community, and I think it unlikely to succeed (Nir, 2004). NYU established the Taub Center for Israel Studies on May 1, 2003. The head of the Taub Foundation asserts that it funded the center to counter the "Arabic point of view" (Cattan, 2003).

Philosophy

The atmosphere in philosophy departments has altered much over my career. For many professional philosophers, what I say may seem outdated. But the general public is still obsessed with the gap between facts and values. They think that, as far as values are concerned, they have a precious possession immune to science and free debate. If values are immune, why debate them?

I refer to false conclusions drawn from the prohibition that you cannot deduce values from facts. At one time this was supposed to show that moral debate was not intellectually respectable. A. J. Ayer (1936) conveyed what dominated our minds when I was in graduate school. Science can test factual propositions and determine whether are true or false; no such truth – test exists for value propositions and therefore, they are mere opinion. If there were a logical bridge from facts to values, the objective status of the facts we agree on might imply values we could agree on. But there is no logical bridge. The moral philosopher will clarify the status and language of values. But when he engages in moral debate, he becomes a mere preacher trying to influence the followers of other preachers through rhetoric.

The antidote to this notion about the role of philosophy is that certain bridges are built, not when we go from facts to values, but when we go from values to facts. And while the connections are not those of logical entailment, they are so essential to a particular morality that if logic or science invalidates them, the morality is crippled (see Box 4).

Box 4. Subjectivity and objectivity in ethics.
As for those who wish to examine this controversy for its own sake, they may wish to read Flynn, 2000, 2012c, and 2018. I have argued

> that while there is no ethical truth test that can convert someone like Nietzsche to adopt humane ideals, there is a common agenda we both must argue over and that at the end of that debate, he will have to acknowledge that his morality is purely personal rather than socially significant.

Values and bridging propositions

I want to distinguish between our "value proclivities" and the "bridging propositions" that elaborate them into a socially relevant morality. On the personal level, our value proclivities are vitally important. When people saw blacks suffering under slavery, it made a crucial difference whether they felt sympathy or indifference.

These are the seeds from which a humane or a racist morality may grow, but they take on social relevance only when connected to the real world through bridging propositions: either recommend that we must end chattel slavery or hold that blacks are deficient in a way that make them natural slaves and, anyway, that they are better off as slaves than they would be as workers in Northern factories. These recommendations make certain assumptions that have consequences that make them empirically testable. In other words, no racist runs through the streets shouting "I hate the color black," a peculiar quirk but not of much interest in general. Hating black people may be the psychological basis of racists' ideology, but they link it to the world by assumptions about genetics (race – mixing debases the offspring), history (if only blacks had existed, the human race would never have become literate), human potential (black immigrants will always be a burden on the public purse), and so forth.

Marx had a proclivity to admire the proletariat, but he did not just run through the streets shouting, "I love workers." This would have put him on a par with someone who says, "I hate my boss" – a sentiment significant to him but to few others. Marx is not like a Frenchman who goes berserk every time he hears the word "camel." The latter may have some entertainment value but his behavior will not be easy to convert into moral advice. What Marx did was give his value proclivity significance through a theory of history that gave the working class a crucial role in progress toward a humane society. That put him at the mercy of evidence.

Student romantics cannot just run about campus shouting, "we love equality." They must assert at least one bridging proposition between their value proclivities and the real world: they love equality, so universities should adopt speech codes to keep everybody from being discomfited by words they find they offensive. Then they must weigh up the consequences of that maxim. Does it prevent the university from researching and discussing fundamental questions? Does it prevent students with the right opinions from attaining knowledge because they cannot defend their ideals? Does it therefore not rob them of autonomy? Does it not breed an atmosphere fatal to free speech, the best road toward discovering truth, and turn one's beliefs into a dogma that breeds intolerance? Does it not keep you from rendering your ideals into something more sophisticated when you graduate and try to alter the real world? After all, when you leave university you must assess a host of bridging propositions: does the welfare state, or affirmative action, or the minimum wage promote human equality, or are they actually counterproductive?

If students really want to deliver good things to all other students without exception, they will not be solaced by the fact that they are dooming all students to suffer equally from these evils. There is nothing wrong with their value proclivities in favor of equality and justice (although they should be balanced by other proclivities such as toward the pursuit of truth, valuing human autonomy, and so forth). The only thing that has been discredited is their naive bridging proposition. One hopes they will retain their humane ideals and, with more knowledge, link them to the real world with propositions that create as good a society as we can get.

I hope it is clear that every fellow feeling we may have for humankind is a mere proclivity until it is connected to the larger world. It is up to us to make sure that in the process we assert no claims that cannot survive the tests of logic and evidence. If you believe in your ideals only because you think every worker noble, or every woman would be perfect unless debased by the company of men, or that all races must have no real genetic differences, you will not last long in moral debate. Nietzsche asserted that Dickens had never painted a picture of someone who had a "good heart" without describing a fool.

When philosophers debate substantive questions of morality, as they often do today, they realize they need to know social science to do it. To debate with Jensen I had to leave philosophy to learn some psychology, sociology, and genetics. No one can ignore free debate and the evidence it brings to bear by hiding behind the fact/value distinction. There is no exception for unexamined "intuitions" about the "equality" of races, genders, and ethnic groups. Holding unexamined values is no more excusable than holding unexamined facts. Science does not give you your ideals. You must have a good heart, but you use science to operationalize and defend your ideals. Nothing, absolutely nothing, is exempt from free debate.

University presses and scholarly journals

Scholars advance by publishing. Academics serve university presses as editors and act as referees to help determine whether a book deserves publication. They run scholarly journals. Censorship of other scholars on ideological grounds exists but it is usually hidden behind the usual language of rejections: this paper is very interesting but not for us.

In March 2007, Rebecca Tuvel published an article entitled "In Defense of Transracialism" in *Hypatica*, a feminist philosophy journal. It argued that a person who identifies with a race not in accord with how society classifies them (on the basis of ancestry) should have the right to change their race. For example, some light – skinned "blacks" pass for white. On May 3, 2017, *Hypatica* received a letter signed by hundreds of academics asking that the article be retracted on the grounds that its "continued availability causes further harm" to marginalized people.

As Justin Weinberg (2017) said, if one reads the published article, every criticism made of its content is false or misleading. To get a notion of the rhetoric of its detractors, listed to Nora Bernstein on her blog post: "[Travel] uses the term 'transgenderism.' She talks about 'biological sex' and uses phrases like 'male genitalia … She [does not] cite or engage with the work of Black trans women who have written on this topic." On this last point, Weinberg notes that none of the critics has been able to name any Black trans woman who has actually written on the topic (Weinberg, 2017).

On April 30, one of the journal's editors, Cressida Hayes wrote an apology from the members of the Board of Associate Editors: "Clearly, the article should not have been published ... publication ... should have been prevented by a more effective review process." The abuse to which the author is being subjected is "both predictable and justifiable" (Singal, 2017), despite the fact that Tuvel was dealing with a wave of online abuse and hate mail. As for the review process, Weinberg inquired and was told that the paper had been reviewed like any other.

When a controversial paper appears in print, withdrawing it from the internet can erase its effect. It creates a terrible dilemma: death threats coerced a journal for "understandable" reasons. But what happens when the intolerant realize that all they have to do is issue death threats to get their way?

In 2007, Bruce Gilley published a paper defending colonialism. As an aside, who can doubt that there have been some good consequences: without the British, India might well be without a sense of nationhood (be as divided as Africa), have no common language among its educated elite, and have no notion of democratic government or an impartial civil service. When the *Third World Quarterly* published his paper, the journal was not intimidated by academics who objected that it was historically inaccurate and that it ignored the literature on colonialism and colonial – era atrocities. It had gone through the usual double – blind peer review process. However, the journal was intimidated when the editor "subsequently received serious and credible threats of personal violence." Giley himself asked that the article be withdrawn, regretting "the pain and anger that it has caused for many people" (Haidt, 2017).

As Flaherty (2017) has observed, death threats against academics are now common: Tommy J. Curry at Texas A&M for talking about violence against whites in a 2012 podcast interview; Keeanga – Yamahtta Taylor of Princeton for criticizing President Trump in a 2017 commencement speech at Hampshire College (she cancelled a schedule of public talks); Johnny Eric Williams at Trinity College in Connecticut after news websites showed Facebook posts he made about race (he fled town); Matthew Hughey of the University of Connecticut after his views on racialized messages in the 2016 election were misrepresented (he had to ask the police to patrol his home); George Ciccariello – Mather at Drexel (Al – Gharbi, 2018) for saying that white patriarchy lay behind mass shootings and that deference to men in uniform struck him as symbolic of blind support of wars abroad (he resigned fearing danger to his family).

Peter Wood, the president of the conservative National Association of Scholars, called upon *Third World Quarterly* to restore Gilley's article (Flaherty, 2017). All very well until someone is killed. It may be that editors and scholars of integrity will have to accept intimidation and a higher level of personal insecurity, rather like journalists who investigate corruption or the mafia. Neither the left nor the right has a monopoly on using the social media to intimidate, although the more "respectable" merely demand dismissal rather than a death penalty.

As for university presses, they almost never make censorship explicit. But I can report one case that was an exception. In 1990, I was under contract to publish a book with one of the best university presses in the world (it was not any of the presses on my vita). It showed that Chinese – Americans outperformed white Americans academically and in terms of occupational status even when they were equated for IQ. Every chapter had been approved but the press wanted me to write a final chapter explaining why this was so. I argued that thanks to their history and social psychology, Chinese – Americans had the most educationally efficient homes and the highest aspirations, while Irish – Americans performed less well due to a history of alcoholism, family violence, and bias, while African – Americans were repeating the Irish experience under even worse conditions including drugs, worse violence, and stronger bias. I thought this was reasonable, but the press objected, arguing, "You can't say this. We might have a riot in our lobby." I said that if there was a riot we might sell a million copies but the press was humorless and unrelenting. Eventually, a different publisher produced the book without any violence.

Commonality and difference

Many of the Walden Codes have one thing in common: they stem from a denial of differences. They attempt to equate groups and individuals by way of an empty "tolerance" that forbids negative assessments of anyone. In fact, the only way to inject commonality despite differences is *actually to make* cross – cultural and cross – personal assessments of a humane – egalitarian sort. These have to do, respectively, with humanity, one's society, and the members of one's society.

First, one must judge all human beings as worthy of moral concern regardless of their culture, nationality, ethnicity, race, or SES (Flynn, 2000, 2012c). Second, humane egalitarianism follows Aristotle on the nature of civil society: every society must try to offer a cherished way of life rich in ceremony, sport, humor, art, and craftsmanship. A citizen is true citizen only if he participates in that way of life (Aristotle, *Politics,* III, cha 9, 1280a – line 31 to 1281a – line 1). Third, if people are barred from participation through no fault of their own, that is a denial of justice. Everyone should feel personally affronted when anyone else is so deprived.

Remember (Chapter 2): the cherished way of life must seek the six great goods: happiness, justice, the pursuit of truth, the creation of beauty, human autonomy, and tolerance. Even within the best society, there will be different balances of the great goods (there are inevitably trade – offs between them). But when an advanced society tramples them thanks to the interests or ideology of an elite, we must try to alter that culture rather than refrain from cross – cultural judgments. It is interesting how many such societies self – destruct either through aggression (Hitler) or internal recognition that the ideology is bankrupt (Soviet Union). None of this, by the way, commits me to something called "the politics of difference" (Flynn, 2000, Cha. 9).

I reiterate: most of those who impose Walden Codes on the social sciences are inspired by humane ideals. But there is no connection between humanism and adopting some sort of Walden Code.

Tolerance and tenure

My case against what I see as counterproductive Walden Codes is filled with opinions about method that some will dispute. To be clear, I do not wish to see those who disagree with me expelled from academia or public life. I want to debate with academics who endorse cultural relativism, love SES, hate IQ tests, think the race and IQ debate unscientific, and favor Israel or Palestine. Even postmodernism should have a voice because it is an important intellectual influence that students should know about, although I hope it will rapidly recede to the place in the curriculum occupied by, say, Hegelianism and other antiquated schools of thought. I simply ask that those who hold these views extend to the rest of us the tolerance we extend to them.

Does tolerance have limits? I would not hire those who lecture about aliens and crop circles, inject politics into their physics lectures, or deny the Holocaust. I am happy to allow them to give a series of lectures on campus (if a student group wants them), advertise lectures near campus if they wish, or disseminate their literature. They will have to get a lot more traction from scholars before they get a place in the curriculum (other than as interestingly wrong).

What of those who turn toward propaganda or idiocy after they get tenure? Sowell (1993) believes that abolition of tenure is the best way to eliminate them, and that tenure is not necessary to protect academics from arbitrary dismissal because of their views. He points to institutions like the Hoover Institution or the Brookings Institution, which, despite not offering tenure, are homes for those who may have been fired elsewhere for political reasons. I disagree. When I was fired twice because of my politics, I was only 28. Understandably perhaps, I did not have the credentials to qualify for any prestigious institution. Bereft of an academic post, I had little chance of enhancing my credentials. I could, of course, have accepted an undemanding job as a night watchman, subjected my family to near poverty, and tried to do research without library privileges, support staff, and the stimulation of colleagues and students.

Even if we keep tenure, certain reforms can limit the irresponsibility of academics. Tenure decisions, and even significant

advancement up the lecturer salary scale, can be postponed until an academic has shown that he has developed the habit of research. Those who cease to be productive after getting tenure still want promotion and are adverse to humiliation. They can be denied leave as well as research grants. At my university in New Zealand, we found it salutary to treat all applicants for promotion to Full Professor as if they were applicants for their present post of Associate Professor: they were taken seriously only if they came out near the top of their junior colleagues.

I had other ideas for reforms that were not introduced. Promotions above the career rank (Senior Lecturer in our case) might be made for only five years and reviewed. Those who fail can keep tenure but their salaries may be reduced to match the top of the career scale. Voluntary retirement and resignation are of course options. There is no shame in giving a Professor who has run out of steam at 60 administrative duties that leave her status uncompromised. In extreme cases of academic irresponsibility, calendar descriptions can be amended: "Accounting 204 – an introduction to accounting as practiced in small businesses with frequent references to American foreign policy."

In New Zealand, the grades in all courses are subject to review at a departmental meeting to see if there is consistency across students taking several courses. Universities could do the same for all students who take courses across departments. In other words, grade inflation by an individual lecturer or department students can be regulated by institutional practice.

Such measures are double – edged swords in that they add to what can be done to the unpopular. Nonetheless, the fact that you cannot be fired for your views is some protection, enough for the really principled.

What we do to ourselves

Many academics are aware that free speech at universities is restricted in practice by outside opinion, the educational bureaucracy, governments, and students. They are less happy that they themselves do not really believe in free speech whenever their own Walden Codes are threatened. This chapter has, I hope, made it clear that the faculty is often its own worst enemy. When they lament that they have failed to educate their students about the value of free speech, they might begin by educating themselves.

The Walden Codes may play an even greater role in suppressing free debate on campus than student outrage. Nonetheless, they are often not as deeply rooted as student dogmas about race and gender, and they usually have no constituency outside of academia, except for the ban on contentious political issues. This means that a debate internal to university staff could soften them. Such a debate might become a training ground for staff to develop a real commitment to free speech the better to resist student pressure. I welcome that conservatives now rally around the banner of free speech, and suspect that they find some of the present Walden Codes obnoxious. It disturbs me that they are not vocal about economics departments that have a Walden Code defining free market economics as the only real economics and do not urge that students have the option of hearing the economics of the left from those who really believe in it. We will know how deeply committed they are if history puts conservatives back in control on campus. I no longer trust anyone who says they are in favor of free speech when it is primarily their free speech that is being violated, unless I know them reasonably well. I trust Charles Murray.

Part 4
What academics do to students

11
The teaching of teachers

Academics, whether in education departments or teachers colleges, do lamentable things to their students. These students play a vital role in society. They go out and teach in our schools. Schoolteachers shape the minds of students who go on to university, which affects the campus environment. As we have seen, the teachers of teachers today hold the most extreme form of the egalitarian dogma. They are reluctant to acknowledge the role of genes concerning individual differences within groups. It is no accident that, like Black Studies and Women's studies, they see themselves as recruiting a cadre to reform the world. Their first priority is to reform the schools by turning them into a replica of what the larger society should be like.

We thus have a clash between the ideal and the real. The ideal school system would have teachers of the highest quality possible teaching children the skills they will need at university, when they try to earn a living, and when at least a few seek the autonomy that comes with critical intelligence. They would tailor what they teach to the hierarchy of potential with which they are confronted, students ranging from those whose genes pose the problem of how to function in everyday life to those who can become notable for their intellect and creativity. No child would be neglected, but no opportunity would be missed to take advantage of individual differences in talent.

The actual system tends toward a staff whose skills are inadequate partially because of selection and partially because they have not mastered the subject matter they should teach. They teach children how to cooperate in an atmosphere of mutual empathy with the ultimate aim of producing another generation of missionaries for equality as they define it, with individual differences denied as far as possible in favor of an inflexible egalitarian ideal.

A graduate of Ithaca College

Jordan Alexander Hill (2016) has reflected at length on the MAT (Master in Teaching) course he took at Ithaca College (New York):

> When someone made a comment … not in line with the department's politics, a meeting was often called to 'unpack' the statement and heal … We returned from our trip to Harlem, having taught students at Frederick Douglass Academy for nearly a week. The principal gave an inspiring talk about his mission to help students escape poverty, rise up, and find success in life (often outside of Harlem). When we returned, the education department held a meeting about how 'problematic' the principal's statements were; how he should have been celebrating Harlem and its diversity; how his attitude was insensitive, classist, and possibly racist … During student teaching the criticisms … were almost always about some 'implicit bias' or slip of the tongue, some unconscious stereotype or micro – aggression. I would share the specific criticisms, but they are so numerous and frankly peculiar that I am afraid nobody would believe me … I was once even accused of 'gender bias' for using the grade – level designation 'freshman' … Then, at the end of the program we were required to put together an 'eportfolio' explaining, defending, and essentially swearing an oath on the core values of the Ithaca College education department, with special emphasis throughout the program placed on the standards related to diversity and creating a safe learning space … To even be considered for the MAT program I had to take a prerequisite course for which the primary text was a book called *Teaching to Change the World*.

Hill had hoped to learn something about what to teach (exposure to a wider range of American or British literature) or how to communicate better with his students. Instead, he learned a great deal about how Black English has its own grammar, which, he was assured, often improves on that of Standard English.

A teacher of physics

Does this kind of conditioning affect teachers? Moses Rifkin (who teaches Physics at University Prep in Seattle) tells us how he triumphed over adversity: "I care deeply about making the world a better place but felt that as a science teacher, my opportunities to do so were limited … I've found a way to introduce my students to the ideas of racial and gender privilege … The project revolves around a question: why are there so few black physicists? 4.2% of physicists self – identified as black as of 2012 (yet) 12.0% of the population aged 25 – 64 identified as black." He does try to conduct a wider ranging discussion than most, for example, whether there is a difference in racial IQ (Rifkin, 2015).

Rifkin has a captive audience based on his credentials. What exactly qualifies him to believe that he is competent to illuminate these questions? I suspect he would hesitate to teach his physics students about memory, French literature, or judicial reform, if these were amateur interests of his. I suspect it is because, like the educationists at Ithaca, he thinks that the answers are relatively obvious once the questions have been posed: that America is racist, sexist, and so forth, and we all ought to examine our consciences – as if that gets us any nearer to real solution to lack of equality in US society.

Columbia Teachers College

You might think that Ithaca College is an outlier, so we will look at Columbia Teachers College, the flagship of US teacher education, and how its Walden Code translates into teaching. Sol Stern has written two articles on this subject.

His first article begins with Maxine Greene's lectures at Columbia. Greene urges teachers to make children see the evils of the existing social order. They should portray homelessness as a consequence of the deprivations of landlords, the arms buildup as a consequence of corporate decisions, and racial exclusion as a consequence of a private property owner's malicious choice. The radical activist Bill Ayers was her student in 1984 and was inspired. Today his website outlines a course for teachers on homelessness, crime, racism, oppression (Stern, 2006). Ayers gets a hero's welcome when he visits Columbia: "A man sporting sunglasses, an earring in each earlobe, khaki pants, a sweater and tweed jacket strode purposefully past the entry and down the hallway toward the auditorium ... His intensity and passion were tangible in the way he walked through the crowd." Ayers and Greene have cooperated on a series of books published by the Teacher's College Press on how to teach science for social justice (Stern, 2006).

Eric Gutstein, Ayer's colleague at Illinois, describes the kind of class he teaches to seventh grade math students. One lesson presents charts showing the US income distribution, aiming to get the students to understand the concept of percentages and fractions, while simultaneously showing them how much wealth is concentrated at the top in an economic system that benefits the superrich. After the calculations, Gutstein asks: "How does all this make you feel?" He reports that 19 of 21 students say that wealth distribution in America is "bad," "unfair," or "shocking." He quotes the comments of one student: "Well I see that all the wealth in the United States is mostly the wealth of a couple people not the whole nation" (Stern, 2006).

A pause for reflection

What ten to 14 – year – olds make of this, except to feel outrage at the cruelty of history, is unclear. In a course called "Justice, Race, and Class," I try to illuminate some of the problems Ayer and Gutstein strive to get primary school students agitated about. This requires a lot of analysis and information. I use the Gini coefficient to compare nations whose income distributions have grown more unequal with those who have remained stable. I look at housing through the lenses of how the market is affected by regulation, rent controls, rent supplements, state housing, the pressure for subprime mortgages, and of course the politics of who exercises more power than whom. I recommend courses and assign books that offer a more conservative set of assessments than I do.

Beyond Colombia

The ideology of Columbia breeds intolerance. In 2003, at San Jose State, Steve Head saw a video about institutional racism against immigrants. He suggested that most immigrants came here because they realized they would be better off, including the advantages of healthier race relations. According to his sworn affidavit, his professor responded that any one holding such opinions was clearly "unfit to teach." He further infuriated the professor by suggesting that the class read conservative black social scientists like Thomas Sowell and Walter Williams. Head received an F, was not allowed to enroll in the student teaching class, and was thus blocked from getting his teaching certificate (Stern, 2006). In 2007, a U.S. district court held that the university had the right to exclude students on dispositional assessment. Head had paid legal fees for three and a half years and appealed for help. I can find no evidence that the lower court ruling was reversed (Langbert, 2007).

The ideology of Columbia is duplicated elsewhere. Stern (2006) offers a sample of education schools ranging from New York to California. Brooklyn College (CUNY): "Our teacher candidates and other school personnel are prepared to demonstrate a knowledge of, language for, and the ability to create educational environments based on various theories of social justice." Marquette University uses education "to transcend the negative effects of the dominant culture." Kansas's education school declares that, "addressing issues of diversity includes being more global than national and concerned with ideals such as world peace, social justice, respect for diversity and preservation of the environment." Claremont not only requires teacher candidates to commit to social justice teaching but also screens applicants to make sure they have the essential "disposition." Humboldt State: "It is not an option for history teachers to teach social justice and social responsibility; it is a mandate."

Columbia and New York City schools

Stern's second article gives a recent history of how teachers college ideology has affected New York City public schools. It wants to turn the school itself into a non – hierarchical structure, an anticipation of the new social order

As interpreted by Columbia and the near – by Bank Street College of Education, progressive education endorses the "child – centered" approach to classroom instruction. Children are natural learners and, with some guidance from teachers, can construct their own knowledge. It is wrong for teachers to communicate knowledge directly (impart "mere facts"). Progressivism damns the kind of education that once dominated America's schools: a coherent, grade – by – grade curriculum that not only taught reading writing and arithmetic but also passed on our civilization's inheritance in the form of its literature, civics, and history, with exposure to languages considered of historical importance (Latin) or as international means of communication (French, German, Spanish, later on Chinese, Japanese, and Portuguese). This kind of "drill – and – kill" teaching is supposed to rob children of their imagination.

Between 1987 and 1997, Stern visited P.S. (Public School) 87, a very good school with a mainly middle – class clientele, which his own children attended. There was no common curriculum or essential texts. There was one fourth – grade teacher who taught history, assigned required books, and demanded book reports. Another fourth – grade teacher required pupils to calculate the exact percentage of Arawak Indians living on the island of Hispaniola who perished after Christopher Columbus's arrival. The assignment ended by asking the students to answer: "How do you feel about this?" Most teachers meandered from one subject to another, preferring "hands – on" projects. A third – grade teacher devoted months to building a Japanese garden, the only math instruction for the duration. Stern was told that the students were doing "measurement" (Stern, 2015).

Between 2002 and 2013, Michael Bloomberg was mayor of New York City and Joel Kline was Schools Chancellor. Initially, two progressive educators (Dianna Lam and Carmen Farika) were appointed in turn to the crucial post of Deputy Chancellor for Teaching and Learning: "Your students must not be sitting in rows. You must not stand at the head of the class. You must not do 'chalk and talk' at the blackboard. Your students must be 'active learners' and they must work in groups." Inspectors visited schools to ensure that every classroom in the early grades had rugs on the floor, which helped create the "natural" conditions necessary for young children to learn (Stern, 2015).

By 2006, New York City had 15 high schools called "social justice schools." Stern visited one of these (the Leadership Institute) in the Bronx. The school had replaced hierarchy with democratic decision – making. When asked what was the most oppressive thing they could think of, the students decided it was the dress code and other classroom regulations. The sense of order and decorum necessary for any serious academic effort had unraveled, and teachers and administrators seemed powerless to repair it (Stern, 2006).

Joel Kline eventually acknowledged that leaving the schools in the hands of Lam and Fariña was the biggest mistake he made as Schools Chancellor. In 2009, he set up a study comparing ten schools using the Hirsch curriculum in Kindergarten through Grade 2 against a demographically similar group that followed the standard program. The Hirsch curriculum is knowledge – based grade by grade. History and social science begin with the background to the Declaration of Independence. It assumes that students must master a broad range of background knowledge if they are to achieve advanced reading comprehension. The results showed a statistically significant gain in reading comprehension for students in the schools that used Hirsch, that is, offered explicit teaching of knowledge through a planned curriculum.

Unfortunately, Kline resigned in 2010. Even by then, about 70 elementary schools had adopted Hirsh's Core Knowledge curriculum. This is a handful given that the Teachers College ideal remains in about 700. The prospects are not good. In 2014, Bill de Blasio was elected mayor and chose Carmen Fariña as his Schools Chancellor (Stern, 2015). New York was back to the same person who helped "progressivize" the New York schools in 2002. Fariña resigned in 2018, but her successor Richard Carranza has been criticized for scrapping New York's academically selective specialized school exam amid charges that the decision reflects an anti – Asian bias.

Beyond Columbia revisited

Although the ideology of Columbia is everywhere, its effects on the public schools are not. New York City is not America, and primary and middle schools are not a replica of how high schools are run. When ideology is at odds with the real world, it affects language much more than practice. One could tell the people that ice burns and fire cools and declare that anyone who says the contrary will be frozen at the stake. But no one cooks his dinner by putting it in the fridge. Nevertheless, how do intelligent people come to hold an ideology so much at variance with the real world?

The roots of the ideology

Like all ideologies, the ideologies of social justice and child – centered education did not develop in a vacuum. I will argue that the combination of history (a persistent "over" demand for teachers) plus institutions (the teachers college monopoly of supply) debased the product (the quality of teachers). This in turn dictated a certain psychology (a crisis of self – esteem) that could be assuaged only by a sense of moral superiority. Finally, this kind of moral superiority could be sustained only by a combination of extreme egalitarianism and the doctrines of progressive education.

Supply and demand

The best book on the American market for teachers is David Labaree's (2004). Alan Barcan (1993) strikes the same theme in his book on Australia since 1949. The demand for teachers for America's public school system escalated after the Civil War. By 1870, there were 200,000 public school teachers; by 1900, 400,000; by 1930, 850,000; by 1960, 1.4 million: by 1980, 2.3 million; and by 2015, 3.1 million (NCAES, 1993, Table 8; NCES, 2016, fast facts). Throughout American history, the escalation of demand has been huge.

The rapid expansion of the school system left teachers in short supply. The quality of aspirants to teach was lowered by competition from many other professions that offered higher rewards. No aspirant could be wasted, which affected the standards of entry and the achievements that teachers colleges could demand. Poor students attracted poor staff, according to the prevailing criteria for good academics, so education departments had low status. Those staff that could do so distanced themselves from teacher education, as the kiss of death, toward academic research about education. By 1921, teachers colleges and schools of education had gained a virtual monopoly on supply and could keep their monopoly only by diluting quality. Professions are generally ranked in status by how difficult it is to qualify.

The fact that almost anyone could be a teacher was a guarantee of low status (Labaree. 2004, pp. 22 – 24).

This was not a normal market situation. In most areas, there is a minimum standard for performance (carpenters must be able to build a saleable product) and increased demand will attract increased capital. In the case of teachers, cash investment was limited by the fact that costs were borne by the locality and state, neither of which wished to face a taxpayer rebellion. To this day, over 90 percent of funds for public school education comes from local and state sources with the US federal government playing a minor role. There was strong resistance to paying teachers higher salaries and lavishing large sums on teacher training. Moreover, teacher performance (unlike carpenter performance) could be compromised without clearly visible disaster.

Teachers colleges had to meet huge demand cheaply: the obvious thing to give was quality. Here you had an intake whose quality did not match those of other professions. All you need is a rationalization. Despite a lack of literacy and numeracy, there was no need to fail a student teacher because content is less important than imparting "skill." It is disheartening to find a trainee teacher who has done no math with her students and breaks into tears when she admits, "I can't do arithmetic," but not everyone has to teach arithmetic – and she may have mastered "how to teach" and may be attitudinally empathetic with children.

A personal note about quality

Teaching low quality intake in courses empty of content attracts low quality faculty. Failure to meet academic standards of publication becomes a virtue.

At our local teachers college, the principal called academic publications an "ego – trip." At a just transformed teachers college at which I first taught, when the question of shorter hours was discussed, someone would say "but then they might expect us to publish," which sent a shudder throughout the room.

The crisis of self – esteem

Teachers college faculties suffer from pervasive derision and can experience low self – esteem. Often, they could not assuage this by intellectual achievement and therefore had to turn to *moral* superiority. They would promote social justice, leaving other academics to lengthen their publications lists. They would foster the education of children in a way that uncomprehending colleagues would never understand. They would treat children with respect, as equals eager for knowledge, and not like the students that fill the typical lecture hall.

Ideology to the rescue

The fact that education is the home of the most extreme of the egalitarians, those who deny that genes differentiate even individuals within groups, fits perfectly. You believe that the fact that one child forges ahead or falls behind another in mathematics or science is a mere aberration, something to be explained by arbitrary differences in how they are treated. Treat every child as of equal promise. The fact that the most talented may begin to compete with one another to be best is suspect (it was a powerful motive in every school I attended: who would win the math medal). Even in sports, competition should be discouraged.

If you think this absurd, if you think that no one could ignore the truth that we should tailor education to the natural ability of the child, here is an interview of Charles Murray by Deborah Solomon, a *New York Times* reporter. *Solomon*: "I believe that given the opportunity, most people could do most anything." *Murray*: "You're out of touch with reality in that regard" (Solomon, 2008). It is only fair to note that Solomon's view has deep historical roots that go back to Rousseau. Sir Peter Newsam (1999) quotes a nineteenth – century educator: "All can walk part of the way with genius."

The ideology is in such conflict with reality that the schools themselves have been reluctant to put theory into practice. Larry Cuban (1980) and Arthur Zilversmit (1993) found that prior to 1960, child – centered education had only a very modest effect. John Goodlad (1984) found the same thing as late as the early 1980s. But as the twentieth century waned, progressive education found a new and potent ally: a social justice movement that believed the main job of education was to provide all of America's groups with institutions in which they all felt equally welcome and never faced microaggressions, a new category that included academic failure.

Elsewhere, teachers have resorted to ideology to alter classroom practice, but evidence of its general effect is lacking. Romantic egalitarianism offers a powerful mutually reinforcing cluster of ideas: every teachers college student is precious; every child is precious; every member of society should be freed from oppression. At every step humanity prevails: nurtured teachers nurture schoolchildren, and nurtured schoolchildren will populate America with ideal citizens rather than with greedy racists. Ideology is self – vindicating: the more you reject genetic differences between individuals (regardless of evidence), the more moral you are; thus the moral superiority of the teachers of teachers is taken for granted.

The darker side of the ideology

The progressive ideology dominant in teacher training commits its greatest sin in systematic bad advice to apprentice teachers about how to teach. It dictates a role that is totally mismatched to the caliber of those who must play it. It assumes that everyone can be a super teacher: charismatic, imaginative, broadly educated. One is to diagnose and relate to the interests of children and use that interest to introduce academic subjects. The reality is that graduates of teachers college are at best a random sample of people often without specific training in individual subjects. They need to be drilled in their subjects. Most have no special charisma, an abstract quality that may be difficult to learn. They need automatic status to get ascendency over their pupils, though traditional methods, such as requiring students to rise when a teacher enters a room, are now hopelessly old fashioned. They need a stern principal who will back them up.

The basic problem teacher training must solve is not what might work with a cadre of super teachers, but what kind of classroom will maximize what average (and not very gifted) teachers can achieve with average (and not very gifted) children.

Other factors

Teacher turnover is extreme: every year 15 percent must be replaced to allow for retirement and abandonment. The work is hard: the stress of keeping discipline; parents and therefore your principal never satisfied; the exhausting schedule of preparation, teaching, and marking. In Eastern Kentucky, ex – coal miners who had gone into teaching told me: "The mines were tough but I was never as exhausted as after a day's teaching – I could barely walk to my front door." The pressure from parents has increased over time. Until about 1950, the typical parent had less education than the teacher. After that, well – educated parents multiplied and they tended to consider teachers to be their inferiors (Riesman, 1958, p.126). Automatic backing for the teacher when children complain has yielded to a significant degree to automatic suspicion that the teacher is at fault.

What is to be done?

The basic tactic must be to increase the supply of good teachers beyond demand. This will mean making teaching a real profession, which will not be cheap. It also means seizing control of the public school system to introduce schools that will challenge progressivism and break the monopoly of the present suppliers, the teachers colleges or, what is today prevalent, the colleges of education within the universities.

Finland and its schools are often used as a mirror to critique the American school system. Finland is the only Western nation that has been at or near the top consistently in the rankings published by the OECD (Organization for Economic Co – operation and Development), an intergovernmental economic organization with 36 member countries. The OECD (2015) also makes a strong case that money invested in enhanced education will be recouped by a stronger economy.

Finnish youth adore teaching. More young people aspire to teaching than law or medicine. Finland's Board of Education is overwhelmed with applicants from excellent universities. The Finns accept only ten percent of the applicants for class teachers (generalists who teach the first six years of school). All above that level are called subject teachers and must have a master's degree: depending on the subject, the ratio accepted varies from ten to 50 percent (Ministry of Education and Culture, 2016).

How might the status, self – image, and credentials of American (and Australian, and New Zealand, and Canadian) teachers be enhanced? The targets are clear, although meeting them will take time:

(1) Class teachers (first six years). All must have a major other than education. Education courses would not be required: such courses would have to attract both teachers and would – be teachers on their merits. The higher standards of non – education university courses would immediately upgrade quality and provide teachers with a better chance of being numerate and literate.

There are initiatives afoot that are encouraging. In 2015, the Council for the Accreditation of Educator Preparation began to advocate that teachers training institutions admit only students with at least a 3.0 average GPA (a straight B) and test scores in the top 50 percent nationally and in the top third by 2020 (Morella, 2014). Some Boards of Education are sympathetic. In 2006 the Massachusetts Board voted to create a 40 – item math test that all elementary and special education teachers must pass in order to earn a license. It became the first state to seriously assess the mathematics knowledge of prospective teachers (Stotsky, 2007).

(2) Subject teachers (after the first six years of primary). All must have a master's in the subject area they teach (math, science, history, and so forth). Once again, higher standards for entry into teaching would be automatic.

(3) Salaries. Starting teachers' salaries could remain at the present level, but should match the average income of all full – time employed university graduates by the eighth year and thereafter. Over the first six years, all student debt up to a reasonable level would gradually be forgiven.

(4) Conditions. The seventh year would be a full – paid sabbatical year to be spent as desired: at home, travelling, upgrading credentials, or preparing to change professions. They

could go to law school: after all, they have a good degree in a non – education area. To get more education, they would once again be eligible for loans. Financed sabbaticals could be repeated every seventh year thereafter.

Aside from rising standards of admission, I anticipate several advantages. No one would have to look upon teaching as a life sentence to an undesirable career. Many idealistic young people who are at present reluctant to enter teaching would be happy to try it as a "first" profession and see if they liked it. They and others would be attracted by the status and self – respect created by new conditions. There might be a transitional period during which the desired surplus applicants do not materialize. If so, governments might keep raising salaries until the applicants appear.

Breaking the monopoly

This discussion may seem to evade an important prerequisite for progress: how to break the monopoly of those who teach teachers and how to break the power of those who try to organize schools around progressive social justice ideology.

Charter schools

The further one goes down the administrative hierarchy of school administration, the more progressivism wanes, and the more teachers and parents are more likely to favor a "content oriented" curriculum over a "child centered" program. In America, a charter school is a public school that opts for local control. Parents, community leaders, social entrepreneurs, businesses, teachers, school districts, and municipalities can submit a charter school proposal to their state's authorizing entity. They must demonstrate performance in the areas of academic achievement, financial management, and organizational stability, or risk being closed.

The charter school is still funded by the state and tuition is free. Federal legislation provides grants to help charter schools afford start – up costs. To avoid charter schools selecting an elite student body, they are often required to select students through a random lottery in their area. Usually, they can choose teachers without the education course credentials demanded in most states. Charter schools can go some way toward favoring teachers over administrative staff. There is no barrier to choosing to be more progressive than the usual public school, but overwhelmingly the choice runs in the opposite direction.

In 2015 – 2016, charter schools comprised eight percent schools of public schools (kindergarten through high school) and served six percent of total enrollment. Their effect varies widely. Over one – third of all public school students in Washington, DC attend charter schools, while about 25 percent in Arizona do so (Reuters Staff, 2017). Only ten percent of New York City's enrollment is in charter schools, but the number is growing thanks to their success. In 2015 – 2016, 19 of the top 50 New York schools were charter. Their students' success rates in reading and math were 43.0 and 48.7 percent, respectively, compared to citywide rates of 38.0 and 36.4 percent (Chapman, 2016).

Public schools

The charter school is a promising option but we should not give up on fighting to reform the rest of the state system. New York City almost showed the way. We should replicate the study Joel Kline launched in 2009, which compared ten schools using the Hirsh "content oriented" curriculum against a demographically similar group that followed the "child centered" program. I suggest that there should also be ten new ordinary (not charter) public schools organized around Hirsch from scratch. The principal would be dedicated to a Hirsh – type curriculum. He or she would recruit a staff that, as far as possible, met the new credentialing requirements, non – education degrees for all, MAs for all senior teachers in their subject matter, and no preference given for education graduates.

When middle class and professional parents abandon the public schools, Albert Hirschman (1970) describes the consequences. They are no longer willing to pay taxes for a service that they no longer use or value. Their exit also has implications for voice. When they participate in the system, they can keep it on its toes by internal criticism of performance and can make their voices heard in politics. Once they leave, they leave behind a clientele that is more uniformly lower class and thus makes the public school's task more difficult. It leaves them with worse teachers because teachers try to escape to better schools.

The university and the schools

In terms of enhancing the larger society, one of the most important things a university does is teach teachers. It should stop doing such a bad job. It will not be easy for education staff to agree on a scenario for a better school system. But certainly, we can begin by critiquing the romantic image that dominates our teachers of teachers at present. This will not take us far unless we create a large oversupply of high quality students who want to teach. That can only be done by making teaching a profession, and making schools a place where a sane person would want to be, and making possible an exit when the fervor for doing this tough job wanes.

Any university that really wants to improve teacher education must promote all of these things. I know that there will be limits to the resources that the university can devote to lobbying for better schools but there are some allies out there. At any rate, if we are serious about teacher education, the lobbying we would do is no less necessary than lobbying the state for better funding of universities. How well would we teach in our law schools if lawyers were obsessed with avoiding microaggressions, and raising self – esteem?

12
The whole man: Critical skills

Virtually every university and liberal arts college has a mission statement that says that teaching students to think critically is the principal aim of undergraduate education. They state two objectives. The first is to enhance skills that will be rewarded in the labor market, which I will call workplace competence. The second is to foster development of the whole man, particularly to produce citizens who can play a critical role in a democracy, which I will call human – autonomy competence.

In fact, the universities succeed only to a very modest degree in enhancing the skills valued by employers, that is, producing students who have the kind of critical intelligence, knowledge, verbal skills, and writing skills valuable in the work place. They do virtually nothing to produce individuals who can transcend government and media attempts to define their world and who can take an independent stance on both important personal and public issues. I will address workplace competence in this chapter and human autonomy competence in the next.

Critical skills on the job

Arum and Roska (2011) do an excellent job of measuring the extent to which the typical student who goes through universities or liberal arts colleges adds to his or her workplace critical competence. The results are depressing. They show that during the 1980s universities were adding value at twice the rate of 1990 – 2010. Their measurements take the competence of the entering class as a given and merely plot how much better students do at various points. If students make no gains at all, they would simply duplicate a freshman class comprised of themselves.

Their findings would be less significant if the competence of entering freshmen increased over time. Assume that 2010 students out of high school were well ahead of those in 1980. Although the university added only half the value at the end of the period as at the beginning, the students graduated might be at the same level of competence. It would still be shocking that universities could not do more with a superior intake but at least the average level of competence would be the same. It might seem relatively simple refute this hypothesis. Just give the test that seniors took in the1980s to the seniors of the 1990s. Unfortunately, altered test content made this was impossible.

We can at least cast doubt on this happy correspondence. College – bound high school students virtually all take tests (though there is some pushback now that the testing system is thought to be biased on the basis of race and class), and these scores were constant between 1980 and 2010. If the college – bound high school students registered no change over those three decades, the university intake was probably of much the same quality throughout.

The competence of the university intake was constant

The Scholastic Aptitude Test (SAT) gives results for three subtests, but the Verbal Test is by far the most relevant as far as workplace competence is concerned. Today it is called the critical reading test and it measures critical thinking, vocabulary, and sentence level reading. All universities use the Verbal score as indicative of the viability of their freshman class, though an increasing number no longer requires the SAT at all. The Mathematics score measures arithmetic, algebra, geometry, and statistics. The Writing Test score, which has replaced an earlier logical reasoning test, measures grammar and diction.

Universities have good reason to doubt Writing Test results. In March 2005, Les Perelman analyzed 45 essays and found that in over 90 percent of cases, the essay's score could be predicted from simply counting the number of sophisticated words (Winerip, 2005). He then trained high school seniors to write essays that made little sense but contained words such as "plethora" and "myriad." All of them received scores of "10" or better, which placed the essays in the 92nd percentile or higher (Jaschic, 2007).

An accolade to American public schools: between 1980 and the present, the ethnic composition of those who take the SAT has widened to include more students from lower performing ethnic minority groups.

Despite this, Verbal scores have increased slightly, so the fact that universities have a broader intake has not diminished the academic promise of that intake. The schools have actually improved basic mathematical performance over time, an achievement more impressive than maintaining a relatively static verbal performance.

The American College Test (ACT) also measures a range of results, but the most relevant score is that on its Reading Test. The Test consists of five passages from the humanities, social studies, natural science, and literary fiction. It measures the ability to isolate the main theme, interpret selected words, phrases, or passages, particularly in the context of the whole, and decide what inferences can be drawn.

Table 1 evidences the fact that the college intake has remained constant in quality over time. It gives average SAT and ACT scores over time for appropriate years. The scores for 1992, 2004, and 2005 have been highlighted. They refer to college bound high school students who actually fed into the relevant entering classes of students: the ones whose progress was measured as they passed through university. The fluctuations for the SAT may look important and those for the ACT may look trivial. This is entirely due to the fact that the SAT scores candidates from on a scale from 200 to 800 while the ACT ranks them from 1 to 36. To allow for this, I have translated them both into a common measure familiar to many, namely, into what the differences would be if expressed in IQ points with an SD of 15 (rather than the huge SAT standard deviation or the small ACT standard deviation).

Table 1. Caliber of university intake for selected years. As measured by the SAT (Scholastic Aptitude Test – Verbal) and the ACT (American College Test – Reading) scores of high school seniors

Scholastic Aptitude Test			
Years	SAT – V Score	Gains SAT points compared to 1980 (SD = 110*)	Gains IQ metric compared to 1980 (SD = 15)
1980	502	– – –	– – –
1990	500	– 2.0	– 0.27

1992	500	– 2.0	– 0.27
2000	505	+ 3.0	+ 0.41
2004	508	+ 6.0	+ 0.82
2005	508	+ 6.0	+ 0.82
2010	501	– 1.0	– 0.14

American College Test			
Years	ACT – R* Score	Gains ACT points compared to 1980 (SD = 6.6*)	Gains IQ metric compared to 1980 (SD = 15)
1980	21.2*	– –	– –
1991	21.2	0.00	0.00
1992	21.1	– 0.1	– 0.23
2000	21.4	+ 0.2	+ 0.45
2004	21.3	+ 0.1	+ 0.23
2005	21.3	+ 0.1	+ 0.23
2010	21.3	+ 0.1	+ 0.23

    * The ACT – R score for 1980 has been translated into the current metric. The test at that time was called the Social Studies Test. SAT scores are all in the current metric. The Verbal test is now called "Critical Reading." The standard deviations used to convert to IQ scores are slightly larger than those given by those tested. They are estimates of what the SD would have been if all students were tested rather than a moderately elite sample (the college bound high school students).

    Sources:

    SAT: Google SAT Wikipedia

    ACT: Google ACT score averages by sex 1970 to 1997; ACT score averages and standard deviation, by sex and race 1995 through 2009; The Condition of College and Career Readiness – 2011 – National ACT (see p. 16).

    Two things are evident: the SAT and ACT trends are very similar, and the fluctuations amount to little, none being as much as a single IQ point. Having concluded that the competence of university intake has been roughly constant, the decline in university added value suggests that there has been a dramatic loss in the absolute critical competence of university graduates.

Measuring the decline

The results of Arum and Roksa are only as valid as their samples and tests. The sample was excellent. It numbered over 2,300 students from 24 four – year institutions that were representative in terms of liberal arts colleges vs. research – oriented universities, gender, geographical spread, and race/ethnicity including both traditionally black college and mainly Hispanic institutions. The sample was representative as measured by the SAT and ACT scores of entering freshmen. Their two studies of how students fared at university examined them on the College Learning Assessment Test (CLA) in these years: the fall of 2005, at the beginning of their freshman year; the spring of 2007, at the end of their second year (Arum and Roksa, 2011); and in mid – 2009, at the end of their fourth and final year (Arum and Roksa, 2014).

The CLA contains both an Analytic and a Performance section. The Analytic section begins with a break – an – argument essay that asks you to critically analyze a case in favor of something. The example given is an argument for enrolling at a particular university based entirely on staff publications, the employment of 75 percent of its graduates, and because two graduates later won the Nobel Prize in Physics (no comparative data, nothing on the quality of undergraduate education). Next one writes a make – an – argument essay. A few sentences detail a point of view ("specialists of all kinds are highly overrated") and the tested student must take a position and argue for it. The test does not administer the Analytic section, which is a pity because it looks a bit broader than the Performance section.

The examples of the performance tasks focus more on what I call workplace competence. DynaTech wants a small plane so its sales representatives can travel to reach customers. After consulting a "document library" consisting of letters, memos, photographs, charts, newspaper articles, the student must write a memo as to whether the company should buy a Swift Air 235, a plane that has recently crashed. The memo should weigh each piece of data in terms of whether the 235 is really more likely to crash than other light planes, particularly about whether the circumstances of the recent crash really count against it.

Another example involves advising a politician who promises to increase the number of policemen. His opponent: (1) uses a chart that shows more crime in areas where the ratio of police to people is higher; (2) uses a chart that shows more crime in areas with more drug addicts; and (3) concludes that any extra money spent should be on drug treatment rather than more police. This may seem to trespass on the skills someone would need to be a good citizen. However, note that the student is forced to focus on the issue as presented rather than identifying it himself and is handed all the relevant information on a plate, rather perceiving what is relevant and ferreting it out.

At much the same time, during 2006 – 2010, the Center of Inquiry at Wabash College did a parallel study, the Wabash National Study of Liberal Arts Education. Its sample was of comparable size and quality except that it included an oversample of Liberal Arts Colleges. The timing of the examinations was slightly different: beginning of the first year (the same), the end of the first year (rather than the end of the second), and the end of the fourth year (the same). Half were randomly assigned the Collegiate Assessment of Academic Proficiency Critical Thinking Test (CAAP – CT) and half the Defining Issues Test (DIT); each group took the same test throughout subsequent years.

The CAAP – CT is very similar to the Arum and Roksa critical thinking test. It is a 40 – minute, 32 – item instrument designed to measure a student's ability to clarify, analyze, evaluate, and extend arguments. There are four passages in a variety of formats (case studies, debates, dialogues, experimental results, statistical arguments, editorials). Each passage contains a series of arguments that support a general conclusion followed by a set of multiple – choice test items. The DIT measures levels of moral reasoning: the extent to which an individual uses principles to resolve moral dilemmas and rejects ideas that are simplistic or biased (Pascarella, et al., 2011).

The choice of the CAAP links the Wabash Study to earlier data. Pascarella and Terenzini (2005), using the CAAP and much the same kind of sample, tested the entering class of 1992 in that year and in 1995 or their final year. The results were quite similar to later studies, but they were radically worse than what Pascarella and Terenzini (1991) found in their literature search of studies done in the 1980s. The 1980s studies showed a university – gain of one SD: a value that is double the 0.50 from recent studies. It is true the earlier studies used the Watson – Glaser test, but it is very similar to the CLA and CAAP. It is most often used by employers who value the ability to consider arguments and propositions critically, such as law firms or consulting firms. The test offers statements accompanied by inferences that must be critically evaluated.

A sample item: "Studies have shown that people who live in England are more likely to own their own homes than people living in Scotland, although there is little difference in the rate of home ownership amongst people who have the same level of educational achievement. The average level of educational achievement is significantly higher in England than Scotland." It is followed by three possible inferences: (1) People with high educational achievements are in a better position to buy their own homes than people with low educational achievements (TRUE); (2) There is a lower rate of home ownership in Scotland among people with relatively high educational achievements than among people in England with much lower educational achievement (FALSE); (3) People with higher levels of educational achievement are more likely to own their own homes, since they earn more money than those with lower educational achievement levels (PROBABLY TRUE).

How large was the decline

The contrast between the results Pascarella and Terenzini got in the 1980s and those the Wabash Study got in 1995 may seem to show just when universities began to add less value to critical thinking. But could the decline have actually begun earlier? Huber and Kunce (2016) did an analysis of all critical thinking tests from studies published between 1963 and 2011. They show that gains may have begun to slip as early the 1960s: they were 1.12 SDs then, a bit worse than our value of 1.00 SD in the 1980s. But the difference is too small to be certain. Their results for recent years were even more alarming: only 0.33 SDs gained from their last study published in 2011, much lower than the 0.50 SDs that seem to prevail beginning with the 1990s.

They also found that longitudinal studies (following students as they went through university) gave lower gains than cross – sectional studies (comparing freshmen and seniors in the same year). All of our studies from 1990 on are longitudinal. It would be risky to date the decline earlier than during the 1990s. This is not crucial: the contrast between the 1980s and thereafter is the striking result.

Table 2 compares results from all of our studies. It offers a choice between measuring university added gains in standard deviations or percentile levels (what percentile the average final year student would attain were he or she still a freshman) or an IQ metric. The results are remarkably consistent as far as workplace critical thinking is concerned. Seniors gained 7.5 "IQ points" on freshmen after 1990 as compared to 15 points gained prior to 1990; seniors attained the 68th percentile of freshman after 1990 as compared to seniors that attained the 84th percentile of freshmen prior to 1990. These results show that something is very wrong today.

I should note that "Moral reasoning" gives better freshmen to senior gains in the Wabash study (2006 – 2010) than do recent standard critical thinking tests. But they are still far below the 1980s. The gain over four years stands at 0.58 SDs or the 72nd percentile or 8.7 IQ points. The surplus is due to an atypically high gain during the first year, albeit with a lower rate of gain thereafter. Perhaps this is because when students enter university, they generally encounter an atmosphere unfriendly to racial or gender bias and a wider range of ethnic groups than at high school. It is a pity we have no more data on moral reasoning this is a trait that would transcend enhanced workplace competence and might have more positive implications for the good citizen.

Different students, universities, and majors

When they isolate elite students, those whose scores on the CLA were in the top ten percent, Arum and Roska (2011, p. 56) disperse some of the gloom. On average, these elite students scored 1.755 SDs above the typical freshman. By the end of their second year, they had gained 1.50 SDs, while a typical freshman gained only 0.18 (Table 2, line CLA, value for year 2), giving them a net gain of 1.32 SDs. They had thus risen to 3.075 SDs above the typical sophomore (by the end of the second year). We do not know how they scored at the end of their final year but it was unlikely that they had lost ground.

Table 2. Gains in critical thinking at university

Test & source	Period	University year 0	1	2	3	4
		Standard Deviation (SD) gains				
Misc. tests	Circa 1960	– –	– –	– –	– –	1.12
W – G (P&T)	1980 – 89	– –	– –	– –	– –	1.00
CAAP (P&T)	1992 – 95	– –	– –	– –	– –	0.50
CAAP (Wabash)	2006 – 10	– –	0.11	(0.22)	(0.33)	0.44
CLA (A&R)	2005 – 09	– –	– –	0.18	(0.33)	0.47
Morality (Wabash)	**2006 – 10**	**– –**	**0.32**	**(0.41)**	**(0.49)**	**0.58**
		Percentile levels				
Misc. tests	Circa 1960	– –	– –	– –	– –	87
W – G (P&T)	1980 – 89	50	– –	– –	– –	84
CAAP (P&T)	1992 – 95	50	– –	– –	– –	69
CAAP (Wabash)	2006 – 10	50	54	(59)	(63)	67
CLA (A&R)	2005 – 09	50	– –	57	(63)	68
		Total "IQ point" gain after entry				
Misc. tests	Circa 1960	– –	– –	– –	– –	16.8
W – G (P&T)	1980 – 89	– –	– –	– –	– –	15.0
CAAP (P&T)	1992 – 95	– –	– –	– –	– –	7.5
CAAP (Wabash)	2006 – 10	– –	1.7	(3.3)	(5.0)	6.6
CLA (A&R)	2005 – 09	– –	– –	2.7	(5.0)	7.1

Values in brackets are interpolated to allow for comparisons.

The Morality test is in bold because it measures moral reasoning (see text), something different from work – place critical competence. Tests and sources:

(1) Misc. tests; Huber & Kunce (2016).
(2) W – G (P&T) – Watson – Glaser Test of critical thinking; Pascarella & Terenzini (1991).
(3) CAAP (P&T) – College Assessment of Academic Proficiency; Pascarella & Terenzini (2005).

(4) CAAP (Wabash) – College Assessment of Academic Proficiency; Pascarella et al. (2011)
(5) CLA (A&R) – College Learning Assessment Test (performance task only); Arum & Rosca (2011 and Arum & Rosca (2014).
(6) Morality = DIT (Defining Issues Test – from Wabash); Pascarella et al. (2011).

This does not mitigate the fact that in all likelihood they were not as good as the top ten percent in the 1980s. But even so, does not a cadre of ten percent of graduates whose workplace critical competence is as high as this give us an elite that has human – autonomy critical competence? Does it not give us an elite that can penetrate the fog of what their leaders and the media tell them? They at least should punch above their weight, attain a standard that signals intelligent opinion by office holders, journalists, and pundits of all sorts. This may seem plausible but wait and see.

Naturally, the top ten percent of entrants overall are concentrated in elite universities and colleges. As a criterion of highly selective institutions, Arum and Roska (2011, p. 56) stipulated that the 25th percentile of the entering class must have a combined SAT score (verbal plus math) above 1,150. This is not a radical elite. All of the top 100 US universities and colleges qualify. What one would like is a better breakdown: take the top ten percent and compare university added value when they go to highly selective institutions with university added value when they go to others. But this is not given. Assuming that they do fare better at elite universities, we would have to determine whether this was because whatever members of the top ten percent are present at elite universities were less handicapped by background variables that affect added value. I refer to race/ethnicity, parental education and profession, English as first language, urban or rural, one or two parent homes.

Reverting to the total sample, different majors give different results. Adjusting for the CLA score of their intake, the added value from entrant to the end of the second year is doubled for majors in science/mathematics and social science/humanities; it is about average for engineering/computer science, communications, and health; and it is well below for education/social work and business (Arum and Roska

(2011, Table A4.3). Perhaps the fact that science/mathematics is a bit larger than social science/Humanities shows that the intellectual rigor of what is taught outweighs content. After all, in terms of content, the humanities teach skills that are more akin to what is measured in the CLA performance test: the ability to write a memo in readable and coherent English prose about statistical data typical of the social sciences. Somehow this seems to make no difference.

What has gone wrong: Student effort and rewards

Since 1961, there has been a massive decline in the hours per week university students spend studying. Babcock and Marks (2011) give 25 hours in 1961, 17 hours in 1981, 17 hours in 1988 (the link between 1981 and 1988 is uncertain), and 15 hours in 2003. Arum and Roska (2011, p. 2) seem to put the last estimate at 13 (perhaps I am in error). At any rate, their comprehensive survey from 2007 shows 12.

Worse, only 8.5 of these study hours were hours studying alone, while 3.5 were hours studying with peers. The two are simply not the same: studying alone is beneficial, while studying with peers is not (Arum & Roska, 2011, pp. 68 – 69 and 100 – 101). The latter involves too much chitchat and when it is dominant, it is negatively associated with improved performance on the CLA. Universities have encouraged peer group study in recent years. This practice was almost unknown in the 1960s, aside from study dates, which paired the sexes.

My guess at trends for serious study runs from 25 hours in 1961, to 17 hours in the 1980s, to little more than 8.5 in the most recent data. Perhaps the notion that critical thinking was already in decline between 1960 and the 1980s deserves more credence than I have given it. At present, only a lesser portion of study hours are devoted to preparing for class: 37 percent of students spent fewer than five hours per week (the rest goes on homework or essays); the value for the average student is not given but could not be above six or seven hours. At highly selective institutions (top 100), students spend an extra five hours per week studying for a total of 17. During this period, the total invested time of all students on academic pursuits has fallen from 40 hours per week to 27 (Arum & Roska, 2011, pp. 68, 70, and 97; Babcock, P., & Marks, M.,

2011*)*. This drop of 13 hours allotted to academic pursuits is exactly the same as the 13 – hour drop in studying (25 down to 12 of which some is "peer study").

Babcock and Marks found that the decline in study affected all students irrespective of ethnicity, gender, outside jobs, and quality of the institution. There was no marked decline with the introduction of computers, the internet, or social media. A new psychological problem had emerged: 33 percent of students now found they "struggled" frequently or all the time with not knowing how to sit down and study. How do they spend their new leisure time (the extra 13 hours per week)? Mostly on socializing and recreation: a recent University of California study found that they spent 12 hours per week socializing, 11 hours using computers for fun, six hours watching television, five hours on hobbies, and three hours on other forms of entertainment – a total of 43 hours compared to 13 on studying.

Grade inflation

Despite all of this, the average student has been rewarded with higher and higher grades. Between 1983 and today, at all four – year colleges and universities, the average GPA (Grade Point Average) has risen steadily from 2.83 to 3.13, or from about B – to B+ (Jashik, 2016). Indeed, the most commonly given grade today is A – (the average is driven down by the few failures). The very elite institutions tend to give the highest grades, often with the justification that students must have been special to get in (at Brown University in 2010, two – thirds of students had an A average).

The reader may wonder how professors can give such high grades when students do so little work. One answer is that it has become easy for students to write a final exam that looks like they have learned something when they have learned almost nothing. A formulaic final exam repeats much the same questions every year: the student need answer perhaps three out of 12. Course readings give the substance of all your lectures, and it is easy to see just which pages you need to memorize to get a good mark on a particular question. Why spend more than 12 hours studying even over the course as a whole? That should be enough to memorize as much as you need.

Why go to class except for entertainment? To get decent attendance, professors show overheads, films, and videos and try to make their subjects "fun." The more responsible ones summarize the course book briefly and then hold a largely uninformed discussion (few students will have actually read the course book in advance). It is also now popular to have the class break down into little discussion groups as an alternative to the lecture. It would be too cruel to ask colleagues to tape what is said in these groups. In passing, when students have recordings of lectures by lecturers who do not offer a detailed course book, this poses a problem – see Box 5.

Box 5. If they have recordings, how to give a decent lecture in say the humanities.

When you lecture on Plato (a thinker no student can understand just from reading the text or the text of last year's lecture), be lively and extemporaneous as if understanding him for the first time. Show them a visible example (perhaps the first they have ever seen) of someone who takes ideas seriously. Make explicit the assumptions behind your interpretation and challenge them. Refer to live issues – how just would Plato think our society is today, for example. Does he solve the problem of induction? Does Aristotle really have a criterion of what way of life maximizes eudaimonia? Given that the international scene today (nuclear weapons) duplicates Hobbes' state of nature, why is there no world sovereign? See Flynn, 2018 for a "text" that exemplifies the strategy.

When professors teach students something that they really must learn (Chemistry, Physics, Anatomy, logic or math), they offer classes that have more substance, demand more time, and grade more harshly, particularly at the pass/fail level. Another thing that has altered over time is cheating. McCabe et al. (2001) did a study of nine colleges and found that students who admitted copying from others on tests rose from 26 percent in 1963 to 52 percent in 1993. This makes sense. If university has become a game of how to buy good grades while paying minimum effort, cheating cuts costs by reducing effort.

What has gone wrong: underlying causes

The law of compromised judgments states that when those assessed become more powerful than those who assess, criteria will weaken. This is particularly true when the roles of assessed and assessor are reversed. When American investment banks that issued securities became more powerful than the agencies that rated securities, the later watered down their criterion for a triple – A rating – a factor that helped cause the financial crisis of 2008. Some of the investment banks actually owned stock in the rating agencies, paid fees only if they liked the rating, and kept a blacklist of those who disagreed, allegedly warning them they would never get a job on Wall Street (Flynn, 2012d). When Protestant churches gave congregations the power to hire and fire ministers, the criterion of entering heaven collapsed and the notion of hell was almost abandoned. Catholic priests not dependent on their congregations did a much better job of holding the doctrinal line.

As universities and university departments became more and more dependent on attracting students, they have allowed themselves to be defined by the preferences of undergraduates, now a massive market force. The universities of today provide state – of – the – art gymnasiums, dorms, cafeterias, athletic spectacles, and counseling for psychological wellbeing. They no longer treat students as naïve young people whose preferences are to be formed in the direction of taking truth seriously, but as consumers whose preferences are to be satisfied. The latter dictate that universities should be less severe in assessing academic performances and resist demands and expectations that students resent. Even Harvard has to keep an eye on Princeton, Yale, Chicago, and Stanford and needs to be perceived as no less student – friendly than these rivals. Even top students do not like to be treated more harshly than they were in high school, and the internet is full of complaints that X university makes students work harder to get top grades than Y university.

Every department chairman knows that if the department gets a reputation for low grades or being too demanding, the consequent loss of students will make cutbacks inevitable and personnel changes likely. Parents now pay huge sums for university credentials and expect their children to get them, often without regard to performance. At some universities, professors who fail too many students or are too harsh in other ways can expect unfriendly interviews with deans or, worse, allegations of discriminatory misconduct that are given every credence, often in the absence of evidence, and often with serious consequences. The publicity of universities moves closer and closer to that of retirement homes, i.e., just relax and have fun within increasingly circumscribed limits. Over the years, my own alma mater's bulletin has trashed the nerd image of Chicago students and publicized the fact that even nerds can have a wonderful time. In sum, the rise of the *student – centered university* has engendered a kind of uneasy *non – aggression pact.*

The non – aggression pact

The terms: if you do not menace us students with poor grades or "unreasonable" demands on our time (cognitively demanding thinking, reading, essays, exams), we will not plague you professors by avoiding your courses, writing bad student evaluations (there is a strong positive correlation between low grades and low evaluations), or filing complaints with your ever more censorious superiors.

Today these terms have a special appeal for faculty members. They can offer courses while doing as little as possible. To assign a tough set of essays means planning, setting new topics every year, checking bibliographical references, offering more help to students, more grading, and more complaints. To set a good exam means even more teaching, advising, grading, complaints, and the terror of bad evaluations and reduced research output, which interfere with promotion and tenure. How easy to give classes when classes have become irrelevant to the learning process, when you can take a holiday any time you like by screening a film rather than analyzing a topic. Today academic staff are far more harassed than 50 years ago: more students, much more supervision, more hours applying for research grants, far more administrative duties, far more administrative intrusion. Evading teaching becomes a test of political skill. Its status is such that "adjunct professors" offer more undergraduate lectures than permanent staff. Without tenure, badly paid, sometimes teaching at several institutions to scrape together a decent salary, it is not surprising that they fail to develop loyalty to institutions that treat them so badly.

The trend among students in general to want an easy time has not eliminated individual students who are eager to learn. Thanks to a six – fold enrolment at my university since 1967, I have more students today who are keen and sometimes hear from them that they are surprised by how little is asked of them.

The student – centered university

When universities make student satisfaction the primary goal and accept this non – aggression pact, they create a culture that students find nearer to ideal. From surveys, Arum and Roska (2011, pp. 4, 76, & 81 – 82) cull interviews that reflect current values and expectations. Here are a few slightly edited:

> I hate classes with a lot of reading. Any class where a teacher gives us lecture notes and a worksheet is better. Something that I can study and learn from in five minutes. I rarely do reading assignments, which is a mistake, I am sure, but it saves a lot of time.

> University really is not much different than high school, except the professors have Ph.Ds [sic] instead of being like regular people [a perceptive comment]. I hate learning, I hate sitting in classes. I just do it for the grades, work enough to get an "A."

> Honestly, I feel like nothing I have learned in the classroom will help me do what I want to do in the end. It is the people I meet, the friends I make that really matter.

> Student advice about courses: Professor Jones is the man to see when you want an A – Don't take 302 with Smith because you can't understand what he wants you to know and he doesn't give As – 145 sucks, never take it, you do three times the amount of work for the same credits and lower grades – Sign up for 235, the course is boring but it is easy as hell, and there is tons of extra credit – I love 101, it was so fun and easy – Take 298, its [sic] so easy.

Imagine what such students hate most: bad grades, flunking out, demanding courses, a lot of reading, and writing long essays. Then look at the trends over the past 50 years, in which the worst consequences are sharply curtailed and the hardest requirements are now softened. This not to deny that some students want to work, even do hard work, especially if it has a vocational pay – off: they do not want to seem ignorant when they join a law firm, be at a loss when they have to perform surgery, be humiliated in graduate school, or need to show that they can do math.

13
The whole man:
Critical minds

Universities aim not only at upgrading workplace critical abilities but also at upgrading human – autonomy critical intelligence. The objective is admirable: educate the whole man into citizens who can play a critical role in a democracy; citizens who can see through the noise with which their leaders and the media bombard them and reach intelligent opinions about public affairs.

The universities fail at attaining this objective almost entirely. The falsifying evidence is of several sorts: what students say of themselves after completing university; what students do after leaving university; and test results that show that graduating students lack the critical skills they need. Why is general education so ineffective? What might be done to make universities better? What might be done to encourage students to read and think more intelligently throughout their lives?

After university

In 2011 Arum and Roska interviewed almost a thousand members of their sample two years after graduation. Only 16 percent discussed politics frequently, and only 33 percent read newspapers daily either online or in print as compared to non – graduates at about 25 percent. On the other hand, 75 percent of the graduates of highly selective institutions reported at least some involvement with newspapers or political discussion.

It is possible that graduates share the plight of the true philosopher in a defective society. Plato advised them to be silent critics who stand aloof from the corrupt politics of the day, which could only tarnish them. It would be understandable if American university graduates have reached similar conclusions (Flynn, 2008). But that is not what they say. Right across the university spectrum, they have a pessimistic view of their country. But they do not withhold wisdom, rather they confess a sense of futility, confessing, "I can't form a really solid opinion;" " I think that getting out of wars would help, but I guess I don't know enough to say very surely what would happen;" or "I don't know what direction the country should go, let alone what direction it will go" (Arum and Roska, 2014, 85 – 86 & 99 – 105).

The very variety of "news" sources available: newspapers, television, radio, internet, blogs, social media, and so on is bewildering. Worst of all, within whatever college they choose, there is no correlation between CLA scores and civic or political awareness. In other words, graduates do not appear to have applied whatever workplace critical competence they may have acquired to the citizen's role of political and social commitment.

Reading after university

Perhaps sampling graduates only two years after university was misleading. Universities may provide only the foundation, and, with employment worries and early career jitters distracting them, it may take some time afterwards for graduates to develop the skills to filter news for reliability and learn enough about various nations and their histories to develop a personal stance on basic issues. However, trends show that just as Americans have given up on reading at university, so are they beginning to eschew reading throughout their adult lives. Between 1982 and 2015, the percentage of adults who read for pleasure (novels, short stories, poems, or plays) fell from 57 percent to 43 percent. Men stand at only 36 percent (National Endowment for the Arts, 2016). This is despite the fact that the percentage of adults with a bachelor's degree almost doubled over that period. Reduced reading reduces empathy in favor of narcissism: 75 percent of students rate themselves as less empathetic than the average student of 30 years ago (Konrath, 2011; Twenge & Campbell, 2011).

Reduced reading includes biography and history. Orwell thought a government had to censor history – to "control the past" – to produce people who were uncritical about their political elite and the media, and

therefore control the present and future. All you really need is an a –
historical generation. The mean IQ has risen in the twentieth century as a
result of more education, but this has little effect when it is accompanied
by the rise of factual ignorance (Flynn, 2010; 2016c).

But what of those whose workplace critical competence puts
them in the top ten percent? For all we know, they are deeply involved in
American politics and social criticism. They have a CLA measured
critical competence at least three SDs above the average graduate.
Compared to the total college population, already somewhat superior,
university – added value takes them from a "critical competence" IQ of
126 to 146. I have acknowledged that they are a potential elite that might
penetrate the fog of what their leaders and the media tell them, while
others have argued that the top ten percent of modern society already is
an elite distinct from the bottom 90 percent. If they are setting a standard
of what can pass muster as intelligent opinion by office holders,
journalists, and pundits of all sorts, they may be leading us to a better
world. Perhaps they can do what informed opinion did to the cause of
slavery in nineteenth – century Britain: set standards of values and
behavior that made its defenders feel humiliated in their own homes and
embarrassed among their associates. Our elite now sets itself apart by
eschewing tobacco, consuming organic food, avoiding single – use
plastics, driving hybrids, acknowledging gender fluidity, practicing
"mindfulness," and signaling what it believes to be progressive virtues in
other ways.

The bridge that does not exist

But if they are to play this kind of a benevolent role, they will
have to somehow leap the wide gap that separates workplace competence
from human – autonomy competence. There is no "natural" bridge
between the two. Recall the limitations of what CLA – type tests
measure: whether one can use critical intelligence in a work structured
situation. You are *told* to be critical, you are *presented* with all you need
to know to reach a conclusion, and you are *directed* to spell out the
conclusion in writing. I have no doubt that American universities are
graduating an elite that can, under these conditions, write excellent
memos on whether to buy a light aircraft such as the Swift Air 235.

However, none of this translates into what a good citizen, as opposed to a highly competent functionary, must do: keep an eye on current events; decide what may be true or false; take the initiative to formulate a critical position; acquire the relevant information; and most of all, use the tools necessary to arrive at an intelligent conclusion.

To do the latter one must actually have these tools: a critical perspective on the nation and its history; knowing that all governments lie when they think they can get away with it; a lack of presumption of what to do to foreign nations without knowing their histories and seeing the world through their eyes; a basic framework for understanding international politics; a basic grasp of market economics; knowledge of the various kinds of flawed moral arguments; a basic knowledge of statistics and what a scientific study should look like; a reasonable picture of the world as revealed by science; and an awareness of why no other approach can match it. Our university has faculty of about 1,500 and a graduating class of about 5,200. But how many of them have this full toolkit?

It may be heartbreaking to interact with a top lawyer who graduated from a leading law school who advocates rent or price controls as an ever – present remedy, who does not realize that the balance of military power in the Middle East is directly relevant to "negotiations" about Israeli expansion, who takes American exceptionalism seriously, who endorses the latest crusade to "nation – build" in a troubled country, who thinks that climate change is a conspiracy, who thinks that history is merely a narrative, who believes that evolution is merely a theory, who thinks that "intelligent design" can afford a causal explanation, who thinks that what gays do is "unnatural," or who believes that the satisfaction of human demand is equivalent to the common good.

In principle, none of these condemned views discriminates between the intelligent left and the intelligent right. Climate change skeptics are more plentiful on the right, but even here the sophisticated conservative will not deny the facts, merely dispute the severity of their implications or what might be done about them (Flynn, 2016b). The point is that if the elite had the tools necessary to do real critical thinking, its members could at least communicate in a manner appropriate to the whole man or the good citizen, without resorting to empty dogma. When this happens, the right and the left begin to grope their way toward some consensus, as they did, for example, in formulating centrist policies in earlier decades that would be unthinkable in America now.

Measuring human – autonomy competence

By their final year, have university students acquired human – autonomy competence: the tools that would allow them to do more than be bombarded by current opinion? To find out, I designed "Flynn's Index of Social Criticism" (FISC).

Here are some representative items. Collectively, they have been compared with the test as a whole to ensure that they are of equivalent difficulty. The examinee is presented with a statement and five alternatives with the warning that only two of them are legitimate inferences from the statement:

Economics – Statement: A city finds that its poor citizens are paying a high proportion of their income in rent. It identifies the properties the poor inhabit and establishes a board to fix rents at a certain level year by year. Alternatives: (1) The rents the board sets will tend to be below what unregulated rents would return; (2) The city will house its poor more adequately; (3) Rent control properties will give a more reliable flow of income; (4) Landlords will find that they have difficulty selling their rent – control properties; (5) Rental properties will tend to expand at the expense of home – ownership properties.

Social Science – Statement: President Kennedy was told that that how well children did in school was directly related to the size of the vocabulary used in the home. He said that there was an obvious solution, namely upgrading the vocabulary to which the low – SES pre – school child is exposed. Alternatives: (1) SES is sufficient to explain why some children do poorly in school; (2) Parental vocabulary is sufficient to explain why some children do poorly in school; (3) Some common factor might explain both home vocabulary and school performance; (4) Other people using a large vocabulary is unlike your parents using a large vocabulary; (5) In all probability vocabulary is one of the factors influencing school performance.

Science – Statement: The hawk moth caterpillar has a rear end that looks like a snake. Alternatives: (1) God explains this because He can make nature as complex as He wishes; (2) Evolution explains this because birds feed on these caterpillars and are afraid of snakes; (3) Scientific explanation must tell us not only how nature evolved but also why it evolved as it did; (4) The moth's instinct for survival caused it to evolve this characteristic; (5) If the moth lived in an environment without birds it would not have developed this characteristic.

Conception of Science – Statement: The world is a blank slate on which every person writes his or her own narrative. Directions: Here you are to assess whether the statement is true or not. Therefore, select the two options that are the closest match for your positive or negation assessment: 1) The narrative in an up – to – date bus timetable is more useful than the narrative in an out – of – date timetable; 2) This is true because each generation of scientists creates a new paradigm of the world as the old one goes out of fashion; 3) Every time I put on my spectacles I prove that there are accurate and inaccurate narratives about the world of vision; 4) We are not passive creatures presented with the same 'sense data' but rather create what we see and each of us sees something different; 5) The fact that scientists admit they have no final and certain truths shows that science is just one narrative among many.

The FISC is meant to provide an *absolute* criterion of critical competence, but this entails an appeal to the reader's judgment. It poses questions that can be answered by anyone who is aware of the law of supply and demand, the primary factors that cloud our analysis of social behavior, clear examples of flawed moral argument, and a coherent concept of scientific explanation. I believe that any student who cannot get most of the items correct simply lacks the skills we expect of a good citizen, skills which build on the competencies tested. If anything, I think it is not rigorous enough because it does not include testing for a coherent concept of international behavior or wide reading or some depth of historical knowledge. If readers think it too rigorous or irrelevant, and still think so after reading the book – length defense (Flynn, 2012d), I have nothing more to say except to ask them to spell out just how a citizen could get such questions wrong and get current issues "right."

FISC studies

The FISC has been administered at seven institutions. I will begin with "Gene Debs University" because of its distinction and the quality of the sample. "Gene Debs" is an alias for one of America's great state universities. In terms of "best undergraduate teaching," it ranks easily in the top ten alongside Princeton, Dartmouth, Brown, Michigan, Stanford, Duke, and Yale (US News and World Report, 2017). It was kind enough to allow a sample of its senior class to take the FISC (Flynn, 2012d).

Gene Debs University

Sample and test. Within two months of graduation, members of the senior class were solicited by email and offered $12 to give an hour of their time. Majors from several areas were targeted: economics, business, mathematics; the social sciences; the humanities; and the natural sciences. The total number who took the test was 185, or 3.22 percent of the graduated class. One student took it twice, perhaps motivated by avarice. The average GPA of the sample was 3.41, as compared to 3.29 for all seniors. The fact that the sample was slightly elite did not affect the results. One of the most disturbing findings was that GPA was virtually uncorrelated with performance on the FISC at 0.06. Whatever earns good grades at "Gene Debs University" does not include critical ability with any broad significance.

The FISC has 20 items. These are evenly divided into four subtests: elementary market analysis and the ability to apply the concept of a ratio (economics); social science methodology sufficient to be wary of flawed studies (social science); flawed argument, including some of the classical errors philosophy has identified (philosophy); and the role and status of science including natural science, history, and social science (science). Each item presents five alternatives, and the student must identify the two that are more reasonable responses than the remainder.

Taking the class as a whole, I put the standard for "coping" with an item at a score of 1.40. If 40 percent of the class could identify both of the correct responses, 30 percent one correct response, and the other 30 per cent were just guessing, they would get an average of 1.415. Or if half knew the two correct responses and the other half knew nothing, they would get 1.40. As this establishes, the standard for the group as a whole has been set rather low but the average puts them midway between zero critical intelligence and the omnicompetence of the whole man.

Class competence by item. Box 6 conveys the content of the FISC items and gives the average performance on each. It shows that more than about half of these subjects are aware of the concept of a placebo and can detect a tautology (circular reasoning). The same is true concerning the relativist fallacy (arguing that all values are relative and then making an arbitrary exception) and the practical syllogism (perceiving that both a moral principle and a fact are necessary to reach a moral conclusion).

Box 6. FISC items and concepts: Gene Debs scores ranked from best to worst.

Concept	No. items	Scores 0.8 = random 2.0 = maximum	Comment
Placebo	1	1.42	Coping
Tautology	1	1.42	Coping
Relativist fallacy	1	1.38	Close to coping
Practical syllogism	1	1.34	Close to coping
Control group	1	1.26	Minority of majors coping
Law supply/demand	3	1.15	Variable coping by major
Purposes in nature	1	1.06	Rejection of purposes feeble
Ratio	2	1.04	Application feeble
Charisma effect	1	1.01	Awareness feeble
Random sample	1	0.96	Aware of its nature & virtues very feeble
Natural = good	1	0.81	Unaware of fallacy of equating natural with good, but stop short of butter is good because it is "more natural"
Butter = natural	1	1.47	

Science unique	1	0.97	Random as to whether science
Scientific history unique	1	0.62	and the historical method are reliable, and as to whether
Soc. science & bias	1	0.78	social science can transcend bias
Sociologist's fallacy	1	0.39	A tendency to believe that equating for one factor always entails comparability for another
Universe blank slate	1	0.25	Strong tendency to believe that no interpretation of reality more objective than any other

Awareness of the need for a control group is true only of a minority, and the ability to use the law of supply and demand variable by major. They are not much better than random about whether nature has purposes (it does not). Most are unable to apply the concept of a ratio or percentage, something that should really give us pause. Their awareness of the charisma effect and the concept of a random sample are feeble. They are unaware that you cannot settle a moral debate by an appeal to nature, but they stop short of the foolishness of endorsing butter as more natural than margarine. They are prone to commit the "sociologist's fallacy" (unaware that matching two groups for one variable can produce a mismatch for another), but that is a rather subtle concept and many university academics do no better.

Most have only random opinions about the role and nature of the sciences. They are strongly prone to deny reality as a check on opinion, which relates to their lack of competence to talk about science coherently. This does not mean that biology majors, for example, would think that what they find in the laboratory is not to be preferred to ordinary opinion. It is just that they have not generalized from what they do as scientists to reach conclusions about science itself.

To isolate and classify those who do seem to have a coherent concept of science, the science subtest asks them to choose between answers that presume a realist concept of science and answers that presume a postmodern concept (that science is in no way privileged). Those with a subtest score of 7.0 or better chose the realist answers at least five times out of ten (perhaps guessing at the rest), and those who had score of 2.0 or worse chose the postmodern answers at least five times out of ten (perhaps guessing at the rest). The breakdown was shattering: 6.5 percent were realists; 69 percent were muddled; and 24.5 had postmodernist tendencies.

Student competence by subtest. As stated, in order to be credited with a reasonable competence in a particular subtest or area, the student had to get a score of 7.0 out of a possible 10.0 (this equals 1.40, or the single item standard, times five). About 17 percent of "Gene Debs" graduates are competent in basic market analysis and the use of ratios, 22 percent in basic social science methodology, and 29 percent in rational discourse about ethics. I suspect that the detection of flawed moral argument is higher because a really bright person can come closer to doing this unaided.

Majors and divisions. The fact that some departments fare better or worse may not reflect on the performance of their faculty. Many departments attempt to develop only very limited critical competence, but this is not reflected in GPAs, which reflect mastery of specific sets of information or skill, however broad or narrow. The seven majors I will discuss had twelve or more students in the sample and unless a follow – up is done with larger numbers, some caution may be in order.

(1) Economics: The benchmark to which others should aspire. It stands first on the economics subtest with its average student at least approaching competence. Its students are not as strong on social science methodology as they should be. Its students are competent at detecting flawed arguments on the philosophy subtest. Given that a bright student can develop this skill without much formal training, variations between majors on the philosophy subtest may largely reflect differences in the quality of their students.

(2) Political Science: Almost equal to economics. It is surprising that its majors come as close to economists on market analysis, but perhaps a lot of them take the introductory macroeconomics course. They perform bit better than economics majors in social science methodology, but no major has a good grasp of this.

(3) History: Bright students, but it is disturbing that its majors have only minimal competence in social science methods.

(4) Neurology: Stronger than expected on social science methods, but does not approach functional competence in any subtest.

(5) Psychology: Surprising lack of competence in social science methods.

(6) English: No real critical competence outside its specialized field.

(7) Biology: No critical competence outside its specialized field. Despite being a science, those few with some kind of coherent vision of science lean more toward postmodernism than realism.

There were only six business majors, but their GPAs were above average. They were worst or next to worst in every area, including economics.

Conclusions

- "Gene Debs University" has a senior class with many bright students.
- These bright students had no real success in developing critical competence outside narrow specialties.
- Only 24 percent of graduates have found their own way to a reasonable level of critical competence in at least two areas out of four.
- Only 6.5 percent of graduates have a coherent realist image of science, while 24.5 percent are at least attracted to a postmodernist concept.
- Apparent differences in critical competence between various majors are large and disturbing, and these should be tested against further data.

Gene Debs compared to other institutions

Altogether, six universities have taken the FISC, but none of the others match the quality of "Gene Debs" in the undergraduate education rankings (US News and World Report, 2017). The other samples are all from advanced psychology classes and vary in size. A full analysis of this data will soon be available (Flynn, in press). To check whether psychology students were better or worse than others, I used the only two samples that allowed for a comparison. At "Gene Debs," 21 psychology students were typical when compared to 163 others; at another university, 35 non – psychology students were typical of 80 psychology students. As usual, I have used pseudonyms to conceal the identity of the universities.

It seemed to make sense to rank the additional universities in terms of their place on the world scale of psychology departments (Quacquarelli Symonds, 2017). This is an elite scale in the sense that it ranks only the world's 300 best (875 universities offer a Psychology MA in the US alone). They include:

Northeast US University: rank = 151 – 200 or very good; sample size = 115.

Southwest US University: rank = 251 – 300 or above average; size = 61.

London Secondary School: very good; all 48 members of final year class.

A London University: rank = 25 – 30 or top flight; size = 32.

UK red brick university: rank = 251 – 300 or above average; size = 30.

Spanish University: rank 101 – 150 or excellent; size = 96.

Postmodern vs. realist. On each of the four subtests, no one matched the performance of "Gene Debs," with the exception of the two UK universities on the understanding science subtest. But this is because UK universities seem to harbor a lower percentage of postmodernists. The percentages are 24.5 and 27.0 in the US, but 15.4 and 10.9 in the UK. These figures are based on isolating individuals that scored 2.0 or below on the science subtest. A postmodern answer gets you zero. The criteria mean that they endorsed somewhere from five to ten of the ten postmodern answers (those who endorsed only five would have got their extra one or two points by guessing at the remainder). The item that actually asks them whether the universe is a blank slate gets a postmodern response (a low score) everywhere. The US and UK scores range from 0.25 to 0.37. Recall that guessing would give a score of 0.80! The Spanish University was worst at 0.12, which probably reflects the fact that postmodernism is pervaise on the continent, with predictable results.

The UK university samples are too small to infer much unless new studies confirm their results. Even if they stand, they do not show that UK university students are scientific realists (the percentages are tiny, at 9.4 and 3.2). The majority (75 to 87 percent) is muddled with no clear concept of science of any sort. There is a positive correlation between being a realist on the Science subtest and your critical competence elsewhere, as measured by your average score on the other three subtests. However, the correlation is small (below 0.300) except at the London University. As distinct from the UK universities, the London secondary school has 37 percent postmodernists, a very much higher figure. However, this may mean little: it is a girl's school and women may be more reluctant to "put down" pre – industrial societies than men. Moreover, as a good independent fees – paying school, half of the 48 students (average age 17.36 years) in its final year are of Korean ethnicity. See Box 7 for all results.

Box 7. FISC performance by subtest, total score, and realist vs. postmodern.

	G. Debs (Very Top)	NE – US (Very good)	SW – US (Above average)	London School	London Univer. (Top)	Red Brick (Above average)	Spain (Excellent)
	On the subtests below 7.0 = coping & 4.0 = guessing						
Economics	5.6	4.5	3.8	4.8	4.0	4.2	3.8
Soc. Science	5.1	4.2	4.8	4.4	5.0	4.3	4.7
Philosophy	6.4	5.7	5.2	5.1	6.0	6.2	5.9
Science	3.7	3.6	3.5	3.1	4.0	3.9	3.4
	On the FISC as a whole 28 = coping & 16 = guessing						
FISC median	20.0	18.0	17.0	17.0	18.5	18.5	18.0
FISC mean	20.8	18.0	17.3	17.3	19.0	18.5	17.8
FISC SD	4.63	3.86	3.05	3.55	4.92	3.78	NA
Number	185	115	61	48	32	30	96
	For criteria of Realist & Postmodern see text						
Realist	6.5 %	5.2 %	NA	2.1 %	9.4 %	3.3 %	NA
Muddled	69.0 %	67.8 %	NA	60.4 %	75.0 %	86.7 %	NA

Postmodern	24.5 %	27.0 %	NA	37.5 %	15.6 %	10.9 %	NA
Correlation	0.285	0.090	– –	0.222	0.460	0.245	– –
	On the items below the average from guessing = 0.80						
Blank slate	0.25	0.31	NA	0.29	0.35	0.37	0.12
Ratio items	1.04	0.90	NA	1.16	0.69	0.78	0.51

Universal deficiency about ratios. Sadly, I chose the London School because so many of its graduates go on to good London universities and I wanted to see whether they profited much from their university years. I wish it were more representative. Its students are better on the two items that test to see if students have grasped the concept of a ratio. The school gets 1.16 when the two are averaged, while students at the UK universities get 0.69 and 0.78 respectively (chance gives 0.80). But the real point is that perceiving the relevance of ratios is deficient everywhere (particularly in Spain). It is not that students are ignorant of what a ratio or percentage is. Rather when a problem calls for "ratio information," they do not spontaneously note its absence. When told that a new contraceptive pill causes more fatalities than pills in use, they do not ask how many more. And they do not ask how much more effective it is as a contraceptive, an abstract question that would take into consideration cutting deaths from abortion and child – birth.

Overall critical intelligence. Box 7 compares all seven institutions in terms of their total FISC score. The pecking order is a mean of 20.8 for "Gene Debs" (rated as a "very top" quality university), 19.0 for London University (top quality), 18.5 for red brick (above UK average), 18.0 for NE – US (very good), 17.8 for Spain (excellent), 17.3 for SW – US (above average), and 17.3 for the London School. The rough correspondence between the FISC Score and the quality of the institutions should not be taken too seriously given the small samples from the London and red brick universities. However, the total array of data at least suggests that no university, even those at the very top in quality, educates the whole person for critical intelligence.

Just to make sure, I assessed every individual's FISC score. No one anywhere showed reasonable mastery, that is, a score of 34 or above (out of a possible 40). A score of 34 indicates that the student knew the two correct responses for 15 out of the 20 items (thus getting 30 points with 4 as a bonus from guessing the rest). At "Gene Debs," only twelve of 185 got scores of 28 – 33, which runs from coping (knowing at least ten out of 20) to getting near – reasonable mastery (knowing 14 out of 20). There were a handful of similar individuals elsewhere (three out of a total sample of 286). I should note that the "Gene Debs" sample was only 3.22 percent of the senior class. If you take the two knocking at the door of reasonable mastery and multiply times 30, you get a total of 60. So 1.05 percent of the total class of 5,739 are very likely to develop overall critical intelligence, assuming they keep reading and thinking. The other 98.95 percent are not despite being elite university graduates.

Reality and rhetoric

Universities do nothing to test whether their graduates attain overall critical competence. Despite this, it is commonplace for US universities to claim that their curricula give graduates a real opportunity to emerge as a whole person. They make this assumption explicit when they justify what they call the "general education requirement" or the "liberal education" program. Here are some examples.

Harvard: "The General Education program prepares one for an *Ars Vivendi in Mundo* – an art of living wisely in the world." It consists of eight courses. First, four "Gen Ed" courses selected from each of four areas: (1) Aesthetics, Culture, Interpretation; (2) Histories, Societies, Individuals (Societies of the World and the US, acknowledging the importance of history); (3) Science and Technology in Society (explicitly places science and technology in a social context); and (4) Ethics and Civics (issues of public engagement and diversity). As to the last, they note that the ethics of self – driving cars may lead to very different conversations than do questions about race and identity in the plays of Shakespeare. In addition, students must take three departmental courses in Arts and Humanities, the Social Sciences, and the Natural Sciences, respectively. There is also a course in empirical and mathematical reasoning. These eight courses comprise 25 percent of the 32 – course degree (Harvard, 2016).

Yale: "Yale is committed to the idea of a liberal arts education through which students think and learn across disciplines, literally liberating or freeing the mind to its fullest potential. The essence of such an education is not what you study but the result – gaining the ability to think critically and independently and to write, reason, and communicate clearly – the foundation for all professions." Yale leaves students "free to choose from among hundreds of humanities, social science, and natural science courses throughout their undergraduate years" (Yale, 2017 – 2018). Nonetheless, Yale does require "breadth." Students must take at least two courses in the humanities and arts, two in the sciences, and two in the social sciences (rather than one each as at Harvard). They must also take two courses in quantitative reasoning, two courses in writing, and courses to further foreign language proficiency, which, depending on their level of accomplishment in foreign languages at entry may number one, two, or three courses. The average looks like a total of twelve courses, or 33 percent of a 36 course degree (Yale, 2017 – 2018). The main difference between Harvard and Yale is that the latter has no specific "Gen Ed" courses designed to get you to think across disciplines. But it fills the gap with more departmental courses that make one step outside a major and has an extra course in quantitative reasoning, adds two courses in writing, and includes a language requirement.

Princeton: "Princeton is committed to offering an academic program that allows each student to achieve a truly liberal education … all students [must have] a common language and common skills. It is as important for a student in engineering to engage in disciplined reflection on human conduct, character, and ways of life or to develop critical skills through the study of the history, aesthetics, and theory of literature and the arts, as it is for a student in the humanities to understand the rigors of quantitative reasoning and to develop a basic knowledge of the capabilities and limitations of scientific inquiry and technological development" (Princeton, 2017). Princeton's liberal education requirements resemble Harvard's. I was glad to see the inclusion of a course on epistemology and cognition. Like Yale, it has a language requirement and a writing requirement. I make the total number of courses students take outside their major fields at about eleven, or 35.5 percent of a 31 – course degree

These elite institutions all profess faith that their general education requirements will produce the whole person. If they are correct, they are far superior to what the other universities (at least those that have taken the FISC) can achieve. Virtually all American universities parrot this sort of rhetoric. Just why is it, then, that general education requirements fail?

Story of the Key Concepts

In my opinion, one cannot have the sort of critical intelligence required unless he has mastered certain "Key Concepts" that share a property virtually requiring critical analysis. There are other concepts that superficially resemble the Key Concepts but are actually wolves in sheep's clothing. They pretend to offer a method of analysis, but the method is either mere words or bankrupt in some other way. I call them "Anti – Keys" because, either by accident or design, they discourage use of critical analysis, usually by disparaging science because their users are uncomfortable with it or misunderstand it. Here is a brief list.

(1) **Universalizablity** (moral philosophy). One must state moral principles with logical consistency: one cannot praise generosity one day and condemn it the next. This may sound very humdrum, but it is surprising how well it clarifies moral debate. For example, it puts classical racists in an impossible position. They must either say that they would be subhuman if their skin turned black, or that they are superior to black people for some trait like intelligence, which invites evidence to the contrary.

(2) **Tautology/falsifiabilty** (logic). We abuse logic when we use it to give a fraudulent defense of something. This is done mainly by deceptive tautologies, that is, statements that appear to be claims about facts but actually banish facts from consideration. Take the claim that the Scots, unlike the English, are a noble people. If you point to a Scot who is a liar and a villain, you may be told, "Ah, he is nae a true Scot." The tautology, only good Scots count as Scots, is implicit. The honor of any group can be defended by a definition of the group that excludes the wicked. Nothing counts against the goodness of Scots. Karl Popper (1902 – 1994) used the concept of falsifiability to expose the misuse of tautologies. If anyone makes a claim of fact, ask him what evidence would count against it. If they say nothing counts, it is just empty words.

(3) **Naturalistic fallacy** (moral philosophy). As we have seen, one should be wary of arguments from facts to values. For example, the

mere fact that execution does not deter potential murders (if it is a fact) does not entail that capital punishment is wrong. You may have values (an eye for an eye) that render the fact indecisive.

(4) **Tolerance school fallacy** (moral philosophy). Perhaps you have heard someone say, "Do not be judgmental." This makes tolerance the supreme virtue, which is very odd given all the behavior we should not tolerate such as profiting from human misery. There is a fallacious argument that lends such an attitude respectability: that we should respect whatever anyone values because we cannot show that any value is better than another. It makes the attempt to justify your ideals suspect as a supposed source of intolerance. At present, postmodernists propagate it and seem to think they have invented it. It surfaced in William James and was embraced by anthropologists such as Ruth Benedict.

(5) **Contrary to nature.** This is an "Anti – Key." If you really grasp the naturalistic fallacy, you may be already immune to it. But it deserves analysis because it does so much mischief. By calling something "unnatural," the speaker labels it intrinsically wrong in a way that is supposed to bar investigation of its consequences, including beneficial ones. Nature never tells us that something is either right or wrong and, as Yuval Hariri points out, anything that can occur in nature is by definition "natural." Nature cannot condemn gays, but humans can.

(6) **Random sample** (social science). People are often skeptical of a poll because the sample is relatively small. They are mistaken. If the sample is truly random, it does not have to be very large. A random sample is one selected strictly according to chance. If it seems odd that this makes it reliable, note that the only alternative to chance is to introduce a bias. In 1936, the *Literary Digest* conducted a huge telephone poll showing that Alf Landon was going to beat Franklin Roosevelt for President. However, in those days, few other than the affluent had home telephones, and the affluent favored Landon. The less well – off were for Roosevelt, who won in a landslide.

(7) **Intelligence quotient or IQ** (social science). I include this because there is such a strong liberal bias against it. Recall the discussion of why educationists hate it – it ranks people hierarchically. Yet it is used

as a criterion (with the justification that it is better than any alternative) that determines the fate of many people, ranging from convicts on death row, to those who need a disability benefit, to those who want to be classified as gifted. To evaluate IQs, you will have to learn what a correlation is. And that is founded upon a concept called "regression to the mean."

(8) **Placebo** (medicine). Merely being given a sugar pill (that the patient hopes will work) often relieves the patient's symptoms. A placebo is something that has no beneficial effects aside from those conferred by the subject's faith in it. Without the notion of a placebo, a rational drugs policy would be overwhelmed by the desperate desire for a cure by those stricken with illness.

(9) **Charisma effect** (social science). When a technique is applied by a charismatic innovator or disciples fired by zeal, it may be successful for precisely that reason. Patients or students feel that they are being noticed and are inspired simply by the excitement of something new and positive.

(10) **Control group** (social science). A confounding variable is anything that may blur what you are trying to assess. We introduce an enrichment program for pre – school children at risk of being diagnosed as mentally retarded. They go to a "play center" each day that gives them "games" designed to raise IQ. Assume that at the end of the program, they have higher IQs. The question arises, what has raised their IQs? Was it really the educational program? Or was it all the other things that were done, such as getting them out of a dysfunctional home for six hours each day, the lunch they had at the play center, or the continual exposure to IQ – type tasks? The only way to nullify the effects of confounding variables is to use a control group. You must select a group from the same population and subject them to everything except the enrichment program. In passing, placebo and charisma effects are special cases of confounding variables.

(11) **The sociologist's fallacy** (social science). Sometimes we think we have made a fair comparison between groups but they become mismatched because they are part of a larger group. For example, we find that the IQs of professionals have dropped from one generation to

the next and assume that the professions have lost some of their allure (bright people are beginning to prefer other jobs). This ignores the fact that percentage of professionals has risen dramatically over 30 years: say it has increased from the top ten percent of the population to the top 30 percent. The top 30 percent cannot have the same intelligence advantage over the average person that the top ten percent does. So the decline in the IQ of professionals may have been precisely because more people wanted to be professionals while the number of people (and professionals) who can fit into the top ten percent is finite.

(12) **Percentage** (mathematics). It seems incredible that this important Key Concept made its debut in educated usage less than 150 years ago. The concept of a percentage is an introduction to the closely related concepts of a rate and a ratio. Its range is almost infinite. Recently in New Zealand, there was a debate over the introduction of a contraceptive drug that kills some women. It was pointed out that the extra fatalities from the drug amounted to 50 in one million (or 0.005 percent) while without it, an extra 1000 women (or 0.100 percent) would have fatal abortions or die in childbirth. It was heartbreaking how many journalists never got beyond telling their audience that it was a "dangerous" drug.

(13) **Market** (economics), which is essentially the law of supply and demand, provokes a deeper analysis of innumerable issues. If the government makes university education free, it will have to budget for more takers. If it approves a minimum wage, employers will find unskilled workers more expensive to hire. They may replace them with machines that employ skilled workers instead. This is not to imply that minimum wage legislation is wrong, but merely that it has to have advantages that outweigh its unwelcome consequences.

(14) **Reality is a text.** The phrase behind this Anti – Key comes from Jacques Derrida (1930 – 2004) and sums up the anti – science of our time. Those who use it are reluctant to state what it means because its plain meaning is ridiculous: that the physical universe is a blank slate on which we can impose whatever subjective interpretation we like. The evidence against the assertion, that all theories are equally explanatory/non – explanatory, was refuted every time Derrida put on his

spectacles. The theory of optics explained why they worked. This Anti –
Key distracts us from what science does (explaining the real world) into
the blind alley of classifying the different kinds of texts we "impose" on
the world. They are all supposed to be merely subjective, as if the text of
an up – to – date telephone book were not more valuable than the text of
an out – of – date one *because* it tells the truth about something, namely
the phone numbers people actually have. If all of this sounds absurd, that
is not my fault.

(15) **Alternative histories.** One Anti – Key leads to another. If
telling the history of the physical universe is subjective, why should not
the history of various peoples be subjective? We accept the history of a
people according to how they tell it, giving us black history, Maori
history, and so on. Political correctness gives this notion extra fuel. It is
considered demeaning if you tell a pre – scientific people that a scientific
approach to its past was more authoritative than their own legends. This
is enforced despite the fact that we smile condescendingly at individuals
who give us what we know are self – serving or garbled histories of their
own lives.

(16) **Alternative sciences.** This Anti – Key introduces confusion
because it says that the nature of science varies with the identity of who
does it. In fact, no matter who does it, there is only one scientific
method: understanding the universe and human behavior by using
theories, predictions based on those theories, and attempts at falsifying
those predictions by evidence. The Nazis spoke of Jewish physics as if it
was methodologically tainted. It was not. Radical feminists speak of
male science as an unacceptable symptom of patriarchy. It is not. Both
examples are simply physics done by Jews or males.

(17) **Intelligent design.** This Anti – Key tries to use God (or
gods) to explain what we see in the physical universe in general and the
variety of living things on earth in particular. As an alternative to
evolutionary biology, it is entirely counterproductive. It pretends to be a
method of investigating nature that discloses signs of order imposed by a
rational agent. In fact, it adds nothing to our knowledge of nature.
Whenever science is unable to give a full explanation of something, we

get nothing better than a monotonous refrain: "God designed it that way," however "intelligently."

(18), (19), & 20). **National interest** and **national affinities** and **national identity** (social science). If you wanted to understand a person's behavior, you would have ask yourself at least three questions. What does his self – interest dictate? Does he always seek his interests, or is he sometimes swayed by friendship (or enmity)? Or perhaps he is swayed by his self – image, whether he thinks of himself as unusually virtuous or knowledgeable or both? Theories of international relations ask the same questions about nations, and often all three must be answered to understand national behavior. The self – interest of Israel dictates survival and, if only power counted, absorbing the whole occupied West Bank. The national affinity between Israel and America is far greater than that between America and the Palestinians, which leads the US to support Israel even if one could argue that it is not in its interests to do so. The national identity of Israel is based on its own historical narrative of persecution and dictates (sometimes correctly) the expectation that any of its neighbors, if it could, would exterminate the Jewish people.

The knowledge trap

If these are the keys to functioning as a whole person, how can general education fail? To illustrate this point, I wish to offer on exactly what a particular Harvard major in History & Literature actually took throughout her scholarly career:

(1) Five courses in French literature from the Middle Ages to the present covering literature, the novel, art, and film with a course on David Foster Wallace.

(2) Four history courses with emphasis on the US and Latin America, Poland, and the Russian Empire and Eurasia.

(3) Four government courses about how to analyze politics, comparative politics, the military and foreign policy, and Central Asia and the Caucasus.

(4) Seven courses that took her well out of her major, in this case, principles of economics, introduction to psychology, African Studies, Francophone studies, and human rights, an ethics course on the existence

of God, a science course on Darwin, and some sort of course on the art of "noticing."

(5) A required writing course.

(6) A language requirement (Russian). And

(7) A course in empirical and mathematical reasoning.

These courses look wonderful and certainly every Key Concept I have listed would likely be covered in one course or another. But that is the problem. I will illustrate what I mean by recalling my own experience at the University of Chicago. It prided itself on its great books program, books that exposed all undergraduates to philosophy, history, social science, natural science, the humanities, and so forth. Its faculty had a coherent notion of what an educated person should know and adopted a curriculum that forbade too much specialization. The lecturers were themselves critically aware and made sure that all students were exposed to the concepts they needed at some point in the collection of courses they took. However, even this university failed to educate properly.

The problem is that professors commendably eager to impart knowledge and the Key Concepts may well get lost in the sheer volume of that knowledge. I am guilty as well. When I teach an introductory moral and political philosophy course, I do discuss the pitfalls of tautologies and the naturalistic fallacy. But there are so many fascinating things to teach about Plato's theory of being, his theory of knowledge, his psychology, and his theory of tyranny. And then there is Aristotle and Hobbes and Marx and Nietzsche. A colleague teaches students history with due emphasis on what distinguishes real history from mere tradition or self – serving myths. But there are the fascinating events that led to World War I, and how the class system structured strategic thinking and made the lives of ordinary soldiers cheap, and why the League of Nations was doomed.

Even if professors have identified the Key Concepts collectively (most unlikely), and even if each lecturer advises students to note and treasure the Key Concepts as he discusses them, they simply do not stand out from the background of the total content of the course, all of which will be on the examination. The concepts of one course do not appear in the next course, and those encountered in one year are absent the following year. Students would have to keep a special Key Concepts diary, to be compiled and consulted for its own sake, to be added to on the rare occasion when a new concept is encountered; they would have to sustain this as a regular chore throughout their undergraduate experience. What university actually advises this, rewards it, and keeps track of whether it is being done?

I am sure that general education is a good thing and should be retained. But what does it look like when translated into what an actual student takes? Look back at the student transcript: what she gets is a wonderful but uncoordinated smorgasbord.

Universities should offer a voluntary minor that any student can elect to take along with their major. Universities differ in terms of whether their undergraduate degree is three or four years, so I have sketched a three – year program.

Year one: Two specially designed courses from history and world literature, respectively. I would have the history course focus on how powerful nations affected weaker ones and the European wars of religion, beginning no later than 1600 to accommodate the Thirty Years War. The course would be skewed toward Europeans (who became powerful at that time) but also cover Ottoman expansion and introduce East Asian states as they became more powerful. The contemporary Middle East would serve to update the theme to the present. The literature course would select novels, poems, and popular history that expose students to the traditions, self – written history, experiences, and points of view that vary from culture to culture.

Crucial for each year: right from the start, the students would be told exactly what tools are essential. They would be told that the whole point is to absorb the seminal concepts that are capsule methodologies for critical analysis. Right from the start, they would keep a Key Concepts diary and all along these would be read and criticized.

Year two: Four specially designed courses, including moral philosophy with emphasis on flawed moral arguments; economics with emphasis on market economics as a tool of social analysis; social science methodology to learn a bit of real statistics and modeling; and international politics to learn how nations formulate foreign policy in terms of national interest, affinity with other peoples, and their self – image of their own history. There would now be even more material in the Key Concepts diary.

Year three: (the last year before graduation): A capstone course (worth double credit) that brings all of this together. It would actually use moral philosophy, social science, economics, and international politics to identify the kind of mistakes people and societies are prone to make (that something is natural, that rent controls make sense, and so forth). It will also discuss why the scientific method is preeminent in establishing factual and causal proposition and critique those who challenge its status. In addition, each department should include a capstone course for its own majors (most of whom will not have taken the minor recommended). It would focus explicitly on how their discipline can illuminate problems in areas usually considered outside its province.

Is there any chance that such a Key Concepts sequence could be adopted, as a general education requirement for all students: not at all. Academics are eager to attract students, and people "left out" of such a sequence would rave. Critics could be quite right in the sense that any list of Key Concepts is incomplete, and they could make a good case for another list that includes their own courses. But it should be feasible to sneak it in as a minor that would be entirely elective, like the rarely selected but historically important Politics, Philosophy, and Economics sequences.

Does this not mean we are settling for very little? Given how universities are constituted, the only realistic goal is to try to educate at least a few more students for critical intelligence (five percent would be a wonderful achievement). This can only be done in a series of courses that have the "key concepts" as their foundation and ever – present objective. Behind all the rhetoric of "all students" this and "all students" that, the universities are actually graduating almost no "whole individuals" at all.

Homily

The theme of this chapter is so important that I will risk making the moral explicit: The critical skills that mark the whole person must be taught as such. They must be taught: they will not take root simply because they appear in the curriculum, whether labeled general education or not. Indeed, often the "general education" label is off – putting to students who prefer to focus on courses in their majors or that interest them, while instructors tend to prefer to teach courses in their specializations rather than prescribed courses assigned to them.

Preparing for after graduation

We cannot tolerate the fact that more and more students graduate without the habit of serious reading. Universities should offer all students incentives, and perhaps more importantly, the time to develop the habit of reading books for pleasure: perhaps make up a list of a 1,000 books of substance, mainly novels but including poetry, films, and good books of popular history (Flynn, 2010, 2016c). Students would be examined each year (after their other exams are over) on say 20 books. Googling book plots should not be enough to pass and earn the incentive. A student who passed the exam each year would get a fancy "L" on their diploma standing for "literate." The record of their performance would go on their transcript year by year (pass/fail) and if they earn it, the transcript would state that they have received a "certificate of literacy."

The trip to Mars

Many of our students will advance truth, create beauty, fight for justice, practice tolerance (as they see it), and add something to the sum total of human happiness. Very few will achieve the great good of human autonomy. Few will acquire the tools to rise above what their leaders and the media do to define them and the world in which they live. Few will become either whole men or good citizens.

American universities have a problem that does not exist in any other advanced nation. They are presented with many students whose minds are more akin to those of the late nineteenth century than to those conditioned by the rise of the scientific ethos over the last 150 years. Recent polls show that 42 percent of Americans think God created humans in their present form within the last 10,000 years: no change since Gallup first asked the question in 1982. People are investing millions in theme parks that show humans and dinosaurs coexisting. In 2016, no candidate for the Republican nomination for President dared to say that he believed in evolution. This antiquated mentality used to exist in all nations but was eroded by modern science: today you can find only a few such people in England, France, Spain, Italy, Canada, Australia, and New Zealand, and they are marginalized eccentrics.

What happened to America? Why did the old mindset persist deep in the psyches in a large minority of Americans while it died elsewhere? If I can find no explanation in the literature, I intend to address this problem in another book.

I have emphasized the critical skills our graduates lack. However, I have merely mentioned in passing that they can have these skills and still be deficient in the knowledge that must accompany them: the knowledge that comes from a postgraduate experience of reading history and across cultures. In the next chapter, I will try to show why this is so necessary. I will also try to defend something I have assumed all along by referring to human autonomy as a great good: that it actually exists.

Part 5
Justification and advice

14
In praise of autonomy

Free speech inclusive of freedom of inquiry is the best road to knowledge, particularly the kind of knowledge that gives individuals autonomy. This assumes that "autonomy" is a worthwhile goal, which presumes that the concept has been fully clarified and justified. I have examined it only on the psychological level, where its justification may seem self – evident: it allows us to rise above the indoctrination of time and place and make up our own minds about what is important. I will now analyze it on three levels: the psychological, the sociological, and the ontological. The last will mean some excursion into philosophy proper. Readers who have no soul may wish to skip it as "irrelevant." But even on the psychological level there is more to be said.

The psychological level

Recall the recent graduates we quoted in the last chapter: "I can't form a really solid opinion;" " I think that getting out of wars would help, but I guess I don't know enough to say very surely what would happen;" "I don't know what direction the country should go, let alone what direction it will go." On many subjects, they have no more autonomy than a medieval serf: "I think I am treated rather badly. But the Church says God has ordained that I will be saved if I do my duty as a serf. Sometimes I wonder if this is true but it bewilders me to try to think about what the world would be like without serfs."

Graduates have no real autonomy if, in area after area, they cannot criticize the narrative that their political leaders and the media feed them about the contemporary world. These students may well be more cynical than serfs about what they are fed ("they are all liars") and thus more prepared to be autonomous. But, as we have seen, they lack the tools they need to be critical.

Here I want to explore another facet of psychological autonomy: the students also need some knowledge to go with those tools. They can have them all and be ignorant of relevant cross – cultural and historical knowledge. They may have taken world history as part of their general education requirement, but it was just a story about the past with nothing highlighted as important for critique of the present. They probably do not remember much of it, much less developed the habit of applying its lessons to the contemporary world.

The knowledge elite

Perhaps only a small intellectual elite can have critical intelligence. But does America have even a small elite that advises presidents, runs the State Department, edits and writes for the media, and punches above its weight when conversation turns to public issues among university faculty, school teachers, corporate leaders, lawyers, doctors, and so forth? Remember how potent elite opinion can be in terms of what is possible for a nation. In nineteenth century Britain, it became almost impossible to find a dinner table at which a defender of the slave trade was not on trial. Despite the spread of tertiary education, I believe that America by and large lacks the kind of elite that is capable of critical intelligence beyond narrow vocational problems.

I have chosen the Middle East to dramatize the role played by ignorance of history and literature. Prior to the invasion of Iraq in 2003, how many Americans had read contemporary novels from the Middle East or even a popular history of Western interventions in that area? How many could even find it on a map? When asked to support the huge cost and loss of life (mainly slaughter of the peoples of the Middle East but several thousand American soldiers as well), the best of our citizens might actually want to know something about that area.

The role of history

I will portray how a properly educated person might reject US policy, which means arguing a case against it. This case is meant to show *only* how the government would have to debate with a critically minded citizen rather than manipulating a mute and pliable one. They would say that a little knowledge is a dangerous thing. That assumes they have knowledge that will overcome mine as the debate proceeds. If they can do that, they can still thank me for helping them to move toward knowledge from right opinion. They will be happy that they can answer all objections to their position.

Knowledge of the Thirty Years War of 1618 – 1648 would be a good starting point. Germany was divided into many smaller states, some ruled by Catholic sovereigns, others by Protestants. From city to city both sides committed unspeakable outrages against dissidents as well as costly military campaigns. Half of Germany's population had been killed by the war's end. Posit an enlightened Turkish Sultan in Istanbul who, unlike actual Sultans, did not want to conquer Europe for annexation, but simply wanted to do good. Why not send in a Turkish army to punish the worst offenders, teach Catholics and Protestants to love one another, and nation – build? When you describe this possibility to students, some say, "Well gee, if the Turks could do all of those things why not?"

Anyone asked to support US policy should be able to name at least one Western intervention in the Middle East that did more good than harm. This means that they should have answers to Robert Fiske's theme in his *The Great War for Civilization: The Conquest of the Middle East* (2005). America is fighting the fifth Afghan war. The first four, three incursions by the British, one by the Russians, killed many Afghans and quite a few Europeans (the Russians lost 13,000 soldiers killed). When these nations departed, they left hardly a trace. Afghans went right on having their own history.

The Pashtuns live in the South (Taliban country), the Tajiks, Hazaras, and Uzbeks in the North, all of whom have little love for the others. If America knows how to nation build there, it has learned a trick that the Afghans have never learned: "Me against my brother, my brother and I against my cousin, my cousin and I against the world." The Afghans have never imagined anything as bizarre as a democracy: the notion that my tribe will be voted down simply because there are more people in another tribe is absent. An Afghan faction is happy enough if foreign troops strengthen its hand in the short run. If they stay too long, they are universally hated.

A properly educated person should know the history of "American exceptionalism," America's conviction that it is a uniquely virtuous nation whose behavior does no harm as long as its motives are pure. Has any nation, other than by invading and slaughtering the population, done more harm in recent years than America has done to Iraq? It had a dictator (Saddam Hussein) who was a Sunni and disliked by the majority Shiites. He had to buy acquiescence. He resorted to repression, of course, but mainly he used oil money to promote policies that at least maintained stability and achieved such feats as the improvement of women's rights, education, health care (he was given UN awards for his performance).

America supported his attempt to add to his luster by attacking Iran, connived in and lied about his use of chemical weapons, and after he had been fought to a stalemate, decided he was a potential source of terror, and levied economic sanctions. As usual, these sanctions left the elite unmoved but did harm to the people they ruled. The economic burden of sanctions plus the cost of the war meant that Saddam Hussein had less money to buy tolerance and he became increasingly repressive. By invading Iraq, America started a civil war that has cost perhaps one million deaths before leading to the rise of ISIS. For detailed documentation of lives lost, see Flynn, 2012b, pp. 124 – 130. This nation has literally been set back a generation or two in terms of economic development.

The role of literature

Reading some literature from the Middle East helps one picture what the people of these nations experience, rather than our seeing them as anonymous human beings likely to resemble Americans in the near future. Qais Akbar Omar's *A Fort of Nine Towers* (2013) tells the horrible history of atrocities that divide the Afghan ethnic groups. In Kabul, when they could not shoot each other in the streets, they shot people at random and even shot stray dogs, just for fun. The hero laments the end of communist rule and Taliban rule as periods of relative peace.

Isaac Bashevis Singer's *The Slave* (1963) and Amos Elon's *The Pity of it All* (2002) tells you what Jews experienced in Europe and Germany long before the Holocaust. Amos Oz's *A Tale of Love and*

Darkness (2004) is indispensable for understanding the passion, blood, sweat, and tears that went into founding the state of Israel in 1948. These books help explain why all negotiations to limit the expansion of Israel are fruitless – see Box 8 below.

Box 8. Without any affinity between Israelis and Arabs, and with mutually antagonistic narratives about their history, both pre – modern and recent, there is no trust. At present, the only thing that can check Israeli expansion is countervailing power. Only one Muslim nation in the Middle East has the size, unity, and economy to break Israel's nuclear monopoly and rival her conventional armed forces – enter Iran. We now see why so many want America to bomb Iran to rubble. My policy: Leave the Shiites (led by Iran) and Sunnis (led by Saudi Arabia) to fight it out in the Middle East. Over the next 30 years, they may get tired of it just as the Catholics and Protestants eventually did. If the Russians are foolish enough to intervene, let them. Send no troops; no bombing; no arms to anybody; and tell Israel to exit the West Bank (with an absolute guarantee of security against invasion) or go it alone. Once again, my suggestions are subject to rebuttal in the light of better knowledge. But knowledge is the key word. Ignorant sentiment will not do.

David Grossman's *The Yellow Wind* (1988) tells you how horrible it is to live as an Arab in the Israeli occupied West Bank. Sayed Kashua's *Let it be Morning* (2006) gives a nuanced Arab perspective on how Palestinians living in the occupied territory differ from those living in Israel. Orhan Pamuk's *Snow* (2005) lays bare the depth of the sectarian versus religious division that troubles Turkey.

Congress is now outraged at Saudi Arabia because of the brutal murder of a journalist. If any of them had read Robert Lacy's *Inside the Kingdom* (2009), they would never have thought of that nation as benign. The notion that we side with the good guys in the Middle East and oppose only the bad guys has suffered a blow. As it is, we are complicit in the terrible suffering Saudi Arabia has inflicted on Yemen: at least 10,000 killed, cholera (at least 2300 dead), two million children with acute malnutrition, 85,000 children under the age of five starved to death thus far, a total of 8.4 million Yemenis on the verge of starvation.

If you want more books that might compromise our "innocence," Flynn (2010 & 2016c) gives a list of 400.

Message

This should be enough to show that knowledge of history and literature is no hindrance to being a good citizen. Even a graduate capable of critical intelligence must love to read widely. The basic tools of moral debate, social science method, market analysis, international politics, and reverence for science are not enough to make a good citizen. But there is no reason why learning should stop at graduation. On the psychological level, gaining autonomy is not easy. But it undeniably exists. On the next two levels, I will examine points of view that tend to ignore or devalue psychological autonomy entirely.

The sociological level

Social science partitions individual differences in intelligence between genes and environment. It uses either the twin method (identical twins raised apart in different families) or the age – table method (Flynn, 2016a). Both of these show a similar progression as children age. As children enter school and make friends with other children, two things happen. Family environment fades away in favor of current environment. And current environment becomes more and more correlated with genes, as school sorts children out in terms of genetic promise and as the children show like being attracted to like (bright children associate with brighter peers).

If social science shows that for every person, genes achieve a perfect correlation with the current environment, what is left of human autonomy after that? All of our conduct is determined by the combination of genes and environment; we do not choose our parents (our genes); we do not choose our environment (our genes choose it for us). Anyone familiar enough with the twin literature should be a genetic determinist.

The answer lies in a factor that is undervalued because it is dismissed as luck. At all ages, the correlation between genes and current environment is not really perfect because of the luck of life history. Being bright is no guarantee you will not be dropped on your head and being below average is no guarantee you will. At 18, you can be drafted out of an environment commensurate with your genes and thrown into the inferior environment of cutting throats in the forest. There is also good luck: happening to marry a partner who lifts you into a new peer group that takes you to an environment that is superior to one commensurate with your genes. Therefore, at all ages, there is an unshared environment that explains 20 percent of IQ variance (Flynn, 2016a, p. 22; Haworth et al., 2010). This is in advanced nations: in Syria with its wars, in the Sudan with its famines, life is much less secure and the frequency of chance events that determine one's fate is much higher.

But as long as this is labeled a luck factor, it seems to have nothing to do with autonomy. Pure luck at least just happens to you and is not under your control. But it is wrong to think of this 20 percent as mere luck. We do not know how to partition it, but at least half of it may reflect human autonomy. When a professor volunteers for the army, he has *chosen* an inferior environment. When someone who did poorly at school and is trapped in a humdrum environment decides to go back to university at age 35, he has *chosen* a superior environment.

Message

Assume that the school leaver's genetic promise would put him at an IQ of 130 (top two percent) were he to have a matching current environment (also top two percent) and that life history leaves him stuck in the average environment. Then his current environment is at least 30 IQ points below his "target" on the environmental scale. If the correlation between environment and IQ is 0.33, he has lost ten IQ points (30 x 0.33). That correlation is dictated by ten percent of IQ variance explained (the square root of variance equals the correlation; and the square root of 0.10 is 0.33). Therefore, if going to varsity affords him a commensurate environment, he will go from an IQ of 120 to 130.

His voluntary action has allowed him to leapfrog from the 90th to the 98th percentile, or over four – fifths of the people who were above him. Despite the dominant role of genes in twin studies, human autonomy is alive and well. If you try less than most people, you will handicap yourself with a worse current environment. If you try harder, you will reap the advantage of a better one. I have chosen intellectual abilities as an illustration because we have the data, and because they are the principal ones we use to acquire knowledge.

The ontological level

How do we know that what we do on the psychological level, all the trying and not trying to attain autonomy, is not really determined after all, perhaps by deep causes buried in our brain physiology?

The present self as caused first cause

The issue of free will turns on whether the present self makes morally significant choices. By the "present self" I mean you at this moment deciding whether to visit a sick friend or go to an escapist film. As Kant pointed out, on the conscious level, you must make your choices as if you were free. You cannot just sit and wait for a billiard ball to knock you towards the hospital or toward the movie theater. But is that mere appearance? The question is whether all such appearances are deceptive because an underlying reality determines all of our decisions; perhaps it is our brain physiology. I contend (along with Kant) that if we are determined, we cannot be praised or blamed for our decisions. For example, we do not blame a clock for striking the hour ten minutes early. Even if it had a conscious life and the illusion of free choice, I would not blame it.

Ever since Gilbert Ryle coined the phrase, those of us who believe that people make choices that are not determined have been accused of believing in a "ghost in a machine." We are supposed to turn the conscious mind into a thing of mystery that lives in the brain but has no connection with it except to give it orders. This is not the case. I believe that the human mind is a functional system with both unconscious (whatever is going on in the brain) and conscious (whatever you are thinking about at this moment) components Sometimes my brain is active when I am not aware of it: whole pages of a book break through to consciousness already composed. Sometimes what is going on in my consciousness, like anger, has effects it cannot control throughout my body, such as stomach pains. But the concept of free choice does mean this: my brain is capable of causing states of mind that have the peculiar attribute of autonomy.

I see nothing odd in this because the stuff out of which the physical universe is made has sprung many surprises as it has evolved. At one time, it was too hot and active to allow for matter in the form of things made out of compounds. Then long – chain carbon compounds came along that were self – replicating, alive. Then some organisms composed of the right compounds achieved consciousness. Then some of those achieved a sense of personal identity. Now perhaps some have achieved a conscious personal identity that can make choices without interference (to some degree) from anything else. At every stage, a case for incoherence could have been made: how can inanimate matter possibly spawn something living?; how can matter which is unaware spawn something that is aware?; how can matter which has no "self" spawn something which has self – awareness?; how can something which obeys laws spawn an awareness that is free?

Free choice

The concept of free choice is perfectly coherent and easily stated. Free choice, to the extent that it is real, would be a caused first cause. The state of mind in which I make free choices is an effect of course. My awareness of choices began at a certain age and will disappear when I die. But once it is caused, it has the power to alter the flow of the world from past to future. If free choice exists, the present self has a genuine choice between (at least) two alternatives and creates a future that would not otherwise have existed. If all of us decide to pick up hitchhikers as an act of charity, the world will be different: more hitchhikers will get to their destinations quicker and some extra lives (when hitchhikers kill people) will be lost.

I quote Father Michael Maher (1860 – 1918), the Jesuit psychologist: "Besides the motives felt, and besides the formed habits or past self, is there not a *present self* that has a part to perform in reference to them both? Is there not a causal self, over and above the caused self (the character) that has been left as a deposit from previous behavior?" (Maher, 1940, 410). As this implies, free choice assumes that the will is to some degree "self – generating." This is not to deny that the free choices of the past, along with many other things, affect the performance of the present self. The more good choices I make, the more I enhance "will power," the more the present self will find it easier to choose good over evil. Choices affect character. When I act out of regard for moral principles, I enliven my commitment to them.

Is free will worth having?

Daniel Dennett (1984) argues against the dignity of free will on the grounds that it is irrelevant to what we admire most: someone who always does good. However, we do not always admire a thing that always does good. Aspirin is an almost perfect medication (unless abused by way of an overdose). It does not inspire admiration because it deserves no credit for its effects. I admire people who find it easy to be good but only because they deserve some credit for what they have become. Their present selves over time made a whole series of choices rightly (some of them very difficult), and the result was the strength of will to do what moral principles (more and more deeply ingrained) entail. Thanks to the present self, these decisions are today virtually automatic

The fact that the road to sanctity is paved with free choices is crucial. We take this into account when we give the highest praise to those who had the most difficult paths. For some, raised humanely with few temptations, the road is not easy because it is never easy. But we admire most those who became outstandingly good despite adversity.

Compatibilism

Compatibilists think that they can both explain all human behavior scientifically and still believe in free will, or at least a will deserving of moral praise or blame. They and I have some common ground. We agree that clocks differ from people. Clocks are unconscious, while people are aware of certain thought processes when they make decisions, that is, they entertain considerations, weigh them, know that nothing will happen unless they make decisions and so forth. Where we part company is whether meaningful freedom sets limits on scientific explanation. If I return a borrowed book to a friend, the universe is such that he can read it that night. If I do not return it, the universe is different in the sense that he cannot. Which is to say that a free choice creates a radical discontinuity from one state of the universe to the next, indeed, this is true of every free choice that people make throughout the world. Which is to say that much human behavior and its effects escape causality in the radical sense that they escape any scientific explanation.

Wittgenstein and free will

Wittgenstein asked what value being free possesses in the sense of being able to do other than one does. I refuse a bribe. What would it mean to say I could have accepted it? I could do so only if I were morally corrupt and who would want to be told that? In rebuttal, this is a case in which I did something right. The sterility of being able to do other than one does is less clear if I have done something wrong. Let us say I took the bribe. Would no one welcome the possibility that she could have behaved like a better person? Would no one prefer to believe that the present self had some influence here, rather than believing that this kind of behavior was beyond its control?

Did Wittgenstein never regret anything he did? He was so arrogant that he turned every session of the Cambridge Philosophical Society into a monologue. He ruined the lives of students by advising them to abandon philosophy and become laborers. He wished to add his personal bit of killing to World War I, a war that had little honor on any side. If he did not welcome the possibility of alternatives to his behavior, many others will wish that his "character" had been free to choose otherwise and that he had actually done so.

These philosophers of language do not analyze it very well. The following is a typical example of moral discourse. Imagine I steal something from a friend. He confronts me and says, "I am disappointed in you." Under the presumption of my freedom, the meaning is quite straightforward: "You and I both know you could have done the right thing." It is a clear indictment that I am morally blameworthy.

From Wittgenstein's perspective, the assertion becomes convoluted. My friend should say, "I am disappointed with myself." After all, if my friend had made a proper estimate of my character, the theft was predictable. He is not disappointed in the *real* me at all. He is disappointed in an *illusory* me who never existed. He was only surprised at my decision because of self – deception about my character. Whose fault is that? Certainly not mine. His assertion really means, "I now see you as you really are." However, this does not obviate the fact that he has purged his assertion of moral blame. He now sees he can expect worse acts on my part than he had suspected, but he has been robbed of the ability to say that I made the wrong choice. There was no free choice.

Forever in limbo

What might count as evidence for or against free will? How could science decide the question of whether its own sway is unlimited, or whether it is circumscribed by the existence of present selves creating uncaused outcomes? I suspect that it could do this only if brain physiology came to the rescue and gave us the ability to predict all human conduct, particularly conduct where we have the "illusion" of free choice. I think that all would agree that brain physiology will not settle the question in the foreseeable future.

This creates a problem about what to do on the interim. We must decide whether the moral indignation we feel when someone deceives us about the time is any more appropriate than when a clock deceives us about the time. I frankly feel that to drain the dimension of praise for choosing well and blame for choosing badly from personal relationships would be a charade on my part. I could tell myself I was doing it but only because I did not really feel that I was doing it. But I am not so arrogant as to assume that those who adopt a different policy are acting in "bad faith." It would be just as rational for a couple to regard one another as determined and they might find that amenable. Both members would know that a display of moral indignation should be interpreted as a strong intolerance of the substance of the partner's behavior. Both would know that an apology should be interpreted as a plea that the behavior in question is atypical and unlikely to occur again.

In any event, determinism on the ontological level, say on the level of the deep causes of brain physiology, is an ever – present possibility that we might have to face. And unless the compatibilists are correct, it compromises the value of autonomy: it no longer makes no sense to give people moral credit because their motives are pure.

In praise of trying

We can now pass an overall judgment on the status of autonomy. The key is the distinction between giving an individual moral approval for *their choices* (makes no sense without free will), and estimating the worth of *their behavior* if it seeks a goal that enhances human nature (if its consequences are humane).

Recall Kant's point: whether or not we are actually determined in all our choices, when actually choosing we have no option other than to treat ourselves as if we were free. If you wait for a billiard ball to knock you toward the hospital (to visit a friend) or toward a movie theater (to enjoy yourself), you will do neither. The best example is the "tiger example." You are in a corridor. You perceive a tiger entering the far end of the corridor, and can only escape by running down it to open a door that leads outside. You know the night watchman remembers to lock the door about half of the time. Even though it is determined whether you will escape or not, you had better run in the hope you are destined to escape. In other words, even if we are determined by deep causes, this does nothing to undermine the necessity of trying.

Take the "great goal" of running a marathon. Deep causes may determine how hard you will try every step of the way. But if you want to run a good time, you had better keep trying every step of the way. The same is true when you train for a marathon. If you are running to raise money for the blind, you get no moral credit – the deep causes mean you had no real choice. But you should do it anyway because you have humane ideals. Similarly, when you strive to achieve the knowledge that will give you the autonomy to liberate yourself from your place and time, you get no moral credit. But what a wonderful goal. Failing to try to achieve it is equivalent to assuming you have been determined to be ignorant. Take a chance on trying hard and finding out that you have been determined to achieve this kind of autonomy.

Message

Determinism on the ontological level leaves a moral void. But lack of moral approval does nothing to dim the luster of human autonomy on the sociological and psychological levels. It is good that the twin studies show that lots of people try to add to their mental competence and knowledge and that they are successful. It is good that when you make the effort to learn, you can transcend your place and time. It is good to know that you are at a free speech university, one that gives you the best chance to avoid dogma in favor of knowledge. It is good when you try to rise above the level of a medieval serf.

15
The three frogs

When I discussed the teachers of teachers, I criticized their hyper – egalitarian ideology (denial of human genetic diversity) and their pretensions: that they can produce a super teacher and need not acknowledge the limitations of those sitting in their classrooms. This raises the question as to whether the university as a whole is not guilty of something similar.

Radical reform of the university

In the hard sciences, before students can progress to really demanding courses, they must prove themselves by showing competence in preliminary courses with high failure rates and demanding prerequisites. As signaled (Chapter 1), this book deals mainly with the humanities and the social sciences. These areas offer many courses from which only a gifted student can profit much, and simply ignore the fact that most of the students that pass have learned little or nothing of value. We disguise this absurdity by giving them high grades as if they had learned something. Far more rational would be to treat the first year as an entrance exam and weed out two – thirds of our students on the grounds that that they really ought to be somewhere else.

I am known for higher standards than most. I assign grades as follows: A+/A = may be capable of developing into a university lecturer (often some real breadth of reading and critical intelligence); A – = can read and compare serious material but nothing original; B+/B/B – = can grasp some demanding ideas but with varying degrees of success; C+/C/C – = there is enough to show they made an honest effort; Fail – did practically nothing or (more rarely) clearly lack the vocabulary to read and understand a *New York Times* editorial. Usually my advanced courses have a superior intake. They are not required, so there is self –

selection because of my reputation for demanding something to get a decent grade.

Even so I would say that only one – third (self – selection sometimes increases this) really learn much; and when I taught required courses at the first – year level, the proportion dropped to about one – fifth. How do we actually behave as lecturers? Do not most of us simply "forget" that most of our students lack either the capacity or the interest to learn what we teach and go right on teaching Plato, epistemology, comparative government, Friedman, poetry, literary criticism, historiography, the mechanics of evolution, social anthropology, and so forth?

Most university lecturers know something about genetic diversity. We know in our hearts that most of our students just do not have the capacity to cope with what we offer them. However, we also know that our jobs depend on the size of the student roll. The students in question may be bored but so long as they get a decent grade with little effort, they are untroubled. Some for the first time become thoroughly socialized in the speech and manners of the middle and professional classes, which is a solid benefit that has little to do with learning. The darker side is the money this kind of holiday costs and lecturers just going through the motions. In addition, there is the fact that if the students were elsewhere, they could be learning vocational skills that would give them better job prospects and better meet the needs of the current economy and polity.

Enter Charles Murray and his book *Real Education*. Murray (2008) contends that only about ten percent of the general population can profit from demanding university courses, not just science and math courses but also humanities and social science courses with real content (setting aside all the junk courses in the curriculum). His estimate corresponds to my own: the top 50 percent go to my university, my courses attract the top 30 percent, only one – third of these get B or better, which equals about ten percent of the general population (30 percent times one – third equals ten).

Murray offers recommendations that have the potential to reduce the number of university students. More relevant vocational training could be offered in either high school or vocational schools. Guidance counselors should stop pushing every student to aspire to university and emphasize the pay and conditions that non – elite vocational work provides. Patterned on the bar exam and the CPA (Certified Public Accountant) exams, a whole range of certification exams should be offered nation – wide with standards high enough to satisfy employers. These would range from the skilled trades to lower management (hospital management, management of the judicial system), computer competence, social work, nurses, engineering technology, and so forth. Employers would stop requiring a BA (which for them is simply a guarantee that you are reasonably bright and have some perseverance) in favor of hiring those who actually have proven competence for the job on offer.

Every one of Murray's proposals that offers young people an option other than university should be adopted. But he acknowledges factors that signal that the composition of university students will change only gradually. Young people want the pleasures of that four – year holiday and the prestige of the degree. Their parents will continue to gamble their money on the hope that university just might place their children higher on the occupational status ladder. If economists are right and conceptually demanding jobs are gradually liquidated (Florida, 2014), both may grudgingly face reality. But do not forget deeply ingrained attitudes dating from Thorsten Veblen (1899) to Morton Grodzins (1956). It is not accidental that the middle class wears the white collar (advertising that they do not get their hands dirty) or that angels are robed in white or that those admired most are those who get maximum return for doing the least.

It is not easy to predict the psychological effects of upgrading the academic competence of university students. This is particularly true when it comes to whether students and faculty will tolerate free speech, whether various departments will have restrictive Walden Codes, and whether universities will actually try to educate the whole person. You could make a case for lower levels of tolerance. Therefore, I will take universities and students as they are and ignore what they might become if the university were turned into an honors stream.

Universities as they are

Are the current students who espouse the hyper – egalitarian dogma beyond redemption? Recall our philosophical analysis of how we must defend our ideals (Chapter 11). After students graduate, some will try to link their value proclivity toward equality with the real world by way of bridging propositions: propositions about what would actually benefit people in general. They will find it a sobering experience. Either they cannot do it, in which case their ideals will never become a functional morality; or they will do it, in which case they will have to face the test of science, no matter what they put forward, whether it be the welfare state, or affirmative action, or the minimum wage. For now they can shelter behind the emptiest bridging proposition of them all: would it not be nice if no one offended anyone? As Eugene Debs said, "love one another" may improve manners, but it is utterly bankrupt politically.

Is the university a wounded animal beyond cure? Humanity has invented no other institution in which intelligent debate is more prominent. Participants search for truth under conditions better than anywhere else. But before ills can be remedied, they must be diagnosed. I will not summarize the substance of this book but collect its recommendations.

The whole person

The true goal should be to educate at least a few students for critical intelligence. The universities should recognize that they are not even doing this. If what I have recommended is to do any good, there must be a course or courses explicitly based on the Key Concepts that demonstrate to students their widespread application (see Flynn, *How To Improve Your Mind*, 2012d). I risk repetition by restating the homily from Chapter 14: The critical skills that mark the whole man must be taught as such. They must be taught: they will not take root simply because they appear in the curriculum whether it be labeled general education or not.

Below the best

My homily may be taken to heart only by academics in the better universities. A wise colleague has written me about the limitations that exist below that level.

Aiming at mediocrity. "I meet with great explicit and implicit resistance from colleagues and students when I try to free up the creative process. Indeed, as deputy HOD [head of department] presently, I have noted that all of my ideas in this domain have been deliberately ignored and scuppered by colleagues at the level of program director."

Teaching for mediocrity. "There is a large group of academics who feel that they have failed to make it (otherwise they would be at a better, higher ranked institution) and they carry much bitterness about this. A big chunk of their self – esteem is tied up in denigrating the student intake and claiming they are not capable of anything other than rule following."

Rewarding mediocrity. "Awards are given to the 'best' teachers each year. Without exception those who win are those who court student popularity. The result [in psychology] is students who are chronically anxious about statistics, but who have learnt only how to answer a specific kind of assessment. When they come up against difficult cases they inevitably fail to make any headway with them and often write them off."

Summary. "It is monumentally depressing to watch this, as I have for the last 23 years. I am finding it difficult to like many of my colleagues." As for my personal opinion, the lesson is that each university must decide whether it is going to keep trying or throw in the towel. The latter can still copy Harvard's mission statement about the whole man, but do not pretend that you really believe it.

Colleges of education, Black Studies, Women's Studies.

I have advocated two departments of black studies one controlled by the "radicals" and one by the conservatives. Charter schools are a big part of the answer as to how to break the hold of radical egalitarianism and progressive education on teacher training and the schools. This will not be enough unless we make teaching a real profession and attract a surplus of good applicants rather than a dearth. Something short of a two – departments solution may do for Women's Studies. On the divisional level, there should be provision for a major in Women's Studies that students can take by selecting courses offered by traditional departments.

The appointments committee should approve new staff based on a record of scholarly achievement with other "qualifications" largely ignored. Class representatives should be able to bring forward complaints that some students are privileged over others on arbitrary grounds. There should be provision for anonymous complaints by individuals that go directly to the Divisional level. The latter should be true of all departments, of course.

The Walden Codes

Professional codes are effective in sending deviant staff to Coventry. They reflect strong feelings within several departments. They veto cultural relativism within Anthropology, ethnic causes within Sociology, IQ ranking within Education, and discussion of race and IQ within Psychology. Sending all staff on a course on the history and philosophy of science might bring resistance. The solution lies with hiring better and better staff, staff more likely to be aware of what assumptions and methodology really progress knowledge in their area. This may seem to be an option only for the very best departments, but professors at those departments sometimes tend to dominate the journals and can shift opinion

The student mob

Even if the university adopts a mission statement that endorses free speech, campus culture prevails, as it did at Yale. When students arrive, they are immersed into a student body that knows it can limit free speech whenever it mobilizes itself to do so. This is compounded by the fact that a sizable number of academics do not believe in free speech themselves and lead or at least tolerate the student mob. The minds of both are closed against public debate, open classroom discussion, and research on important questions about race, class, gender, and current politics.

The staff that really believes in a free speech should identify one another and begin the slow process of habituating the rest toward at least tolerance. They would face fierce opposition if they attacked these staff head – on. Following Aristotle, they must begin the slow process of accustoming the recalcitrant toward a new set of dispositions step by step.

The first step would be to establish a tradition of an annual series of lectures. There would be perhaps four, each of which would explore an unmentionable topic: genetic differences between the races; genetic differences between the genders; the nature of ethnicities and subcultures; Israel and settlement of the West Bank. For extra appeal, perhaps one about the thesis that Hitler was unaware of the extermination camps. The committee that selects the speakers might have to be trained by the ACLU (American Civil Liberties Union) or FIRE (Foundation for Individual Rights in Education). Students would at least get used to hearing Charles Murray on campus. I would be happy to take him on for a third time – see Box 9.

> **Box 9.** For the first debate at the American Enterprise Institute on November 28, 2006, google "Flynn versus Murray." For the second debate on December 2, 2007 at the Manhattan Institute, google "Flynn Murray Pro – science: IQ in the *New Yorker*" to get a somewhat pro – Flynn summary. The Manhattan Institute no longer seems to have the video on the net. A pity in that I thought I did better the second time around.

Second, lecturers should confront these issues in their courses and support one another whenever the inevitable complaints occur. I give a course, half of which is devoted to IQ differences between races, the genders, and classes. Other lecturers court controversy. "Colleagues, my PSYC 466 paper involves a debate series in which students bring their new knowledge and research to bear on controversial issues. I invite anyone interested to hear the debate and vote on the winners: 14 September – Are religious people more moral?; 21 September – Does evolutionary psychology provide the best explanation for sex differences in social behavior?"

Some of my students take Women's Studies and some of these are from America. The latter seem interested rather than outraged. They are in a completely different atmosphere: for the first time, they are in an almost free speech university. Some of them remark on this. We do not send them to mind – altering sessions. New Zealand is not America but even in America, academics might be embarrassed to oppose controversial public lectures because they would then have to openly oppose free speech. There is also an instinct of self – preservation that cherishes the right of each academic to design her own courses.

The third step is to get universities to tolerate and even fund research on fundamental issues and this will be the most difficult of all. Nonetheless, we could at least aim at altered conduct so that self – righteous academics did not make their more adventurous colleagues fear they might be run out of town.

Mind – altering sessions

Ideally, mind – altering sessions would be abolished. Whatever good these sessions do is outweighed by the student culture they tend to create: never say anything that might upset blacks, women, or ethnic minorities. Where they exist, there would be overwhelming opposition to abolishing them particularly when they are voluntary. The solution is to accompany them with seminars students can attend without time conflicts called AID (All Issues Discussable). These would not directly challenge the attempt to get everyone to adopt an etiquette that upsets nobody. But each (one on race, another on women, etc.) would address issues that must be subject to scientific inquiry feelings aside. Just as various campus groups contribute to AWARE programs, the committee that sponsored the annual series of lectures on forbidden topics would design these sessions.

I pity those who think that getting students to adopt an elaborate etiquette so no one will ever take offense are doing some great thing. It reminds me of Gogol's *Dead Souls*, which parodies the fact that one gentleman should always usher another gentleman through a door before himself. He describes two such playing out an elaborate pantomime, which delays their actually entering a room for minutes. Every student who cannot face the race and IQ debate outweighs the occasional use of the word "nigger." Chicago in my day was largely free of racial epithets but once in an argument, someone called a black teammate of mine a "black bastard" (and was immediately appalled at himself). Later I asked my friend if he was ok. He said, "don't be silly – what I hear on campus is a thousand times better than what I hear outside – you get angry but if you are not crazy, you just get over it and move on." No longer.

At this point, some of my colleagues ask me if I would really allow anyone to expose the campus to extreme racist views: what about someone who argued that blacks were apes? This kind of thing would not be unprecedented. Until 1900, *Puck* (1980) thought it amusing to run cartoons portraying the Irish as chimpanzees.

If someone handed me a leaflet of this sort, I would no more argue with him than with a member of the flat – earth society. I would add the leaflet to my collection of nut literature, which at present contains cases for simplified English spelling, non – insertive sexual intercourse, and the "flirty fish series" (bringing a young man to Christ by dancing suggestively with him while whispering the Bible in his ear). If state law gives him a right to hold a meeting on campus, I would afflict him with non – attendance and go right on studying for my finals. If he started to shriek at passers – by, I would have the campus police take him into custody for harassment and his own protection. What is to be gained by allowing an attention – seeker to seduce me into a silly drama that is a distraction from everyday life? What is to be gained by showing that I can beat him up (if I can) or that I can drive him off campus?

What disturbs the Romantic left is not this sort of person but Charles Murray: because they have not read him, cannot answer his arguments, and suspect that if they did read him they would be unable to refute him.

The Chicago ideal

The culmination of all of this would be that one's university would not only adopt the Chicago statement but also mean it. Like Chicago, students should be warned in advance that they are coming to a free – speech university and will confront ideas that enrage them. They should be told why there is no speech code with a warning that they are, of course, expected to treat each other with a minimum of courtesy and that actual persecution of an individual or group will not be tolerated. There would be no courses students are forced to take about how to be non – racist: pathological cases can be referred to a clinical psychologist if they so desire. However, there will be a compulsory free – speech course for all administrators.

The ultimate insult

One last appeal to those who wish to eliminate scientific research into group differences. They wish to protect blacks or women or other groups whenever that research examines questions or reaches conclusions that groups find insulting. What lies behind this policy is one ultimate insult: you must not know everything about your group or you might be ashamed. I still have enough group feeling to resent this. If Irish on average have mildly inferior genes for IQ than Jews or Chinese or blacks, if they tend to be more violent than most because of surplus testosterone, if these things are evident in their history, I would not for a moment lose the warm feelings I have for a community that once had me in its embrace. I do not need academics to protect my group from what it really is.

All human groups have the intelligence, creativity, and fellow feeling to fashion rich cultures. Are we to imply that this would no longer be true, unless there were no genetic differences for all human traits? Some groups achieve this despite a larger environment that inflicts systematic injustice. Let us fight injustice wherever it exists (there is plenty of it). But we need not put our brains in deep freeze. If you say that some of the conclusions of Jensen, Lynn, and Murray will obscure the truth, I can only say, "you just don't get it, do you?" We will come closer to the truth if all hypotheses are tested, rather than simply those you think respectable. The application of the scientific method will illuminate every subject it touches. Solace yourself with the fact that for every wound a disadvantaged group may suffer, the racist has suffered a thousand cuts, all due to science.

The idea that group genetic differences might set limits to my personal ambition is absurd. I am what I am no matter what group I belong to. For academics to fear for the youth if they are told that on average women are worse at mathematics, or that blacks are worse at higher education, or that the Irish tend to more violence is to endorse the premise that supports all racism: your group membership defines what you as an individual really are. Every young person should be told that premise is false – not "do not worry, you group is no different from any other." Why qualify what is undeniably true with what may or may not be true?

The third frog

I want to make my own internal psychology clear. I do not commit the sin of racial stereotyping. Every statement that compares racial groups has to do with average differences, recognizing that many individuals within a group may well have traits that are more manifest in other groups. To refuse to acknowledge these differences is either to tell a lie or reveal ignorance. I am not a racist (a stronger claim than "I do not *think* I am a racist"). Being unaware of nuances of speech and behavior that might upset someone somewhere does not make anyone a racist. I consider racism next to sadism as a paradigm of evil.

Race is not a lifelong obsession of mine. I have gone from direct action with blacks as a young lecturer in the South, to using reason to clarify racial issues during my scholarly career, to other issues today. In the few years I have left, I think it far more important to alert people that we are on the verge of irreversible climate change (Flynn, 2016b). However, I still want to learn as much as I can about race and hate whatever stands in the way: "If this be treason, make the most of it.'

This book was written not with the usual sense of achievement at the end but with a rising tide of anger. In *The Informer*, an IRA man calls Ireland a holy church. I feel the same way about the University. How dare they profane it with their ignorance and intolerance?

However, at the end, I do have the usual feeling that I could have put my whole message in a paragraph. Colleagues sometime tell me I have too much confidence in the ability of students to winnow truth from falsehood. I do not have a great deal of confidence at all, but I have a lot more confidence in them that in the self – appointed censors; and most of all, I believe in the scientific method. It is possible that a few harbor the shameful thought that scholars should be able to seek the truth about important questions without interference. How long will we be terrorized by those too terrified to face science? I realize I am offering nothing better than the "three frogs" solution. You may swallow a live frog under compulsion, and then another. But by the third frog, you feel you just cannot swallow any more.

Looming over this whole debate is a terrible temptation: the assumption that since you know that virtue is on your side, truth must be on your side – and that an honest effort to perceive the truth is immoral. This is the surest road to hell for an otherwise honorable human being.

References

Aaron, M. (2017). Evergreen State and the battle for modernity. *Quillette*, June 8, 2017.

AbSpegman (2017). Evergreen settles with Weinstein, professor at the center of campus protests. *The Olympian*, September 16, 2017.

Aby, S. J. (2009). Discretion over valor. *American Educational History Journal* 36: 121 – 132.

Acton, R. (2007). Furor over author Ayaan Hirsi Ali's visit stirs debate on religious freedom. *Pittsburgh Tribune,* April 22, 2007.

Adler, J. H. (2015). Yale students protest forum on free speech. *Washington Post*, November 10, 2015.

Ahren. R. (15 (2011). Jerusalem anti – Semitism scholar backs Yale's move to ax program. *Haaretz,* July 15, 2011.

Al – Gharbi, M. (2018). A scholar is fired for telling the truth about white supremacy and gun violence. *Alternet – education*, February 8, 2018.

Alkalimat, A., Bailey, R., Byndom, S., McMillion, D., Nesbitt, L., Williams, K., & Zelip, B. (2013). *African American Studies 2013: A National Web – Based Survey*. Champaign – Urbana IL: Department of African American Studies, University of Illinois.

Aristotle. *The Politics*. The citation in the text gives the pages and lines of the standard medieval edition, whose page numbers are duplicated in every respectable current edition.

Arum, R., & Roksa, J. (2011). *Academically adrift: Limited learning on college campuses. Chicago ILL: University of Chicago Press*

Arum, R, & Roska, J. (2014). *Aspiring adults adrift: Tentative transitions of adult students*. Chicago ILL: University of Chicago Press.

Associated Press (2000). UT head criticized for canceling Kissinger. *Amarillo Globe – News,* February 23, 2000.

Associated Press (2008). University says sorry to janitor over KKK book. *NBCNews*, July 15, 2008.

Ayer, A.J. (1936). *Language, truth, and logic*. London: Gollancz.

Babcock, P., & Marks, M. (2011). The falling time cost of college: Evidence from half a century of time use data." *The Review of Economics and Statistics* 93: 468 – 478.

Barcan, A. (1993). *Sociological theory and educational reality: Education and society in Australia since 1949*. Kensington NSW Australia: New South Wales University Press.

Barendt, E. (2010). *Academic Freedom and the Law: A Comparative Study*. Oxford: Hart Publishing.

Barmann, J. (2017). Milo Yiannopoulos spent 15 minutes at UC Berkeley, cost them $800,000. *SFist Nerws,* September 25, 2017.

Barreca, G. (2106). Why I'll never give students 'trigger warnings'. *The Hartford Courant,* June 9, 2016.

Beatty, D. (2017). McMaster debate with controversial professor Jordan Peterson disrupted by activists. *CBS (Canadian Broadcasting Corporation),* March 20, 2017.

Belenky, M.F., Clinchy, B. V., Goldberger, N. R., & and Tarule, J. M. (1986). *Women's ways of knowing.* New York: Basic Books.

Belkin, D. (2017). College faculty's new focus: Don't offend. *Wall Street Journal.* February 27, 2017.

Benjamin, R. M. (1993 – 1994). The bizarre classroom of Dr. Leonard Jeffries. *The Journal of Blacks in Higher Education* No. 2 (Winter, 1993 – 1994): 91 – 96.

Bennings, T. (2016). Federal judge denies UT professors' request to block implementation of campus carry. *The Dallas Morning News,* August 2016.

Ben – Porath, S. R. (2017). *Free speech on campus.* Philadelphia: University of Pennsylvania Press.

Bertrand, M., & Mullainathan, S. (2004). Are Emily and Greg more employable than Lakisha and Jamal? A field experiment on labor market discrimination. *American Economic Review* 94: 991 – 1013.

Blatchford, C. (2018). Christie Blatchford sits down with "warrior for common sense" Jordan Peterson. *National Post,* January 19, 2018.

Bodenner, C. (2017). The surprising revolt at the most liberal college in the country: Activists are disrupting lectures to protest "white supremacy," but many students are taking steps to stop them. The Atlantic, November 2, 2017.

Bouchard, T. J. (1998). Intensive, detailed, exhaustive. Intelligence 26: 283 – 290

Bowen, W. G., & Bok, W. (1998). *The shape of the river: Long – term consequences of considering race in college and university admissions.* Princeton: Princeton University Press.

Boyle, K. (2004). *Arc of justice: A saga of race, civil rights, and murder in the Jazz. Age.* New York: Henry Holt.

Brayton, E, (2007). Fired for saying Adam and Eve mythical? *Patheos,* September 25, 2007.

Bromwich, D. (2016). What are we allowed to say? *London Review of Books* Vol. 38 No.18: 3 – 10.

Brown, S. (2017). 'I don't want to back down'. *Chronicle of Higher Education,* April 23, 2017.

Callaghan, G. (2018). Right – winger? Not me, says alt – right darling Jordan Peterson. *The Sydney Morning Herald,* February 8, 2018.

Carter, P. T. (2003*). "Black" cultural capital, status positioning,* and *schooling conflicts* for *low – income African American youth. Social Problems* 50: 136 – 155.

Case Law – Speech Codes, 1989 – 2012: *Doe v. University of Michigan,* 721 F. Supp. 852 (E.D. Mich. 1989); *UWM Post v. Board of Regents of the University of Wisconsin,* 774 F. Supp. 1163 (E.D. Wis. 1991); *Dambrot v. Central Michigan University,* 55 F.3d 1177 (6th Cir. 1995); *Corry v. Leland Stanford Junior University,* No. 740309 (Cal. Super. Ct. Feb. 27, 1995) (slip op.); *Booher v. Board of Regents,* 1998 US Dist. LEXIS 11404 (E.D. Ky. Jul. 21, 1998); *Bair v. Shippensburg University,* 280 F. Supp. 2d 357 (M.D. Pa. 2003); *Roberts v. Haragan,* 346 F. Supp. 2d 853 (N.D. Tex. 2004); *College Republicans at San Francisco State University v. Reed,* 523 F. Supp. 2d 1005 (N.D. Cal. 2007); *DeJohn v. Temple University,* 537 F.3d 301, 319 (3d Cir. 2008); *Smith v. Tarrant County College District,* 694 F. Supp. 2d 610 (N.D. Tex. 2010); *McCauley v. University of the Virgin Islands* 618 F.3d 232 (3rd Cir. 2010); *University of Cincinnati Chapter of Young Americans for Liberty v. Williams,* No. 1:12 – cv – 155 (S.D. Ohio Jun. 12, 2012).

Cattan, N. (2003). NYU Center: New addition to growing academic field. *Forward,* May 2, 2003.

CBS (2017). Pierce College student alleges constitution not allowed to be distributed outside 'Free Speech Zone'. *Columbia Broadcasting System,* March 30, 2017.

Ceci, S J., & Willams, W. M. (2018). Who decides what is acceptable speech on campus? Why restricting free speech Is not the answer. *Perspectives on Psychological Science* 7: 496 – 603.

Chapman, B. (2016). State exam scores soar for New York City's top charter schools. *New York Daily News,* August 3, 2016.

Charles, N., & Coleman, C. (1995). Crime suspect. *Emerge,* 24 – 30.

Chase, S. (2018). Ann Coulter's speech in Ottawa cancelled. *The Globe and Mail,* April 28, 2018.

CHE (2008). College settles with instructor fired for teaching Adam and Eve as myth. *Chronicle of Higher Education,* July 14, 2008.

Chemerinsky, E., & Gillman, H. (2017). *Free speech on campus.* New Haven: Yale University Press.

Chou, V. (2017). How science and genetics are reshaping the race debate of the 21st century. Harvard University: The Graduate School of Arts and Sciences, April 17, 2017.

Coates, T – N. (2013). Black Studies and 'intellectual cowardice'. *Atlantic,* May 9, 2012.

Cofas, N. (2018). From foolish talk to evil madness. *Quillette,* October 1, 2018. Google: https://quillette.com/2018/10/01/the – grievance – studies – scandal – five – academics – respond/

Cohen, J. S. (2015). University of Illinois Oks $875,000 settlement to end Salaita dispute. *Chicago Tribune,* November 12, 2015.

Coleman, N. (2017). On average, nine mosques were targeted every month in 2017. *CNN World*, tally 2017).

Corak, M. (2006). Do poor children become poor adults? Lessons from a cross country comparison of generational earnings mobility. In J. Creedy, & Kalb, G.. (ed.) *Dynamics of Inequality and Poverty. Research on Economic Inequality* 13: 143 – 188.

Creeley, W. (2013). At Brown, free speech loses as hecklers silence NYPD Commissioner. FIRE, October 30, 2013.

Creeley, W., & Harris, S. (2008). The court got it right. *Inside Higher Education*, August 18, 2008.

Crosby, F. J. (2004). *Affirmative action is dead, long live affirmative action.* New Haven CT: Yale University Press.

Crouch, S., & Benjamin, P. (2003). *Reconsidering the Souls of Black Folk.* Philadelphia PA: Running Press.

Cuban, L. (1980*). How teachers taught: Constancy and change in American classrooms.* New York: Teachers College Press.

Damron, A. (2017). Yale "decolonizes" English dept. after complaints about white authors, students no longer required to study Shakespeare and Chaucer. *The College Fix,* October 2017.

De Parle, J. (2004). *American dream.* New York: Viking.

Dennett. D. C. (1984). *Freedom evolves.* London: Penguin.

Derrida, J. (1999). The university without condition. In J. Derrida, *Without Alibi* (trans. Peggy Kamuf). Stanford CAL: Stanford University Press.

Dey, E. L., Ott, M. C., Antonaros, M., Barnhardt, C. L., & Holsapple, M. A. (2010). *Engaging diverse viewpoints: What is the campus climate for perspective – taking?* Washington DC: Association of American Colleges and Universities.

Dickens, W. T., Flynn, J. R. *(*2006). Black Americans reduce the racial IQ gap: Evidence from standardization samples. *Psychological Science* 17: 913 – 920.

Dickerson, D. (2005). *The end of blackness: Returning the souls of black folk to their rightful owners.* New York: Anchor Books.

Duehren, A. M. (2015). Steinberg addresses video controversy at Law School. *Havard Crimson*, April 12, 2015

Eberhardt, J. L., Davies, P G.; Purdie – Vaughns, V. J.; and Johnson, S. L (2006). Looking deathworthy: Perceived stereotypicality of Black defendants predicts capital – sentencing outcomes. *Cornell Law Faculty Publications*. Paper 41.

Economist (2017). Young, college – educated Americans are more accepting of controversial speech: But self – censorship becomes more common as students progress through university. *The Economist*, October 18, 2007.

Elon, A. (2002). *The pity of it all: A portrait of the German – Jewish epoch 1743 – 1933.* London: Penguin.

Ehrlich, J. (2018). A paper on the precipice. *The Chicago Maroon*, May 24, 2018.

Farquhar, S – E. (1998). Teaching: A women – only profession? *New Zealand Annual Review of Education* 7: 169 – 180.

Ferguson, R. A. (2017). *We demand: The university and student protests* . Oakland CAL: University of California Press.

Fernandes, D. (2017). Harvard panel back – pedals on social club ban after backlash. *Boston Globe*, September 30, 2017.

FIRE (2004). Major Victory for Free Speech at Cal Poly. May 6, 2004.

FIRE (Foundation for Individual Rights in Education), 2017. Chicago Statement: University and Faculty Body Support, September 22, 2017.

FIRE (2018). Spotlight on speech codes: 2018.

Fisk, R. (2005). *The great war for civilization: The conquest of the Middle East.* New York: Vintage.

Flaherty, C. (2017). Old criticisms, new threats. *Inside Higher Education*, June 26, 2017.

Florida, R. (2014). Where the good and bad jobs will be, 10 years from now. *City Lab*, February 25, 2014.

Flynn, J. R. (1980). *Race, IQ, and Jensen.* London: Routledge.

Flynn, J. R. (1984). The mean IQ of Americans: Massive gains 1932 to 1978. *Psychological*
Bulletin 95: 29 – 51,

Flynn, J. R. (1987). Massive IQ gains in 14 nations: what IQ tests really measure. *Psychological Bulletin* 101: 171 – 191.

Flynn, J. R. (1991). *Asian Americans: Achievement beyond IQ.* Hillsdale NJ: Erlbaum.

Flynn, J. R. (1993). Reaction times show that both Chinese and British children are more
 intelligent than one another. *Perceptual and Motor Skills* 72: 544 – 546.

Flynn, J. R. (2000). *How to defend humane ideals: Substitutes for objectivity.* Lincoln NEB: University of Nebraska Press.

Flynn. J. R. (2007). *What is intelligence? Beyond the Flynn Effect.* Cambridge UK: Cambridge University Press.

Flynn, J. R. (2008). *Where have all the liberals gone? Race, class, and ideals in America.* Cambridge UK: Cambridge University Press.

Flynn, J. R. (2009). Howard Gardner and the use of words. In B. Shearer (ed.), MI at 25: *Assessing the impact and future of multiple intelligences for teaching and learning* (pp.83 – 99). New York: Teachers College Press.

Flynn, J. R. (2010). *The torchlight list: Around the world in 200 books.* Wellington, New Zealand, AWA Press.

Flynn, J. R. (2012a). *Are we getting smarter: Rising IQ in the twenty – first century.* Cambridge UK: Cambridge University Press.

Flynn, J. R. (2012b). *Beyond patriotism: From Truman to Obama.* Exeter UK, Imprint Academic.

Flynn, J. R. (2012c). *Fate and philosophy: A journey through life's great questions.* Wellington, New Zealand: AWA Press.

Flynn, J. R. (2012d). *How to improve your mind: Twenty keys to unlock the modern world.* London: Wiley – Blackwell.

Flynn, J. R. (2013a). Arthur Robert Jensen. *Intelligence* 41: 144 – 145.

Flynn, J. R. (2013b). *Intelligence and human progress: The story of what was hidden in our genes.* London: Elsevier

Flynn, J. R. (2016a). *Does you family make you smarter? Nature, nurture, and human autonomy.* Cambridge UK: University of Cambridge Press.

Flynn, J. R. (2016b). *No place to hide: Climate change* – a short introduction for New Zealanders. Nelson, New Zealand: Potton & Burton (see second printing 2017).

Flynn, J. R. (2016c). *The new torchlight list: In search of the best modern authors.* Wellington, New Zealand: AWA Press.

Flynn, J. R. (2017). Male and female balance sheet. *Mankind Quarterly* 58: 43 – 68.

Flynn, J. R. (2018). *Homage to political philosophy: The good society from Plato to the present.* Newcastle UK: Cambridge Scholars press.

Flynn, J. R. (2019). My book defending free speech has been pulled. *Quillette*, September 24, 2019.

Flynn, J. R. (in press). *The FISC Manual with Research Supplements.*

Fogg, P. (2005). Harvard faculty votes no confidence in the university's president. *The Chronical of Higher Education*, March 16, 2005.

Fosse, M. H. (1951). *Trends in academic freedom, 1947 – 1951* .Master's Thesis, Illinois State Normal University.

Freud, Sigmund, (1990). *The future of an illusion.* New York: Norton.

Friedersdorf, C. (2016). The perils of writing a provocative email at Yale. *The Atlantic*, May 26, 2016.

Friedersdorf, C. (2018). Why can't people hear what Jordan Peterson is saying? A British broadcaster doggedly tried to put words into the academic's mouth. *The Atlantic*, January 22, 2018

Fuller, T. (2017). Life and combat for Republicans at Berkeley. *The New York Times*, May 8, 2017.

Galster, G. (2012). *Driving Detroit: The quest for respect in the motor city.* Philadelphia PA: University of Pennsylvania Press.

Gardner, H. (1983). *Frames of mind: The theory of multiple intelligences.* New York: Basic Books.

Gardner, H. (1993). *Multiple intelligences: The theory in practice, a reader.* New York: Basic Books.

Gardner, H. (1999). *Intelligence reframed: Multiple intelligences for the 21st century.* New York: Basic Books.

Gardner, H. (2009). Reflections on my works and those of my commentators. In B. Shearer (ed.), MI at 25: *Assessing the impact and future of multiple intelligences for teaching and learning* (pp.83 – 99). New York: Teachers College Press.

Garfinkel, H. (1969). *When Negroes march: The March on Washington Movement in the organizational Politics for FEPC.* New York: Atheneum.

Ginger, R. (1962*). Eugene V. Debs: A biography. New York: Macmillan.*

Glabermaan, M. (1980). Wartime strikes: The struggle against the No – Strike Pledge In the UAW during World War II. Detroit MICH: Berwick Editions

Goebel, B. A. (1993). Diversity, conformity, and democracy: A critique of Arthur Schlesinger, *The disuniting of America: Reflections on a multicultural society.* Google that title.

Gonzalez, M., & Jones, L. A. (2018). Our struggle is my struggle: Solidarity Feminism as an intersectional reply to Neoliberal and Choice Feminism. *Affilia: Journal of Women and Social Work* .Google: https://www.scribd.com/document/ 390022198.

Gonzalez, S. (2016). Is free speech threatened on college campuses? An audience casts its vote. *Yale News*, March 2, 2016.

Goodlad, J. (1984). *A place called school: Prospects for the future.* New York: McGraw – Hill.

Grodzins, M. (1956). *The loyal and the disloyal: Social boundaries of patriotism and treason.* Chicago Ill: University of Chicago Press.

Gross, N. (2013). *Why are professors liberal and why do conservatives care?* Cambridge MA: Harvard University Press.

Gross, N., & Simmons, S. (2014). *Professors and their politics.* Baltimore MD: Johns Hopkins University Press.

Grossman, D. (1988). *The yellow wind.* New York: St. Martin's Press.

Grossman, R. (2005). `I'm not the ideal poster boy'. *Chicago Tribune,* December 20, 2005.

Guardian (2002). Harvard bars Oxford poet. *The Guardian*, November 14, 2002.

Hacker, D., & Theriot, K. (2014). Professor incites destruction of student newspaper while university shrugs. *Alliance Defending Freedom*, April 11, 2014.

Haidt, J, (2017). Professors must now fear intimidation from both sides. *Heterodox Academy*, June 28, 2017.

Hamilton, R. F., & Hargens, L. l. (1993). The politics of the professors: Self – identifications, 1969 – 1984. *Social Forces* 71: 603 – 27.

Harris, S. (2014). Disinvitation season' hits a new low at Brandeis University. FIRE, April 9, 2014.

Harris, S. (2118). Sarah Lawrence's shame: Professor who wrote op – ed urging greater viewpoint diversity finds himself the target of vandalism, anonymous accusations. *FIRE*, November 6, 2018.

Hartocolis, A. (2106). Yale professor and wife, targets of protests, resign as college heads. *New York Times*, May 26, 2016.

Harvard (2016). General Education Review Committee Final Report, January, 2016.

Harvard Crimson (1989). Growing apathy: AWARE WEEK. *Harvard Crimson*, March 2, 1989.

Haworth, C. M. A., et al. (2010). The heritability of general cognitive ability increases linearly from childhood to young manhood. *Molecular Psychiatry* 145: 1112 – 1120.

Henninger, D. (2017). McCarthyism at Middlebury. *The Wall Street Journal*, March 9, 2017.

Hill, J. H. (2016). I see: Social justice and teachers college curriculum. *Heterodox Academy*, July 7, 2016.

Hill, T. P. (2018). Academic activists send a published paper down the memory hole. *Quillette*, September 7, 2018.

Hirschman, A. O. (1970). *Exit, Voice, and Loyalty: Responses to decline in firms, organizations, and states.* Cambridge MA: Harvard University Press.

Holligsworth, P. J. (2000). *Unfettered expression: Freedom in American intellectual life.* Ann Arbor MI: University of Michigan Press.

Holmes, D. (1989). *Stalking the academic communist: Intellectual freedom and the firing of Alex Novikoff.* Hanover CT: University of New England Press.

Huber, C. R., & Kunce, N. R. (2016). Does college teach critical thinking? A meta – analysis. *Review of Educational Research* 86: 431 – 468.

Huber, D. (2017). Following Weinstein debacle, Evergreen State College president kowtows to student demands. *The College Fix*, May 28, 2017.

Hudler, H. (2015). Yale students demand resignations from faculty members over Halloween email. *FIRE* (Foundation for Individual Rights in Education), November 6, 2015.

Jacobson, W.A. (2017). My pro – free speech views made me the target of a smear campaign at Vassar College. *USA Today*, November 5, 2017.

Jaschik, S. (2007). Fooling the College Board. *Inside Higher Education*, March 26, 2007.

Jaschik, S. (2106). Grade inflation, higher and higher. *Inside Higher Education*, March 29, 2016.

Jaschick, S. (2017). Nobel laureate's talk called off over his racist comments. *Inside Higher Education*, May 27, 2017.

Jeffries, L. (1991). Our sacred mission. Google that title.

Jensen, A. R. (1969). How much can we boost IQ and scholastic achievement. *Harvard Educational Review* 39: 1 – 123.

Jensen, A. R. (1972). *Genetics and education.* New York: Harper and Row.

Jensen, A. R. (1973). *Educability and group differences.* New York: Harper and Row.

Jensen, A. R. (1998). *The g factor: The science of mental ability.* Westport, CN: Praeger.

Jimenez, S (2013). *The book of Matt: Hidden truths about the murder of Matthew Shepard.* Hanover NH: Steerforth Press.

Jung, H. (1990). 7 more arrested in Castle abduction. *The Summer Pennsylvanian*, August 2, 1990.

Jussim, L. (2016). Which of these academics got suspended? *Heterodox Academy*, November 1, 2016.

Kabbny, J. (2107). Evergreen official asks student vigilantes to stop patrolling campus armed with bats, batons. *The College Fix*. June 5, 2017.

Kampeas, R. (2005). Campus oversight passes Senate as review effort scores a victory. Jewish Telegraphic Agency (JTA), November 22, 2005.

Kapur,S. (2015). A history of disrupting the peace. *The Chicago Maroon*, November 30, 2015.

Kashua, S. (2006). *Let it be morning*. London: Atlantic Books.

Kaufman, E. (2017). A University stands up for free speech – and itself. *National Review*, July 26, 2017.

Keiler, A. (2000). *Marian Anderson: A singer's journey*. Champaign – Urbana IL: University of Illinois Press.

Keim. K. (2007). James Watson suspended from lab, but not for being a sexist hater of fat people. *Science*, October 19, 2007.

Killane, K. (1990). *Lower than vermin: An anatomy of Thatcher's Britain*. London: Arrow Books.

Konrath, S.H., O'Rrien, E. H., & Courtney, H. (2011). Changes in dispositional empathy in American college students over time: A meta – analysis. *Personality and Social Psychology Review* 15: 180 – 198.

Kors, A. C., & Silverglate, H. (1998). *The shadow university: The betrayal of liberty on America's campuses*. New York: Free Press.

Kotecki, P. (2016). Schapiro to freshmen: People criticizing safe spaces 'drives me nuts.' The Daily Northwestern, September 20, 2016.

Kourany, J. A. (2016). Should some knowledge be forbidden? The case of cognitive differences research. *Philosophy of Science* 83: 779 – 790.

Krupp. E., Onsgard, K., & Pars, M. (2016). Protesters shut down Yiannopoulos speech. *The DePaulia*, May 24, 2016.

Kuran, T. (1995). Private truths, public lies: The social consequences of preference falsification. Cambridge MA: Harvard Univerity Press.

Kurtz, S. (2003). Reforming the campus: Congress Targets Title VI. National Review Online, October 14, 2003.

Kurtz, S. (2017a). Year of the shout – down: It was worse than you think. National Review, May 31, 2017.

Kurtz, S. (2017b). Campus chaos: Daily shout – downs for a week. National Review, October 12, 2017.

LA Times (2017). Students deserve to be punished for shouting down campus speakers, but don't go overboard. Editorial Los Angeles Times , October 19, 2017.

Labaree, D. F. (2004). The trouble with ed schools. New Haven CT: Yale University Press.

Lacy. R. (2009). Inside the kingdom. New York: Penguin.

Ladd, E. C. Jr. & Lipset, S. M. (1975). *The divided academy: Professors and politics*. New York: McGraw – Hill.

Langbert , M. (2007). Steve Head, a man for all seasons, needs legal advice. Mitchell Langberts's Blog, July 4, 2007.

Lanman, S. (1997). 'Water buffalo' case settled. The Daily Pennsylvanian, September 10, 1997.

Lazarsfeld, P. F., & Thielens, W. (1958). *The academic mind: Social Scientists in a time of crisis.* New York: Free Press.

Lehigh, S. (2004). Humor vs. free speech at UNH. Boston Globe, November 17, 2004.

Lesh, M, (2017). Free speech on campus audit 2016. Institute of Public Affairs, December, 2017.

Levesque, G. A. (2009). Comment on McWhorter (2009b). Google "McWhorter, 2009."

Levine, L. W. ((1996). The opening of the American mind: Cannons, culture, and history. Boston MASS: Beacon Press.

Lewy, G. (1990). The cause that failed: Communism in American political life. New York: Oxford University Press.

Lilienfeld, S. O. (2017). Microaggressions: Strong claims, inadequate evidence. Perspectives on Psychological Science 12: 138 – 169.

Loehlin, J. C., Lindzey, G., & Spuhler, J. N. (1975). Race differences in intelligence. San Francisco: Freeman.

Loury, G. Reflections on my interview with Amy Wax. The Daily Pennsylvanian, March 3, 2018.

Lubienski, C. A., & Lubienski, S. T. (2013). *The public school advantage: Why public schools outperform private schools.* Chicago IL: University of Chicago Press.

Lukaianoff, G. (2014). Unlearning liberty: Campus censorship and the end of the American debate. New York: Encounter Books (paperback edition).

Lukianoff, G., & Haidt, J. (2015). The coddling of the American mind. The Atlantic, September 2015.

Lynn R. (1987). The intelligence of the Mongoloids: A psychometric, evolutionary, and neurological theory. *Personality and Individual Differences* 8: 813 – 844.

Lynn, R. 2002). Racial and ethnic differences in psychopathic personality. *Personality and Individual Differences* 32: 273 – 316.

Lynn, R., & Irving, P. (2004). Sex differences on the progressive matrices: A meta – analysis. Intelligence 32: 481 – 498.

Mac Donald, H. (2018). The Penn Law School mob scores a victory. Wall Street Journal, March 19, 2018.

Maher, M. (1940). Psychology: Empirical and rational. New York: Longmans, Green.

Margolin, K. H. (2014). On Ayaan Hirsi Ali and college disciplinary codes. Newton TAB, May 2, 2014.

Mashek, D., & Haidt, J. (2019). 10 colleges where you won't have to walk on eggshells: These schools are seriously committed to civil and diverse debate. Reason, June 2019 issue.

McCabe, D. L., Trevino, L. K., & Butterfield, K. D. (2001). Cheating in academic institutions: A decade of research. Ethics and Behavior 11: 219 – 232.

McCarthy. C. (2005). No country for old men. New York: Vintage.

McConnell, M. W. (2012). You can't say that: 'The harm in hate speech,' by Jeremy Waldron. The New York Times, June 22, 2012.

McCormick, C. H. (1989). This nest of vipers: McCarthyism and higher education in the Mundel Affair, 1951 – 52. Champaign, Ill: University of Illinois Press.

McNeil, K . (2002). The War on Academic Freedom. The year since Congress passed the USA Patriot Act has brought an ever – growing enemies list from our nation's thought police. The Nation, November 11, 2002

McWhorter, J. (2005). Winning the race: Beyond the crisis in black America. New York: Penguin.

McWhorter, J. (2009a). African – American studies – As they should be. The James C. Martin Center for Academic renewal, June 9, 2009.

McWhorter, J. (2009b). What African – American studies could be. Minding the Campus, September 30, 2009.

Mead, L. (1989). The logic of workfare: The underclass and work policy. Annals of the American Academy of Political and Social Science 501: 156 – 169.

Mearsheimer, J. J., & Walt, S. M. (2007). The Israel lobby and US foreign Policy. New York: Farrar, Straus and Giroux.

MEC (Ministry of Education and Culture), 2016). Finnish education in a nutshell. Helsinki, Finland: Ministry of Education and Culure, National Board of Edcuation.

Mill, John Stuart (1859). On liberty. London: Parker & Son.

Miner, J. (2012). Controversial prof Philippe Rushton dead. The London Free Press, October 4, 2012.

Mohan, G. (2001). Graduation speech riles Sacramento. Los Angeles Times, December 20, 2001.

Moore, E. G. (1986). Family socialization and the IQ test performance of traditionally and transracially adopted Black children. Developmental Psychology 22: 317 – 326.

Morella, M. (2014). Standards drive education schools to raise the admissions bar. US News and World Report. March 31, 2014.

Morey, A., & Harris, S. (2017). In anti – intellectual email, Wellesley profs call engaging with controversial arguments an imposition on students. FIRE, March 21, 2017.

Murray, C. (2008). Real education: Four simple truths for bringing America's schools back to reality. New York: Crown Forum.

Murray, C. (2017). Harvard shows how it should be done: Giving a speech on a college campus is easy, if the adults are in charge. The Weekly Standard, September 7, 2017.

Murray, C., & and Herrnstein, R. (1994). The bell curve: Intelligence and class structure in American life. New York: Free Press.

National Endowment for the Arts (2016). Arts Data Profile #10 – Results from the Annual Arts Basic Survey (AABS): 2013 – 2015

NCAES (National Center of American Education Statistics), 1993. 120 years of American education: A statistical portrait. See Table 8. Historical summary of public elementary and secondary school statistics: 1869 – 70 to 1989 – 90.

NCES (National Center for Educational Statistics), 2016. Fast facts.

Nelson, L. J. (2003). Rumors of indiscretion: The University of Missouri "sex questionnaire" scandal in the Jazz Age. Columbia MO: University of Missouri Press.

Newsam, P. (1999). Teaching and learning. Microsoft Encarta Encyclopedia 2000.

Nir, O. (2003). Groups back bill to monitor universities. Forward, March 12, 2004.

Norcross, J. C., Aiken, L. S., Hallstorks, R., & Christidis (2016). Undergraduate study in psychology: Curriculum and assessment. American Psychologist 71: 89 – 101.

O' Brien, M. (1998). Hesburgh: A biography. Washington D. C.: The Catholic University of America Press.

OECD (Organization for Economic Co – operation and Development), 2015. Universal basic skills: What countries stand to gain. E. A. Hanushek, & L. Woessmann (eds.), OECD Library, May 13, 2015.

Oesterdiekhoff, G. W. (2012). Was pre – modern man a child? The quintessence of the psychometric and developmental approaches. Intelligence 40: 470 – 478.

Ogbu, J. U. (2003). Black American students in an affluent suburb: A study of academic disengagement. Mahwah NJ: Lawrence Erlbaum Associates.

Oliver, K. (2106). Education in the age of outrage. The New York Times, October 16, 2016.

Omar, O. A. (2013). A fort of nine towers. New York: Picador.

Ondaatje, M. (1987). In the skin of a lion. Toronto: McClelland and Stewart.

Onsgard, K., & Deppen, M. (2017). Student groups express anger after Yiannopoulos event, call for leadership change. The DePaulia, May 24, 2016.

Oran, D. A. (1986). Joining the club: A history of Jews and Yale. New Haven CN: Yale University Press.

Owens, E. (2016). University Of Florida urges students to report politically incorrect Halloween costumes as BIAS INCIDENTS. The Daily Caller, October 10, 2016.

Oz, A. (2004). A tale of love and darkness. London: Vintage.

Paley, J. (2017). Safe spaces, brave spaces: Diversity and free expression in education. Boston MAS: The MIT Press.

Palmer, T. (2017). Monash University trigger warning policy fires up free speech debate. ABC (Australian Broadcast Corporation) News, March 29 2017.

Pamuk, O. (2005). Snow. London: Faber & Faber.

Paros, M. (2018). Update: The Evergreen State College. Heterodox Academy September 10, 2018.

Pascarella, E. T., Blaich, C. M., Georgianna, L., Martin, G. L, & Hanson, J. M. (2011). How robust are the findings of "Academically Adrift"? Change: The Magazine of Higher Learning 43: 20 – 24.

Pascarella, E., & Terenzini, P. (1991). How college affects students. San Francisco: Jossey – Bass

Pascarella, E., & Terenzini, P. (2005). How College Affects Students: A Third Decade of Research, Volume 2. San Francisco: Jossey – Bass

Patai, D., & Koertge, N. (2003). Professing feminism. Lanham MD: Lexington Books.

Paulson, S. K. (2012). Ward Churchill loses appeal to win back CU job. *Denver Post,* September 10, 2012.

Peterson, G. (2018). Jordan Peterson: 'One thing I'm not is naïve.' *Financial Times,* February 8, 2018.

Piper, G. (2017). Students harass white professor for refusing to leave campus on anti – white 'Day of Absence'. The College Fix, May 25, 2017.

Plato, Republic. The citation in the text gives the pages and lines of the standard medieval edition, whose page numbers are duplicated in every respectable current edition.

Plato. The Theaetetus. The citation in the text gives the pages and lines of the standard medieval edition, whose page numbers are duplicated in every respectable current edition.

Pollak, J. B. (2016). See no evil: 19 hard truths the left can't handle. Audiobook – Blackstone Audio Publisher.

Princeton (2017). General education requirements. Undergraduate Announcement, 2017.

Public Affairs (2017). Milo Yiannopoulos event canceled after violence erupts. *UC Berkeley News,* February 1, 2017.

Puck (1880). See Puck, volume 8, number 191, 3 November 1880, page 150.

Purdy, L. (2008). Getting under the skin of "diversity:" Searching for the color – blind ideal. Minneapolis MN: Robert Lawrence Press

Quacquarelli Symonds (2017). QS World University Rankings by Subject 2017 – Psychology (top 300 ranked).

Reisman, D. (1958). Constraint and variety in American education. Lincoln NEB: University of Nebraska Press.

Reuters Staff (2017). Number of charter schools, students in US rises: report. Reuters, August 23, 2017.

Richardson, R. B. (2017). Trump's attack on science isn't going very well. The Washington Post, August 10 2017.

Rifkin, M. (2015). Guest post: Teaching social justice in the physics classroom. Quantum Progress, February 12, 2015

Riley, N.S. (2012). The most persuasive case for eliminating Black Studies? Just read the dissertations. The Chronicle of Higher Education. 30 April 2012.

Riley, N. S. (2016). The new trail of tears: How Washington is destroying American Indians. New York: Encounter Books.

Roll, N. (2017). More campus speakers shouted down: Columbia students prevent British anti – Islam activist from talking via video; Michigan students block part of Charles Murray talk. Inside Higher Education, October 12, 2017.

Roundtree, C. (2017). College professor is attacked and injured by 'seriously scary' student mob as she escorts controversial 'white supremacist' guest speaker off campus. Dailymail.com, March 4, 2017.

Rubin, M. (2017). Yale surrenders: A faculty that wants to be loved. Commentary, August 29, 2017.

Russell, W. (2107). What do undergraduates learn about human intelligence? Paper presented at the 17th Annual Meeting of ISIR (International Society for Intelligence Research), July 13 – 16, 2017.

Rutherford, A. (2014). He may have unravelled DNA, but James Watson deserves to be shunned. The Guardian, December 1, 2014.

Sachs, J. (2019). Campus free speech under threat from the right. Arc, September 3, 2019.

Salaita, S. (2015). Steven Salaita (@stevesalaita) Twitter. December 22, 2015.

Samuel, E. (2018). Outselling the Bible. London Review of Books, March 15, 2018).

Sargrad, S. (2017). Don't gamble on vouchers. US News and World Report, June 21, 2017.

Saul, S. (2017). Middlebury disciplines student protesters. The New York Times, May 25, 2017.

Scarr, S. (1998). On Arthur Jensen's integrity. Intelligence 28: 227 – 232.

Schlesinger, Jr. Arthur M. (1991). The disuniting of America: Reflections on a multicultural society. Dunbeath, Caithness, Scotland: Whittle Books.

Schlosser, E. (2015). I'm a liberal professor, and my liberal students terrify me. VOX, June 3, 2015.

Schmidt, S. (2017). Professor fired after defending blacks – only event to Fox News. 'I was publicly lynched,' she says. The Washington Post, June 26, 2017.

Schrecker, E. W. (1986). No ivory tower: McCarthyism and the universities. New York: Oxford University Press.

Schrecker, E. W. (1994). The age of McCarthyism: A brief history with documents. Boston MASS: St. Martin's Press.

Schrecker, E. W. (1999). Political tests for professors: Academic freedom during the McCarthy Years. University of California, History Project, October 7, 1999.

Schrecker, E. W. (2010). The lost soul of higher education: Corporatization, the assault on academic freedom, and the end of the American university. New York: The New Press.

Sica, A., ed. (2005). *Social thought from the enlightenment to the present.* Boston MA: Pearson Education.

Simmons, S., & Smiley, W. (2010). The undergraduate psychology major: An examination of structure and sequence. Teaching of Psychology 37: 4 – 15.

Singal, J. (2017). Fordham University's suppression of Pro – Palestinian views shows why liberals should fight for free speech. Daily Intelligencer, April 27, 2017.

Signal, J. (2017). This is what a modern – day witch hunt looks like. Daily Intelligencer, May 2, 2017.

Singer, I. B. (1963). The slave. London: Penguin.

Skinner, B. F. (1948). Walden Two. Indianapolis IND: Hackett.

Skinner, B. F. (1971). Beyond freedom and dignity. Indianapolis IND: Hackett.

Smith, L. (2019). Guest opinion: Ousted professor's free speech was violated. The Daily Iowan, September 10, 2019.

Smith, M. (2018). Going in through the back door: Challenging straight male Homohysteria, Transhysteria, and Transphobia through receptive penetrative sex toy use. Sexuality & Culture, https://doi.org/10.1007/s12119 – 018 – 9536 – 0.

Soloman, D. (2008). Head of the class. The New York Times Magazine, September 19, 2008.

Sorkin, A. D. (2012). Why the National Review fired John Derbyshire. The New Yorker, April 9, 2012.

Sowell, T. (1972). Black education: Myths and tragedies. New York: David McKay.

Sowell, T. (1993). *Inside American education:* The decline, the deception, the dogmas. New York: The Free Press.

Sowell, T. (2004). Affirmative action around the world: An empirical study. New Haven CN: Yale.

Sowell, T. (2009). Applied economics: Thinking beyond stage one (2nd edition). New York: Basic Books.

Sowell, T. (2015). Wealth, poverty and politics: An international perspective. New York: Basic Books.

Spegman, A. (2017). Evergreen professor at center of protests resigns; college will pay $500,000. The Seattle Times, September 16, 2917.

Spiked (2017). Free speech university rankings 2017. Spiked, February 3, 2017.

Starkey, M, (1952). *The devil in Massachusetts: A modern inquiry into the Salem witch trials.* London: R. M. Hale.

Steele, S, (1999). The age of white guilt and the disappearance of the black individual. Harper's Magazine, November 30, 1999.

Stein, M. (2017). Black student group at UC Santa Cruz threatens more campus takeovers if additional demands not met. The College Fix, May 11, 2017.

Steorts, J. (2002). Shades of offense. The Harvard Crimson, April 26, 2002.

Stephens, B. (2017). America's best university president. New York Times, October 20, 2017.

Stephenson, W. H. (1948a). John Spencer Bassett as a historian of the South. North Carolina Historical Review, July, 1948.

Stephenson, W. H. (1948b). The Negro in the thinking and writing of John Spencer Bassett. *North Carolina Historical Review, October, 1948.*

Stern, C. (2018). Charlotta Stern on gender Sociology's problems. With Chris Martin, *Half Hour of Heterodoxy*, October 28, 2018.

Stern, S. (2006). The ed schools' latest—and worst—humbug. Teaching for "social justice" is a cruel hoax on disadvantaged kids. *City Journal*, Summer 2006.

Stern, S. (2015). Twenty years on the New York education beat. What I saw in the schools. *City Journal*, Autumn 2015.

Stoloff, M., McCarthy, M., Keller, L., Varfolomeeva, V., Lynch, J., Makara, K., Simmons, S., & Smiley, W. (2010). The undergraduate psychology major: An examination of structure and sequence. *Teaching of Psychology* 37: 4 – 15.

Stotsky, S. (2007). The power of rigorous teacher tests. *Thomas B. Fordham Institute*, April 11, 2007.

Subotnik, D. (2005). *Toxic diversity: Race, gender, and law talk in America.* New York: NYU Press.

Sugrue, T. (2009). *Sweet land of liberty: The forgotten struggle for civil rights in the north.* New York: Random House.

Sumner, W. G. (1899). The conquest of the United States by Spain. *Yale Law Journal* 8: 168 – 193.

Sun, L H., & Eilperin, J. (2007). Words banned at multiple HHS agencies include 'diversity' and 'vulnerable'. *The Washington Post*, December 16, 2017.

Thernstrom, S., & Therstrom, A. (1999). *America in black and white: One nation, indivisible.* New York: Simon & Schuster.

Trahair, R. (2012). *Encyclopedia of cold war espionage, spies, and secret operations.* New York: Enigma Books.

Treiman, D. (2011). Lipstadt on Yale anti – Semitism initiative: Advocacy sometimes trumped scholarship. *Jewish Telegraphic Agency*, June 16, 2011.

Tuchman B. (1966). *The proud tower: A portrait of the world before the war, 1890 – 1914.* New York: MacMillan.

Turner, C., Weddle, E., & Balonon – Rosen, P. (2017). The promise and peril of school vouchers. *National Public Radio*, May 12, 2017.

Twenge, J. M., & Campbell, W. K. (2009). *The narcissism epidemic: Living in the age of entitlement.* New York: The Free Press.

University of Chicago (2012). Statement on principles of free expression. *UChicago News*, July 2012.

US Department of Education, National Center for Education Statistics (2017). *The Condition of Education 2017* (NCES 2017 – 144), Public School Expenditures.

US News and World Report (2017). *US Ranking for Undergraduate Teaching 2017.*

Veblen, T. (1899). *The theory of the leisure class.* New York: MacMillan.

Vellasenor, J. (2017). *Views among college students regarding the First Amendment: Results from a new survey.* Washington DC: Brookings.

Wachter, K. W., & Freedman, D. A. (1999). The fifth cell: Correlation bias in U. S. census adjustment. University of California, Berkeley, Department of Statistics, Technical Report 570, December 17, 1999.

Waldron, J. (2012). *The harm in hate speech.* Cambridge MASS: Harvard University Press.

Waldron, J. (2018). Brave spaces. *The New York Review of Books*, June 28, 2018.

Wang, Vivian (2018). Once at the center of Yale protests, professor wins the school's highest honor. *New York Times*, August 14, 2018.

Washington Times (2002). First lady objected to as speaker at UCLA. *The Washington Times*, February 26, 2002.

Watkins, M. (2017). How Tech's president juggles free speech and political polarization. *The Texas Tribune*, September 26, 2017.

Watson, J. (2007). Professor allegedly makes racist remarks in class at Brandeis University. *Diverse: Issues in Higher Education*, December 2, 2007.

Wax, Amy (2018). What can't be debated on campus. *Wall Street Journal*, February 16, 2018.

Weinberg, J. (2007). Philosopher's article on transracialism sparks controversy (Updated with response from author). *Daily Nous*, May 1, 2007).

Wheeler, David R. (2015) . At many colleges, budding journalists and their advisers are still fighting for freedom of speech. *The Atlantic*, September 30, 2015.

Wikipedia (2017). Hosty v. Carter, updated through November 1, 2017.

Wikipedia (2018). Jordan Peterson. Accessed November 2, 2018.

Wilkinson, R., & Pickett, K. (2009). *The spirit level: Why greater equality makes societies stronger.* London UK: Bloomsbury Press.

Williams, W. E. (2016). Creators Syndicate, September 21, 2016. Hermosa Beach CAL.

Wilson, Helen (2018). Human reactions to rape culture and queer performativity at urban dog parks in Portland, Oregon. *Gender, Place & Culture*, DOI: 10.1080/0966369X.2018.1475346.

Wilson, J. K. (2014). "A history of academic freedom in America." Theses and Dissertations Paper 257: From Illinois State University.

Winerip, M. (2005). SAT essay test rewards length and ignores errors. *The New York Times*, May 4, 2005.

Winters, M. A. (2012). Better schools, fewer dollars. *Wall Street Journal*, June 21, 2012.

Witek, A. (2107). Dunne, Vincent Raymond (1889 – 1970). St. Paul MINN: Minnesota Historical Sociey (MNOPEDIA).

WND (2003). College cancels Ritter speech: Reverses decision amid disruption caused by controversy. *World Internet Dailey*, January 1, 2003.

Wood, P. (2003). *Diversity: The invention of a concept*. New York: Encounter Books.

Wood, P. (2016). How I would have handled John Derbyshire's appearance on campus. *Chronicle of Higher Education*, March 16, 2016.

Woodward B. (2017). How the shooting at the UW protest of Milo Yiannopoulos unfolded. *The Seattle Times*. 24 January 2017.

Yale (21017 – 2018). The undergraduate curriculum. *Yale College programs of study*, 2017 – 2018.

Young, C. (2012). Liberal intolerance and the firing of Naomi Schaefer Riley. Left – wing academics silence a critic. *Reason*, 16 May 2012.

Zelip, B. (2013). *African American Studies 2013: A National Web – Based Survey*. Champaign – Urbana IL: Department of African American Studies, University of Illinois.

Zilversmit, A. (1993). *Changing schools: Progressive education theory and practice, 1930 – 1960*. Chicago Ill: University of Chicago Press.

Zimmerman, J. (2017). Free speech loses ground as Harvard retracts offers to admitted students. *The Chronicle of Higher Education*, June 13, 2017.

Zimmerman, J., & Robertson, E. (2017). *The case for contention: Teaching controversial issues in American schools* . Chicago: University of Chicago Press.

Zubairi, A. (2016). School of social work director steps down. *Ryersonian*, November 7, 2017.

Index

Name Index

Only the first author of works with multiple authors are indexed. Their pages refer only to their appearances in the text and not to the list of references.

Aaron, M. 115
Abdul-Jabbar, Kareem 99
Abrams, S. 136
Aby, S. J. 74
Acheson, Dean 81
Acton, R. 100
Adams, H. C. 63
Adler, F. 62
Adler, J. H. 133
Ahren. R. 131
Al-Gharbi, M. 204
Ali, Ayaan Hirshi 99-100
Alkalimat, A. 153
Allende, Salvador 100
Anderson, Don 10, 80, 85
Anderson, E. 162
Andrews, E. B. 63
Aristotle 1, 49, 148, 205, 239, 267, 295
Arum, R. 227, 231-232, 235-238, 242, 245-246
Associated Press 28, 100
Auerbach, S. 69
Aurelius, Marcus 8
Ayer, A. J. 199
Ayers, W. 213-214

Babcock, P. 237-238
Bailey, Pearl 164
Baldwin, Roger 70
Barcan, A. 218
Barendt, E. 109

Barmann, J. 102.
Barnes, H. 92
Barreca, G. 96
Basset, J. S. 66
Bassiri, K. G. 119
Bemis, E. W. 64
Ben-Porath, S. R. 24
Benedict, Ruth 262
Benjamin, R. M. 154
Benning, A. 99
Bennings, T. 122
Bernstein, N. 202
Berry, Hale 164
Bertrand, M. 44
Bevan, Aneurin 87
Bilbo, T. G. 69
Bitterman, S. 119
Blatchford, C. 112
Bloomberg, M. 216
Blumenthall, G. 117
Bodenner, C. 119
Boghossian, P. 178, 180
Boozer, C. 95
Bouchard, T. J. 85, 195
Bowen, W. G. 163
Boyle, K. 162
Brand, Chris 109
Brayton, E 119
Brewster, J. 65
Bridges, G. 115
Bromwich, D. 133
Browder, Earl 71

Brown, S. 101
Browne, R. L 164
Bryan, William Jennings 66
Burger, W. 31
Bush, George W. 99-100
Bush, Laura 99

Cabranes, J. 141
Cade, V. 124
Cain, B. 105
Calhoun. John C. 137-138
Camara, K. 141
Campbell, T. 164
Carl, N. 120-121
Carranza, R. 217
Carroll, D. 164
Carter, P. T. 163
Case Law -- Speech Codes 93-94
Castro, Fidel 79
Cattan, N. 199
Cattell, J. M. 66
CBS 94
Ceci, S. J. 30
Chapman, B. 225
Charles, N. 45
Chase, S. 110
Chaucer 140
CHE 119
Chemerinsky, E 24
Chou, V. 142
Christ, Jesus 15
Christakis, E. 17-19, 132-134, 136, 139
Christakis, N. 17, 18, 19, 132-134, 136, 141
Churchill, Ward 109
Ciccariello-Mather, G. 204
Coates, T-N. 158, 159
Cohen, J. S. 106
Coleman, N. 23
Columbus, Christopher 216
Cook, W. M. 164
Coolidge, Calvin 68
Corak, M. 48
Coulter, A. 102, 110

Creeley, W. 92
Cronkite, Walter 84
Crosby, F. J. 163
Crouch, S. 161
Cuban, L. 220
Curry, T. J. 203

Damron, A. 140
Dana, H. 66
Dandridge, Dorothy 164
Danon, D. 104
Darrow, Clarence 70
Darwin, Charles 61, 149, 267
Davis, Angela 90
Davis, H. B. 70
Davis, J. 70
Dawkins, Richard 180
De Blasio, W. 217
Debs, Eugene V. 66, 69, 292
Defoe, Daniel 140
DeGraff, O. 69
DeJohn, C. 92
Dennett. D. C. 284
DeParle, J. 163
Derbyshire, J. 101
Derrida, J. 185, 265
Dersshowitz, A. 104
Dey, E. L. 126
Dickens, Charles 202
Dickens, W. T. 38, 189
Dickerson, D. 162
Dickinson, M. 54
Dixon, M. 86
Drumm, E. 118-119
DuBois, W. E. B. 161
Duchen, A. M. 101
Dunha, B. 70, 87
Dunne, V. 7
Durden, L. 110

Eberhardt, J. L. 45
Ehrlich, J. 94
Einstein, Albert 173
Eisenhower, Ike 80
Elliot, T. S. 140

Ellison, Ralph 161
Elon, A. 278
Ely, R. T. 64-65
Eysenck, Hans 158-159

Falwell, Jerry 94
Farika, C. 216-217
Ferguson, R. A. 24
Field, M. 64
Fields, W. C. 120
Finley, N. I. 87
FIRE 91,102, 106, 124, 141, 295
Fisk, R. 277
Flaherty, C. 203
Florida, R. 291
Flynn, J. R. ix-x, 3, 13, 27, 33-34,
     36, 37-38, 40-45, 51, 57, 74, 79,
     81, 149, 177, 187-188, 192-194,
     196, 199, 205, 240, 247-249,
     251, 256, 270, 278, 280-281,
     292, 295, 299
Fogg, P. 146
Fosse, M. H. 68
Foster, William Z. 69
Freud 11, 74, 158,
Friedersdorf, C. 111
Friedman, Milton 290
Fuller, T. 102

Galster, G. 163
Galton, Sir Francis 195
Gardner, H. 191-192, 196
Garfinkel, H. 72
Garneau, T. 93
Gastañaga, C. 105
Giles, D. 119
Gilley, B. 203
Gilligan, C. 171
Ginger, R. 67
Glabermann, M. 73
Goldberg, S. 118
Gonzalez, M. 180
Gonzalez, S. 17
Goodlad, J. 220
Goodman, S. 115-116

Göring, Herman 191
Gottfredson, L. 108
Gray, H, H. 129
Greene, M. 213-214
Griffith, D. W. 120
Griswold, E. 76
Grodzins, M. 291
Gross, N. 59
Grossman, D. 279
Grossman, R. 110
Gutstein, E. 214

Hacker, D. 125
Haidt, J. 203
Hallinan, V. 80
Hamilton, R. F. 65
Hansel, Charles 1
Harding, Warren 68
Hariri, Y. 262
Harper, W. R. 64
Harris, S. 100, 136
Harrison, Z. N. 161
Harvard 260
Harvard Crimson 141, 143
Hawkins, C. 164
Haworth, C. M. A. 281
Hayes, C. 203
Hays, A. 70
Head, S. 214
Heaphy, J. B. 99
Hegel, W. F. H. 206
Heisenberg, Werner 139
Henderson, D. 70
Henninger, D. 54
Henson, T. 164
Heraclitus, 184-185
Heriot, G. 90
Heying, H. 116
Hicks, G. 70
Hill, J. H. 212
Hill, Joe 65
Hill, T. P. 149
Hindley, D. 106, 119-120
Hinkle, S. 93
Hirschman, A. O. 225

Hitler, Adolf 8, 138, 180, 186, 205
Hobbes, Thomas 267
Hollingsworth, P. J. 125
Holmes, D. 76
Hopkins, N. 146
Horrace 159
Huber, C. R. 233, 235
Huber, D. 115
Hudler, H. 133
Hughey, M. 204
Hussein, Sadam 278
Hutchins, R. M. 13, 69, 76

Irving, D. 20

Jacobowitz, J. 122-123
Jacobson, W.A. 26, 99
James, William 262
Jaschik, S. 110, 228, 238
Jeffries, L. 153, 154, 165
Jensen, A. R. 8, 32-34, 36-37, 50-
    51, 53-54, 73, 85, 143. 181, 190,
    196, 202, 298
Johnson, Lyndon 81, 84
Johnson, O. 70
Jourdan, Louis 164
Joyce, James 140
Joyce, James 69
Jung, H. 123
Jussim, L 98

Kabbny, J. 116
Kampeas, R. 199
Kant, Immanuel 282, 287
Kaufman, E. 104
Kefauver, Estes, 81
Keiler, A. 162
Keim. K. 109
Kelley, M. 95
Kelly. R. 106
Kennedy, John F. 79, 81
Kennedy, K. 99
Kennedy, Robert 81
Khúc, M. 135
Killane, K. 87

Kippis, L. 101
Kirkpatrick, J. 69
Kissinger, Henry 100
Kline, J. 216-217
Klinzman, J. 116-117
Klocek, T. 110
Konrath, S.H. 246
Kors, A. C. 95, 107-108, 123-125,
    143, 155
Kotecki, P. 98
Kourany, J. A. 121
Krupp. E. 102
Kuran, T. 143-144
Kurtz, S. 103-106, 118, 199

LA Times 105
Labaree, D. F. 218-219
Lacy. R. 279
Ladd, E. C. Jr. 59
Lam, D. 216, 217
Landon, Alf 263
Langbert , M. 215
Lanman, S. 123
Lapin, D. 104
Lazarfeld, P. F. 59
Lehigh, S. 204
Lerman, A. 131
Lesh, M, 91
Levesque, G. A. 165
Levin, M. 107-108
Levine, L. W. 13
Lewi, J. L 65
Lewis, J. 164
Lewy, G. 73
Lillenfeld, S. O. 96
Lindsay, J. A. 178
Loehlin, J. C. 37, 177
Loury, G. 124
Ludwig, W. 69
Lukianoff, G. 18, 93, 95, 106, 122-
    123, 130, 133, 142-143, 145
Lynn, R. 32-33, 39-40, 42, 50-51,
    73, 143, 172, 181, 298

MacDonald, H. 104, 124

Mackin, A. M. 122
Maher, M. 284
Mahmood, O. 96
Mallott, D. W. 76
Marcuse, Herbert 11
Margolin, K. H. 100
Marks, J. 31
Martin, A. 155
Marx, Karl 61, 67, 88, 200
Massey, D. 162
Matusow, H. 75
Maurer, L. 69
Maxwell, James Clerk 170
May, K. O. 71
McCabe, D. L. 240
McCarthy, Joseph 10, 61, 75, 77, 81,87
McConnell, M. W. 20
McCormick, C. H. 76
McDonald, H. 104
McInnes, G. 104
McKenna, V. 104
McMillen, L. 156-157
McNeil, K. 199
McWhorter, J. 154-155, 159-163
Mead, L. 161
Mearsheimer, J. J. 197-198
MEC 223
Mencken, H. L. 68
Meyer, M. F. 69
Mill, John Stuart 7-10
Miller, E. J. 107
Miller, H. 69
Milton 140
Miner, J. 107
Mohan, G. 99
Monty Python 175
Moore, E. G. 37-38, 170, 189
Moore, S. 87
Morella, M. 223
Morey, A. 102
Mozart, Wolfgang Amadeus 192
Murray, C. 2, 27-29, 31-33, 43, 46-47, 50-53, 73, 102, 105-106, 110,

143, 147, 181, 196, 208, 220, 290-291, 295, 297-298

National Endowment for the Arts 246
NCAES 218,
NCES 218
Neal, Fred Warner 79
Nearing, Scot 65-66, 68, 70
Nelson, L J. 69
Nesson, C. 142
Newell, S. 140
Newman, C. 111
Newsam, P. 220
Newton, Sir Isaac 173
Nietzsche, Friedrich Wilhelm 200, 202
Nir, O. 199
Norcross, J. C. 196
Novikoff, A. B. 87

O'Brien, M. 79
OECD 222
Oesterdiekhoff, G. W. 186-187
Ogbu, J. U. 163
Oliver, K. 121
Oliver, K. 121
Omar, O. A. 278
Onsgard, K. 102
Orwell, George 246
Osama bin Laden 99
Owens, E. 131
Oz, A. 278

Page, K. 70
Paley, J. 24
Palmer, T. 97
Pamuk, O. 279
Parada, H. 121
Paros, M. 116
Pascarella, E. T. 232-233, 235
Patai, D. 167, 174, 182
Patton, L. 31
Paul 84-85
Paul (Saint) 54

Paulin, T 100, 106
Paulson, S. K. 109
Perelman, L. 228
Perry, T. 164
Peters, B. 164
Peterson, Jordan 111-113, 180
Piaget, Jean 158, 186
Pinker, Steven 180
Piper, G. 115
Pipes, D. 199
Plato 1, 8, 23, 140, 158, 184-185,
239, 245, 267, 290
Pluckrose, H. 178
Poitier, Sydney 164
Pollak, J. B. 146
Popper, Karl 8, 262
Princeton 261
Pryor, T. 97
Ptolemy 173
Public Affairs 102
Puck 297
Purdy, L. 163
Putin, Vladimir 186

Quacquarelli, Symonds 256
Quinn, M. 106

Randolf, A. Philip 71
Reiner, R. 99
Reuters Staff 225
Rice, Condoleezza 99
Richardson, R. B. 60
Rifkin, M. 215
Riley, N.S.
Riley, N.S. 155-159
Ritter, S. 100
Roberts, J. 89
Robinson, T. 106
Rockefeller, John D. 64
Rodgers, H. 64
Rodgers, H. S. 76
Roll, N. 106
Roosevelt, Franklin 263
Roosevelt, Theodore 65
Rosenberg, J. 77

Rosenberg, E. 77
Ross, E. A. 64-65
Roundtree, C. 31
Rousseau, Jean-Jacques 220
Rushton, J. Philippe 107, 110
Russell, W. 196
Rust, V. 95
Rustin, Bayard 71
Rutherford, A. 109
Ryle, Gilbert 282

Sachs, J. 106, 117
Said, Edward 120
Salatia, S. 106
Sands, Dianna 164
Saul, S. 54
Savovey. P. 18-19
Sayre, J. 70
Sayre, N. 68
Scarr, S. 37
Schappes M. 70-71
Schill, M. 105
Schlesinger Jr., Arthur M. 154-155
Schlosser, E. 120
Schmidt, S. 110
Schmieg, J. 94
Scholl, M. 142
Schrecker, E. W. 61, 63-66, 69-71,
76-77, 87, 119
Schuyle, G. 161
Sevy, M. 65
Shakespeare 140
Shapiro, B. 104
Shapiro, S. 79
Shockly, William 102
Sica, A. 65
Sinclair, Upton 120
Singal, J. 106, 203
Singer, I. B. 278
Skinner, B. F. 183
Smith, L. 116
Smith, M. 180
Smith, Will 164
Snipes, Wesley 164
Snow, C. W. 65

Soloman, D. 220
Sorkin, A. D. 101
Sowell, T. 14, 39, 153, 155, 161, 163, 176, 206, 215
Spegman, A. 116
Spenccr, R. 105
Spencer, Herbert 62
Spiked 91
Stalin, Joseph 67, 72, 186
Stanford, J. 64-65
Stanford, L. 64
Stanley, Jason 17, 19
Starkey, M. 26
Steele, G. 64
Steele, S. 161
Stein, M. 117
Steinberg, R. 101
Steorts, J. 141
Stephens, B. 130
Stephenson, W. H. 66
Stern, C. 178
Stern, C. 178
Stern, S. 213-216
Stevenson, Adlai 80
Still, W. G. 164
Stoloff, M. 196
Stone, D. 137
Stone, D. 19
Stotsky, S. 223
Stranger, A. 32
Subotnik, D. 162
Sudhalter, R. 164
Sugrue, T. 163
Summers, Larry 146, 149
Sumner, W. G. 62, 186
Sun, L H. 60
Swamy, S. 142
Syeed, M. 135
Synge, J. M. 140

Taylor, H. 76
Taylor, K-T. 203
Thernstrom, S. 162
Thomas, C. 155
Tkacik, Maureen 120

Tobin, D. 72
Tomasulo, F. 120
Trahair, R. 75
Treiman, D. 131
Trotsky, Leon 72
Trump, Donald 94, 116, 203
Turvel, R. 202, 203
Twain, Mark 120
Twenge, J. M. 246
Tyson, C. 164

US News and World Report 251, 256

Veblen, T. 65, 291,
Vellasenor, J. 125
Venker. S. 101
Victoria (Queen) 15

Wachter, K. W. 43
Waldron, J. 2, 19-25, 28-29
Wallace, David Foster 266
Wallace, Henry 77
Wang, Vivian 141
Washington Times 99
Waters, Ethel 164
Watkins, M. 90
Watson, J. 120
Watson, James 109
Wax, Amy 124-125
Weaver, M. 93
Weinberg, J. 202
Weinstein, B. 115-116
Wente, M. 111
Wheeler, David R. 95
Wiggins, E. M. 70
Wikipedia 112, 230
Wilkinson, J. J. 138
Wilkinson, R. 48
Williams, E. 203
Williams, W. 215
Williams, W. E. 162
Wilson, Helen 178
Wilson, John 61
Wilson, William Julius 162

Wilson, Woodrow 62, 66
Winch, R. 131
Winchell, A. 62
Winerip, M. 228
Winsett, N. 119
Witek, A. 73
Wittgenstein, Ludwig 285-286
WND 101
Wolff, Virginia 159
Woltman, F. 69
Wood, P. 101, 162-163, 204
Woodward B. 102
Wright, Richard 161

Wright, T. P. 76

Yale (2017-2018) 260
Yang, K. K. 135
Yiannopoulos, M. 90, 102
Young, C. 157

Zaccari, Z, 92
Zilversmit, A. 147, 220
Zimmer, R. J. 129-130, 149
Zimmerman, J. 24, 147
Zoellick, R. 99
Zubairi, A. 121

Subject Index

Advice
  University reform 290-293
  Key concepts courses 261-266
  The missionary departments 293- 294
  Walden codes 294
  Educating for tolerance 295-296
  Mind-altering sessions 296-297
  Chicago ideal 297-298
Academic freedom 58-59
Affirmative action 45-46, 164
Australian universities 91, 97
Autonomy
  Liberating 1, 13-14, 275
  Psychological 275-280
  Sociological 280-282
  Ontological 282 -288
  Trying 287
Black Studies
  Mission 117, 160
  Ban on conservative literature 155, 159-164
  Assimilation vs. separation 155, 164-165
  Separate departments 165-166
  The Riley "debate" 155-158
Buffalos 122-124
Canadian universities 110-112

Critical skills
  University goals 3, 227, 259-261
  Job skills (trends) 227-237
  Autonomy skills 245, 248-259, 261-270
  Key concepts 261-266
  Actual performance
  Gene Debs University 251-255
  Six universities 256-259
  FISC (Flynn's Index of Social Criticism) 3, 249-251
Role of knowledge
  Knowledge trap 266-271
  Decline of reading 246, 270
  Role of history 276-278, 280
  Role of literature 278-280
  The knowledge elite 52, 236-237, 247, 275, 292
  (See student culture)
Disinviting (or banning or shouting down) speakers 70, 77, 79, 99-107
Free speech defense
  Mill 2, 7-12, 16,
  Stanley 17-19
  Waldron 19-29
  Debate vs. test of strength 9, 12, 16, 53
  Learning from your "opponents"

8, 32-50, 73-74, 158-159
Loyalty oaths 9-10
Group difference 298-299
Halloween 17-19, 23, 97, 132-134,
    141
Israel & Palestine 107, 120, 131
    132, 197-199
Ku-Klux-Klan 22-23, 27, 105, 158
Loyalty Oaths 9, 61, 70-71, 74, 76,
    80, 143, 145, 212, 215
Men, women & genes 42-43, 146,
    149, 177-178
Meritocracy thesis 46-50
Microaggressions 92, 95-96
Political neutrality of the university
    58-60, 147-148
Publisher bias ix-xii, 202-204
Progressive education
    History & its roots 218-221
    Effect on schools 213-214, 217-
    218, 221
    Columbia Teachers College 214
    New York schools 215-217, 225
    Alternatives 217, 225
    Credentialing 218, 224
    The "super teacher" 221
    Education as a profession 222,
    226, 294
Racism 144-145, 299
Race & IQ debate 14, 27, 33-39,
    53-54,142, 190-191, 193-196,
    295
Re-naming 137-139
Safe spaces 97-99
Sanctions outside university
    Teachers 76
    Students
    Others 72-73, 75, 77, 80, 84, 124,
    157
Speech codes 16, 21, 27, 88-91,100,
    125
Speech zones 88, 89-90, 92, 94
Student culture
    During Vietnam 84-86
    After Vietnam 87

Student opinion 125-127
Decline of studying 237-238,
    242-243
Grade inflation 153, 238-239
The student centered university
    240-243
The non-aggression pact 241-
    242
Decline of reading 246
Shadow of the 19th century 270-
    271
Case for fewer students 290-291
Student mob
    Ignorance 51,
    Egalitarianism 87, 126, 211, 292
    Disinviting speakers
    Classroom invasion 95, 118-119
    Dictating courses 118, 140
    Control of the university 115,
    117
    Violence 115-116, 122-123, 174
    Fear to speak one's mind 127,
    137
Teacher training
    Mission 211, 215
    Student teachers 212, 214-215,
    221
    History 219
    Crisis of self- esteem 220-221
    Loyalty oaths 212, 215
    (See progressive education)
Trigger warnings 95-98, 122
UK universities
Universities (selected)
    Chicago 20, 62, 64, 69, 77, 84,
    86, 91, 94, 129-130, 143, 147-
    150, 297-298
    Delaware 144-145
    Evergreen 115
    Harvard 26, 69, 71, 77, 91, 141-
    147, 259-260
    Middlebury 2, 16, 31-32, 50-51,
    53-54, 91
    Pennsylvania 91, 122-126
    Princeton 91, 130, 260-261

Reed 77, 91, 118-120
Texas Tech 89-90
Vassar 26, 98-99
Wellesley 101-102
Yale 17-19, 131-141, 260
University mission
  Elevating debate 16-17, 28
  Encourage debate 13, 16-17, 28
  (See critical skills)
University newspapers & leaflets
  92-96, 124-125, 142
University staff sanctions
  Indoctrination 96,
  Tenured 62-71, 77, 79, 95-96,
  106-110, 116,1 24-125,142, 146
  58, Untenured 110. 119, 142-143
  Adjunct professors 110
  Fear to speak one's mind 127
  Tenure 206
University student sanctions
  Indoctrination 111, 143-144
  Cleansing sessions & apologies
  93, 122, 296, 296
  Expulsion 69-71, 92, 96
  Probation & suspension 96-97
  Fear to speak one's mind
  127,137
Vietnam War 79-80, 83-87
Walden codes
  Concept 183, 205, 207-208
  Anthropology 184-188
  Education 191-193
  Philosophy 199-202
  Political Studies 197-199
  Psychology 193-196
  Sociology 188-191
  University presses & journals
  202-204
Woman's pay 15, 176-177
Women Studies
  Mission 173-174, 182
  Women's "road to truth" 171-
  173
  Anti-science & social science
  167-170

Postmodernism 173
Classroom practice 167, 174-176
Scholarship 176-178
Women's journals 178-180
Remedy 182

CPSIA information can be obtained
at www.ICGtesting.com
Printed in the USA
LVHW080838060121
675575LV00025B/1501